SOCIALIST RECONSTRUCTION

A BETTER FUTURE FOR THE UNITED STATES

LIBERATION MEDIA

SAN FRANCISCO

Socialist Reconstruction:
A Better Future for the United States

ISBN: 978-0-9910303-9-2

Library of Congress Control Number: 2022941505

Liberation Media

2969 Mission Street #201

San Francisco, CA 94110

(415) 821-6171

books@LiberationMedia.org

LiberationMedia.org

TABLE OF CONTENTS

Acknowledgments

Socialist Reconstruction: A Better Future for the United States is the product of the collective labor of Sohrob Aslamy, Ben Becker, Brian Becker, Richard Becker, Hannah Craig, Jane Cutter, Jodi Dean, Hannah Dickinson, shenby g, Chris Garaffa, Patricia Gorky, Max Greenberg, Ryan Hamby, Kai Heron, Saul Kanowitz, Stephanie Kenific, Katy Lang, Tina Landis, Mazda Majidi, Nadia Marsh, Rob Maclean, Keith Pavlik, Eugene Puryear, Nicole Roussell, Russell Ruch, Marissa Sanchez, Walter Smolarek, Vivek Venkatraman, and Joyce Wilcox.

SOCIALIST RECONSTRUCTION

A BETTER FUTURE FOR THE UNITED STATES

THE THINKING BEHIND SOCIALIST RECONSTRUCTION: A BETTER FUTURE FOR THE UNITED STATES

*T*his book, *Socialist Reconstruction: A Better Future for the United States,* is the result of a three-year-long collective project that began with a discussion and decision by the Fourth Party Congress of the Party for Socialism and Liberation held in 2019.

The Fourth Party Congress discussion revolved around some of the particular ideological challenges facing a revolutionary process in the United States, where anti-communism has long been the unofficial religion, and in the world generally in the post-Cold War era. There is no absence of militant struggle in the United States, but without a simultaneous ideological struggle to revive socialism as the legitimate alternative to capitalism, this will not happen on its own. Socialists cannot expect to make a revolution by being the best and most dedicated organizers in the mass struggles and then hope that one of these mass struggles simply gives way to socialist leadership in a time of great crisis. Neither is it sufficient, given the urgency of the times, to win people over to socialism in ones and twos. A larger cultural shift and acceptance of socialism must be effected and a mass pro-socialist consciousness has to be deliberately cultivated, now and in advance of a revolutionary crisis, if socialists are to successfully seize such an opportunity.

For all these reasons and more, we resolved to write a book that we understood would be unorthodox for Marxists. Among the Marxist left, it has long been a principle that no one can sketch out a blueprint for what a socialist society or government will look like. But that's what the assembled writers have done here—not because we have located a crystal ball, but because it has become politically necessary for our current time.

Previously, we might have argued that sketching out such a blueprint would be an exercise in utopian dreaming. It would be more useful to spend our time organizing and writing around a burning issue of the moment. After all, no revolutionary process follows along ready-made paths. Anything can be written on paper, but in practice, all political processes encounter new variables, twists, and turns that cannot be anticipated. When the working class comes to power, involving millions in the reorganization of society on a practical level, this will produce and generate so many new ideas and solutions; the new power will not be bound by or follow the script of any one book or pamphlet that had been written years earlier under capitalism.

Karl Marx himself declined to describe the details of future socialism, insisting instead that he and the rest of humanity were "uncivilized" compared to the future human beings of highly developed socialism and communism. Future societies would look back at our world and be astonished at how limited our understanding was. The important thing for revolutionaries, Marx and Friedrich Engels established, was to identify the contradictions within capitalism that would spell its downfall, and organize that class that has every interest in such a revolutionary transformation— the working class. Once the working class became conscious of itself as a class, understanding its distinct interests and developing its own yearning for political power, this would set the stage for a socialist revolution. To that end, Marx consciously broke with utopian socialists and focused his intellectual work on a critique and analysis of capitalist development.

A few pages are devoted to a broad sketch of socialism and communism in *The Grundrisse, Critique of the Gotha Program,* and in Engels's *The Housing Question.* His most important work, *Capital,* says very little about these matters. Even *The Communist Manifesto* limits its forward-looking program to a general picture of the rise and ultimate fall of capitalism, forecasting that the working class would overthrow the rule of private property. It includes a series of immediate changes for the first stage of socialism in advanced capitalist countries: the abolition of private land ownership and inheritances, state control of banking and industry, the shared responsibility of all to labor, free education for all, a gradual abolition of the distinction between town and country, and so on. The *Manifesto* provides no further details on what all this looks like and even these measures "... will, of course, be different in different countries."

Since the publication of the *Manifesto* in 1848, socialist and communist parties have mostly limited their publications and presentations in a similar fashion to Marx and Engels. Their programs describe their overall vision, what they are fighting for, and emphasize what immediate changes they would declare right away to remedy the central problems of capitalism. It would be inappropriate for a party program to go beyond this. For political parties, the program represents the essential basis of unity for someone who is considering joining. One can be in the same party, in other words, without agreeing to all the ins and outs of what future socialist living and governance would look like. In the future, such questions may in fact become dividing lines, but for now, the primary task is for the working class to conquer power, and a socialist party must devise strategies and tactics to that end.

The Party for Socialism and Liberation (PSL), which published this book, also has a program which is in keeping with that Marxist tradition and serves as the essential basis of unity for our organization. So why did we also produce this book, which in some ways, breaks with the Marxist tradition of declining to provide a blueprint for socialism?

This book does not substitute for a party program but serves another purpose entirely: to demonstrate, rather than just declare, that there is an alternative to capitalism in the United States, and to start a dialogue with all of society about what such a socialist society will look like. In this project, we have enlisted as writers individual members, and some non-members, who have experience and expertise in particular fields and areas of struggle, and posed to them a singular question: if the working class already had power in the United States, how would it reorganize *society*? Of course, we do not pretend that any of the responses represent the final word or final answer to any of these questions. That can only be shaped in real life. Nor is every major question about what socialism would look like answered. Each chapter demonstrates that another world is not just possible, but quickly achievable once private profit is removed as the engine of society and the existing technology, resources, and power structures are reorganized to meet the needs of the people and the planet.

Our mission with this book is not to convince everyone of every detail, but rather to raise the socialist and communist horizon, to reintroduce that into our day-to-day organizing work, to make socialism vivid and real; to give people a taste so they order a full helping. Much of popular culture today is rightfully understood as a form of escapism, allowing a reprieve from the depressing reality of capitalism. Many contemporary postapocalyptic films and novels attest to the truth that it is now easier to envision the end of the world than it is to envision a new system. This book is an attempt to puncture that. It too is escapism, but of a different type: to escape for a moment from the narrow and horrible boundaries of what appears politically possible at this exact moment; to let our minds jump forward one historical stage and conceive of how much we could achieve under socialism. There is a considerable history of political science fiction, some of it quite sophisticated, which speculates on how future high-tech societies could be reorganized and, in turn, impact social relations. But typically, socialist organizers have only indulged in such conversations over a meal or a drink, perhaps after a meeting or a long day of marching. Here we bring greater systematic thinking and concreteness to these discussions.

Making vivid the socialist future—and getting people to discuss and debate this *now*, under capitalism—is especially important for the development of any revolutionary process in the United States. This is the conclusion that the PSL has drawn after extensive internal discussions about the particular ideological factors that shape our political reality.

It has long been assumed that the irreconcilable contradictions of capitalism will become so pronounced, usually through the combination of a failed war and an economic crisis, that this will cause a revolutionary crisis—whereby the working class and the ruling class can no longer go on living in the old way. The shattering of the capitalist state and its institutional legitimacy will create a breach into which socialists can step, with a forward-looking solution, and lead the working class to power. Until that time, a revolutionary socialist party must focus on winning the leadership of the multinational working class by being the most dedicated fighters in all struggles, big and small, against exploitation and oppression. In addition, in order to seize a revolutionary crisis, to navigate all the tremendous complexity of such a period, and to defeat the centralized forces of the existing state, such a party must have the capacity for concentrated and centralized action, united by its own discipline and revolutionary purpose.

This is basically what happened in Russia before the 1917 Russian Revolution. Socialist parties were the only genuine fighters for workers and for democracy. In a war crisis only the Bolshevik Party consistently represented the urgent demands and interests of the Russian workers and peasants—for bread, land, and peace. The great mass of the population in the Russian empire had not become socialists in an ideological sense, but they wanted the Bolsheviks to take power, or at least would not fight them from doing so. In the socialist revolutions in China and Vietnam, the communists provided leadership to the national liberation movements against colonialism and neocolonialism—which was the engine of the overall revolutionary process that ultimately had a socialist horizon. All these experiences must be studied closely and have universal lessons, but they cannot simply be copied and pasted into our reality.

The liberation movements inside the US (especially the Black freedom struggle) are also an engine for revolutionary and mass struggle, but are operating in a very different context inside an imperialist state. To defeat such a state will require a close alliance with a broad working-class and multinational socialist movement that consciously joins the fight against national and class oppression—in other words, it requires higher political consciousness.

While Russia's example holds true as a kind of general theory of revolution for advanced capitalist countries, there are additional particularities that must be accounted for in the United States. The United States is not at the periphery of the global capitalist system but at its center, where the capitalist ideological institutions are far more entrenched, sophisticated, and durable. When socialism or communism were relatively new ideas to the working class, such as in Russia in the early 1900s, the czarist government's anti-communism could be quickly overcome *en masse* through the process of struggle itself.

Because this country's ruling class has represented the center of global anti-communism, the unofficial religion of the US, this has left a pronounced imprint on all political life and mass consciousness here. Progressive and working-class movements that in most other countries would naturally move in the direction of socialism do not automatically do so here. Even movements in US history that have had socialist or pro-socialist leadership either had their history erased or had self-censored in order to not be crushed or isolated. The imperialist state also has additional resources to co-opt and buy out sections of the working class's leadership, even supporting some of their demands so long as they renounce any pretense of socialism. Compared to other advanced capitalist societies, the ruling-class institutions here have thoroughly marked socialism as illegitimate, not even worthy of consideration and even discussion of it amounting to treason.

In such a climate, the class struggle by itself will be insufficient to overcome anti-socialism in the United States. It is illusory to think that socialists can win over the great mass of the working class by virtue of their good deeds and dedication alone, keeping their heads down ideologically, and then announce themselves as socialists when a revolutionary crisis arises. This will be seen or attacked as a bait and switch and rejected by a majority of the working class if all their prior exposure to socialism is of a negative caricature. In this situation, anti-socialist and even right-wing groups are more likely to emerge as the beneficiaries of the accelerating contradictions of capitalism, since their "solutions" have been more widely in circulation and deemed "respectable." The opposition to and wariness of socialism must be overcome in advance of bigger crises and on an ongoing basis during periods of capitalist stability. Socialists must fight for the battle of ideas now, wherever we can and as openly as is practical, in such a way that links the everyday struggles with the necessity of a new system, socialism, as the only solution to the problems of capitalism.

This has already started to happen thanks to the cascading crises of capitalism, rising popular social movements, and the political breathing room that has opened absent the Cold War context. The fog of anti-communism is already lifting. But unlike an actual fog, it won't go away by itself. Any space that has opened must be fought for and expanded. The historical breakdown between US working-class and popular movements on one side, and the political movement for socialism on the other, can only be overcome by building pro-socialist consciousness on a much larger scale. Political education and exposure to socialism cannot be confined to study groups alone. Transforming mass consciousness will in turn create the political space for more powerful socialist organizations, and for movements and leaders to openly attach their projects to a socialist horizon.

What does the battle of ideas consist of in our moment? Winning a majority of the US working class to socialism, or to be accepting of it, requires contending, above all, with the myth that socialism is a failed project—that socialist leadership and planning lead to economic stagnation or poverty and that socialism is antidemocratic. Socialists in the United States in the 21st century must contend, in other words, with generations of nonstop indoctrination about the actual experience of socialist governments. We do not have the luxury of presenting socialism as just a new idea because, at the end of the day, people have been trained to think that "socialism will not work," even if they like the idea in theory. This book shows how much could be improved once the working class has power; it shows that a new system is both workable and plausible.

The book also takes on a major talking point in anti-socialist indoctrination. In school and in the media, people are given apples-to-oranges comparisons, lining up the average standards of living in the capitalist United States with the socialist projects struggling to overcome underdevelopment and imperialist encirclement. Framed in such a way, where socialism appears to be a material step backward from capitalism, it cannot win a majority of the working class. This false framing always serves to put socialists on the defensive. A true comparison would be to compare a socialist Cuba, for instance, to a capitalist Cuba or other nearby capitalist countries. Here the superiority of the socialist system is evident. The capitalist United States likewise should be compared to what a socialist United States would look like. This book offers a necessary correction to the anti-communists' false framework by laying out what socialism based on high technology and abundance would achieve.

Another reason that this book departs from tradition, in offering a blueprint, is that we recognize that there is an existential crisis of a greater scale that is now upon us: catastrophic climate change. If in previous historical periods, socialists could content themselves with general proclamations of how they would reorganize production once in power, now this will not do. The climate crisis is of such immediacy that people are crying out for specific plans that meet the scale of the problem so that future generations have a planet to inhabit. As argued in a previous PSL publication, *Climate Solutions Beyond Capitalism* (2020), the capitalists have dragged their feet for so long that it is now too late for piecemeal and slow reforms to production, distribution, and consumption. This is especially so in the United States, the world's largest carbon emitter. Specific plans to reorganize the economy are necessary to make clear that the climate crisis is indeed solvable, a necessary antidote to overcome cynicism and apathy. This book demonstrates that drastic action can in fact be taken, once the means of production are subordinated to an economic plan, while still vastly improving the quality of life of the working class in the United States and worldwide. We do not have a "climate chapter" because it requires comprehensive action in all major fields of policy: energy, transportation, housing, agriculture, and so on. Likewise, the other burning struggles of our time over racism, women's oppression and LGBTQ oppression are not separated into issue-based chapters, but instead threaded throughout the book. The answer to institutional and structural oppression is to uproot all those institutions and structures.

Finally, this book also serves as an ideological intervention in a period of general ideological retreat, when many movements worldwide have been generally backing away from the question of power. "Another World Is Possible" is the slogan of the World Social Forum, formed in 2001 by social movements across the world as "a permanent space and process to build alternatives to neoliberalism." But what exactly is the possible other world, the alternative? In the period after the fall of the Soviet Union, a full-scale ideological offensive was launched on the ideas of Marxism and socialism, many left-wing parties disintegrated or became demoralized, and movements rejected the long-held aspiration for the working class to conquer political power. Other ideologies filled the space, and the next generation of fighters that entered the struggles against injustice did so without a clear political horizon or anchoring theory. While millions recognized that capitalism was at the root of so many injustices, if and how capitalism could be replaced remained a giant question mark. This book decisively says: yes, the working class must take power and should have all the confidence to do so. None of the necessary transformations to provide for the people and the planet can take place unless the working class gains power.

If the ideas on the pages that follow entice and engage you—whether you are in total agreement or have another proposal for remedying the crises of capitalism—then you should consider yourself a socialist. That feeling of wanting to reconstruct society, to repair injustices, and to more effectively organize our common world, those feelings represent your deeper hunger for another system. They are in fact cravings for power—not individual but collective power—where the best ideas to serve humanity and the planet can be applied and tested in real life. In the capitalist present, such a world may seem like a dream. But it's not. It can happen here.

—Executive Committee,
Party for Socialism and Liberation

INTRODUCTION

*T*he capitalist system confronts the world with problems that capitalism is unable to solve: mass inequality, climate change, and war. Capitalism can't solve these problems because capitalism causes them. Billionaires get rich while millions sink into poverty. Fossil fuel corporations continue to drill and mine even as temperatures rise across the globe. The US government uses military bases, sanctions, bombs, and threats to pursue an aggressive imperialist agenda, even as it claims to stand for freedom and democracy. For the sake of people and the planet, we need a new system. We need a new society. What may have once seemed impossible is now an imperative necessity—socialism.

This book presents the Party for Socialism and Liberation's proposal for the first decade of socialism in the US in the twenty-first century. In this vision, power is in the hands of the working class. The diverse multinational working class has achieved political supremacy and is actively eliminating bigotry, racism, and national oppression as it expands economic, social, and political democracy. Major industries, corporations, services, and enterprises have been nationalized. Unions, cooperatives, collectives, and voluntary associations work together with public agencies to plan and coordinate production for the benefit of people and the planet. The working class leads the project of reconstructing the United States.

What will life look like in the first ten years of a socialist US? How will socialism be better than what we have now? No one can predict every detail of a future socialist society. But we can demonstrate how socialism enables us to redress wrongs and address challenges, wrongs the capitalist class refuses to acknowledge, and challenges it is utterly unable to address because doing so threatens its wealth and power.

Karl Marx describes the Paris Commune as the form through which the working class works out its own emancipation. Similarly, we think of socialist reconstruction as a framework for how we get free—equally free from exploitation, white supremacy, patriarchy, and imperialism; and equally free to share collective responsibility for meeting social needs and enriching social life. The chapters in this book sketch out central features of this socialist reconstruction: the end of wage slavery and domination by the capitalist market, the dismantlement of the structures of special oppression, the transformation of energy production and use, the provision of universal basic services, the expansion of free time, and the engagement of more and more people in the active reproduction of our common world.

Workers Make the World Run—Workers Should Run the World

Mainstream politicians in the US push a deceptive old Cold War image of socialism as shared deprivation. They want people to think that the capitalist system—where the billionaires get richer while the majority of working people end up struggling to survive—is the best we can do. With their messages amplified by capitalist media, Republican and Democratic leaders alike try to make people think that socialism means the government is going to "take our stuff." What's so laughable about this view is that it's capitalism and the capitalist state that take "our stuff." Workers produce the goods and services necessary for meeting people's needs, but we end up struggling to meet our own needs. Capitalism appropriates our labor, lives, and futures, chewing us up and spitting us out for the private benefit of landlords and owners, banks, and billionaires.

During the first year of the COVID-19 pandemic, working people got infected and died, especially frontline "essential" workers who are disproportionately Black and Latino. We lost our jobs and were threatened with eviction, foreclosure, and homelessness. Hundreds of thousands of women were forced permanently out of the workforce and back into the drudgery of constant cooking, cleaning, and child care. Billionaires increased their wealth by 40 percent, profiting off the devastation inflicted on households and small businesses while intensifying the exploitation of warehouse and delivery workers. Before the pandemic, technology companies like Uber and Airbnb were already transforming the personal property of working people into the means of production for corporations—I drive my car and someone else gets rich. Corporations and the state bombard us all with fees and charges and rents and fines, hounding us to pay money we don't have and threatening us with lawsuits and sometimes even jail when we can't pay. The demands on workers never let up—not even during a pandemic that killed over a million people in the US alone. Forced to labor in crowded and dangerous conditions, we faced the impossible choice between getting sick and infecting our loved ones or sinking into debt and getting thrown out of our houses. Millions of us didn't even have this choice—we lost our jobs entirely.

Together with the Republican Party, the Democrats have consistently betrayed working-class people, built up the massive US prison system, amplified and entrenched racial division and oppression, indebted students and households, pursued aggressive imperialist interventions across the world, and failed to use government to guarantee free and universal health care, education, child care, housing, transportation, and utilities. Much like their Republican opponents, the Democrats have proven themselves more interested in saving the banks than in saving the people and the planet. As long as Democratic leaders are oriented toward the interests—and campaign contributions—of Wall Street and the corporations, they will serve and protect that class, not our class, the working class, the class of those who have to sell our labor power in order to survive. Working people cannot count on the Democrats to have our backs. We can only expect what we have already gotten: stabbed in the back.

Everybody knows that this system of mass exploitation and oppression can't continue. More and more people are using "socialism" as the name for the solution. But what do they mean when they say "socialism"? In history and in the present, there are different versions of socialism. The version presented here begins with the abolition of the tyranny of the market and the emancipation of the diverse multinational working class. Instead of being dictated to by a system rigged in favor of billionaires, capitalists, and landlords, we the people should determine what we need and coordinate a plan for producing the goods and services necessary to meet those needs. Workers make the world run, workers should run the world!

Today, all production is socialized: nearly every product depends on the interconnected skills, labor, and contributions of many people, often from all over the world. It follows that the responsibilities for and the benefits of production should be socialized, too. In the capitalist system, all the benefits are privatized—the few profit off the labor of the many. Decisions are made with an eye to the "bottom line" of making money, making sure that the rich are getting richer. The social and environmental impacts of this compulsion to accumulate are basically ignored. The only way to ensure that production serves people and the planet instead of having people and the planet serve production is to take it out of the hands of the capitalists and owners and place it into the hands of the collective people. Decisions about production and distribution have to be made democratically, by workers and communities, in accordance with a common plan. This is how we liberate ourselves from capitalist exploitation and market dependence.

Too many jobs in the capitalist US are deeply alienating. Just as the assembly line replaced craft work, so today jobs in a wide array of services have taken the place of higher-skilled and better-paid jobs in industry. Whether low-waged jobs in fast food, transport, delivery, retail, warehouses, and call centers or higher-waged jobs in information services, human resources, insurance, or some other bureaucracy, much of the work in the US doesn't feel rewarding to those of us who are doing it. Because work is organized through a capitalist labor market, most of us have to work for wages in order to pay for the things we need to survive—food, transportation, medical care, housing, and so on. While some people are fortunate enough to get paid to do what they love, that privilege is unequally distributed according to class, race, and gender. Under capitalism, the majority of us spend most of our time doing work we hate so that someone else can get rich.

When we are constantly worried about losing our jobs; constantly worried about making rent; constantly worried about making it to the end of the month; constantly worried about a medical emergency that could wipe us out; constantly worried about fires, floods, and weather extremes; we aren't free. But we don't have to let market forces determine our lives and futures. After all, the ruling class doesn't: since they control the state, they find ways to use the state to bail them out. So-called "free markets" are managed by central banks and elements of the state to protect corporations and maintain the position of the ruling class as a ruling class. In a way, this protectionism is already a kind of socialism, but it's socialism for the rich. What we need is socialism led by the working class for the benefit of society as a whole.

People can come together, coordinate needs with the skills and resources necessary to meet them, plan what we should produce, and collectively determine how to do it. Planning already happens at multiple levels and scales throughout society—whether we are talking about the US military, Walmart's massive distribution network, local government, school curricula, or a household's weekly budget. When planning doesn't happen—or when plans aren't followed—the results are calamitous. The preventable deaths of over a million people in the United States from COVID-19 demonstrated the disastrous consequences of the failure to coordinate a centralized response. Countries such as China, New Zealand, Japan, and Cuba didn't experience anything close to the magnitude of death ravaging the US because they combated the pandemic with proper planning, centralized leadership, and mobilized community messaging and organizations.

Climate Change is Class Struggle

The last forty years have made abundantly clear what Marx and Friedrich Engels argued over a century ago: capitalism is as much a system of destruction as it is a mode of production. Profit-oriented production leads to extraordinary excess and waste, squandering natural resources, and devastating the natural world. Overcapacity in some areas of production is accompanied by undercapacity in others. In some places, there is too much, and in other places too little. Competing firms make nearly identical versions of the same commodities, encourage consumers to buy what we neither want nor need, and even end up destroying unsold goods. In search of profit, owners pay workers as little as possible, resorting to wage theft and reducing hours to avoid paying benefits and overtime. Some companies invest in technology instead of people, finding new ways to monitor workers more closely and push us more intensely. Other companies stop making things altogether, preferring to buy back their own stocks and enrich their investors. And still other companies operate like birds of prey, swooping down to buy firms that they tear apart as they sell off the assets and discard the workers. From the demolition of communities, ways of life, and entire industries to the ecological devastation inflicted upon the planet, production for the sake of private profit is incompatible with the flourishing of human and nonhuman life.

The existential crisis facing us all is climate change, the steadily warming climate. The capitalist class can't and won't solve this problem. Decarbonization, eliminating our dependence on carbon-emitting energy sources, is necessary—an absolute imperative if there is to be a future in which the majority of the world's people and species will thrive. But eliminating fossil fuels is only possible if we decommodify and decolonize energy production and use, in other words, only possible if we abolish the profit motive and ensure that all countries and communities have the energy they need to adapt to and flourish on a warming planet. Meeting the energy needs of technologically advanced economies by means of renewables—wind, solar, and hydropower—is already possible, so long as industrial production is substantially reconfigured. We must also change our approach to food production and rebuild our housing and transportation infrastructure in more environmentally responsible ways. Life under socialism won't be the same as the popular image of straight, white, and middle-class life in the late twentieth century US—a way of life only ever available to the few and at the cost of exploiting and oppressing the majority of people in the world. Life under socialism will be better as everyone will be able to count on free health care, education, transportation, utilities, low-cost housing, more free time, and deeper engagement in determining our common futures.

> ## Life under socialism will be better as everyone will be able to count on free health care, education, transportation, utilities, low-cost housing, more free time, and deeper engagement in determining our common futures.

Adapting to the changing climate requires the reconstruction of the economy along socialist lines. A socialist reconstruction will shift from consumption-oriented commodity production to the production of universal basic services. From fundamentals such as free public transportation and guaranteed housing to conceptions of health and education expanded to encompass mental, sexual, social, and cultural flourishing, a socialist economy takes off from and universalizes the gains capitalism hoards for the few. The goal of socialist production isn't private profit or capital accumulation; it's advancing the conditions under which people and the planet can thrive. Instead of capital's world and soul-destroying drive for more money, more commodities, and more accumulation, the motive force of socialist planning will be developing the forms of association that reproduce a flourishing social and ecological world.

Socialism is Possible and Necessary

In the US, we already have the capacity to solve a wide array of social problems. Highly developed logistics systems such as Amazon's can be directed toward the elimination of hunger, with food and other necessities being distributed as needed. The elaborate databases used by real estate companies like Zillow can be deployed to connect houses with potential occupants, enabling us to eradicate the racist legacy of redlining and guarantee secure, comfortable, and attractive housing to all. The practices and infrastructure necessary for socialist planning are already in place, but they are in the wrong hands, the hands of the class of owners instead of the class of workers.

Most contemporary socialists in the US agree with the imperative of ending exploitation and special oppression. They share the goals of providing everyone with reliable access to quality health care, education, and housing. Programs like Medicare For All and the Green New Deal and movements to abolish debt and racist policing have grown in popularity because they articulate real popular demands for systemic change. This book proceeds from the conviction that these demands are realizable here and now. They aren't just a dream. Socialist reconstruction will make them a reality.

What is necessary to make socialist reconstruction a reality is working-class power. If power over the state and economy is not in the hands of the multinational working class, then we will be forever fighting for concessions that the ruling class will do its best to retract. We won't be able to move forward because we will constantly have to defend what we've already won. The capitalists and landlords will continue to invent new ways to keep us distracted, indebted, divided, and insecure, and we will end up forced to acquiesce to ongoing exploitation and oppression. But the crises of capitalism can't be addressed piecemeal—they are all related. Because US social democrats and democratic socialists focus on small gains while leaving the underlying system in place, they don't seem to believe their own program. For them, socialism is the music of a distant future. Along with millions of others across the country and around the world, we hear the music now—and believe we should all join in playing it.

The following chapters show what the first decade of socialism could be like in the US, how it is possible, and why it will create a better future for people and the planet. Anchored in an appreciation of all workers as unique human beings, our vision replaces capitalism's market determination of value via exchange with socialist values of meaningful, unalienated work and expanded free time.

Workers are not line items on balance sheets, although that's what capitalists reduce us to. Workers are unique human beings with hopes, needs, talents, and relationships that must be supported and cultivated. All labor that is necessary for society to function and achieve our collective goals will be recognized as meaningful, thereby overcoming alienation. Forms of labor that are currently seen as less desirable can be better distributed, more widely respected, and better compensated so that the burdens of such labor are socialized rather than foisted onto specific social groups who are underpaid and degraded. The only way to eliminate structural racism and sexism is by changing the structures. When different forms of labor are shared, people learn to see and appreciate them, to understand, for example, where our food comes from, and participate in growing, preparing, and serving it. When everyone has a say in planning what needs to be done and when everyone does our part in carrying it out, we all learn to respect the work that goes into reproducing our society and meeting our needs. We also all get more time to pursue the things we love—as well as more time off.

Meaningful Work and More Free Time

In his classic account *The Origin of the Family, Private Property, and the State,* Engels presents the determining factor in history as the production and reproduction of immediate life. As Engels explains, production involves making and securing means of existence such as shelter, food, clothing, and tools. Reproduction involves "the propagation of the species," that is, the work of caring for children and maintaining community relations. Throughout history, the organization of production and reproduction changes. In fact, history can be understood in terms of these changes. Important for our analysis here is the way that productive work became subject to wages with the development of industrial capitalism and capitalist agriculture. Instead of taking the proceeds of workers' labor by brute force (although this still happens), capitalists purchase the labor power of workers for a period of time (the price, length, and conditions of labor are always a matter of class struggle). Labor under capitalism is "alienated," for the profit of another (the capitalist), and distributed via the market, which means the capitalist wants to buy it as cheaply as possible. The system is so twisted and unjust that some of the hardest and most necessary jobs receive the least compensation and respect.

The rise of industrial capitalism also impacted reproductive labor. The domestic sphere ceased to be a site for the production of basic goods like cloth, soap, candles, and canned goods; these became industrially produced commodities. Since the care work associated with rearing children and tending a household held no immediate value in capitalist markets, women's position vis-à-vis men was devalued. A "cult of domesticity" reduced women's roles to those of wife and mother. That working-class women and enslaved women always worked for others outside their own households—often in grueling jobs requiring great strength and long hours—reveals the contradictory nature of the ideology that "a woman's place is in the home." As the formerly enslaved worker, abolitionist, and women's rights activist Sojourner Truth famously said, "Ain't I a woman?"

Oriented toward the private accumulation of capital, the capitalist system undervalues or devalues most of the labor essential to the production and reproduction of life. From the standpoint of the capitalist, our labor is nothing more than an input into the process through which they make their money. In contrast, socialism recognizes and values as meaningful the work of producing and reproducing our social world. In a socialist US, most people will engage in both kinds of work, ending alienation and the devaluation of reproductive labor.

Under socialism, productive work will be meaningful and unalienated because it will result from planning, that is, from collective discussion of values, priorities, and goals. People will understand work as contributing to larger social aims, such as the provision of healthy food, repair of vital infrastructure, regeneration of land and water, education of children, and enrichment of cultural life. The very experience of work will change as people have more control over their working conditions. Reproductive work will be recognized as occurring at multiple levels: caring for children and others in our households and families of choice, tending to relationships in our community, and organizing and planning our common life. Here, too, planning will affect a revaluation of emotional labor: the fact that we are always connected with others who depend on us and on whom we depend is featured in the ways we organize and socialize the tasks of everyday life. From the length of the workday or workweek, to the provisions for infant and child care, to the cultivation of voluntary associations and the creation of new social forms, under socialism, reproductive labor will be championed as essential and meaningful work.

Like meaningful work, expanded free time—time to do with what we will—is a key component of the vision of socialism developed in this book. Workers, feminists, and environmentalists have consistently advocated for shorter working days and weeks. The labor movement brought us the eight-hour day. Shorter working days enable greater work-life balance, diminishing pressure on parents in the labor force, and improving physical and mental health. Reductions in labor time have environmental benefits as they lead to decreases in carbon emissions and energy demands.

Advances in technology and automation should have already led to shorter working days, a shorter workweek, and months of paid vacations.

In some European countries, the efforts of labor unions and social democratic parties have secured these benefits for many workers. This has not
been the case in the United States, largely due to the particular ferocious-
ness of the US capitalist class and its attack on anything that smelled of
socialism. Because automation is developed under capitalist control, it
hurts US workers more than it helps us. Exploitation and unemployment
increase as some workers labor longer and longer hours, and others don't
work at all. Instead of more free time for everyone, the result of capitalist automation has been a larger reserve army of the unemployed and a
smaller but overworked labor force. The dirty secret of the technology
sector is that it runs on far fewer workers than the industrial economy
required. Socialist planning will eliminate this contradictory and unfair
approach to work. The benefits of automation will be extended to all
workers, decreasing the amount of labor time necessary for the production of goods and services. At the same time, the priority of involving
everyone in production for the good of all, of letting everyone share in
meaningful work, will have the happy effect of increasing the amount of
time available for us to do with what we will.

A Better Future Under Socialism

A socialist reconstruction is possible in the United States—here and
now. The technological and scientific means of production have advanced
beyond what was scarcely imaginable one hundred years ago. The problem
is that they are confined within capitalist property relations; they are conceived as private property owned by the few. The very idea that a company
or corporation is "private property" conceals its relationship to all sorts
of people, practices, and resources outside its legal scope. For example,
a company like Amazon relies on public goods and services like the US
Postal Service, roads, and the internet. It presupposes that someone has
paid to educate the people who come to be its employees. It also depends
on someone somewhere finding something to do with all the boxes,
packing materials, trash, and envelopes its service generates, what econ-
omists refer to as "externalities" for which the company doesn't pay but
which have costs nevertheless. To use another example, pharmaceutical
companies like Pfizer and Moderna received billions of dollars in public
funding to develop coronavirus vaccines. Yet they patented the vaccines,
claiming as their own private property not only what is clearly vital to the
global common good but what was paid for by the tax dollars of working
people. Relying on public money to fund private capital accumulation

is standard operating procedure under capitalism. Risk is socialized and reward is privatized. The next and necessary step is to socialize rewards so that everyone benefits, not just the few. And this means abolishing the legal form of private property that distorts collective ventures and socially produced knowledge into means for private capital accumulation.

A socialist reconstruction is possible in the United States—here and now.

Across the United States, interest in socialism is growing. People may not know exactly what it means but most recognize it as the answer to the problems capitalism poses but cannot solve. The vision of socialist reconstruction presented here supplies a framework that demonstrates how socialism enables us to get beyond the contradictions of capitalism by decarbonizing and deprivatizing the economy and by reorienting production around universal basic services, meaningful work, and greater time to do with what we will.

CHAPTER 1

SOCIALISM IN THE UNITED STATES

The Socialist Revival

"Socialism is making a comeback in the United States." That statement, presented by one of the speakers at a 2016 conference in Los Angeles attended mainly by very young, working-class socialists, might have seemed bewildering to many in the crowd. It would likely be bewildering to many of their parents. Comeback from what and from when? The statement implies that socialism was once popular in America. If the older parents of the young conference attendees had lived their lives in the US, most would have no such memory of socialism ever being popular. The memory of socialism and its immense contribution to progressive struggles for social and economic rights inside the United States was essentially extinguished—or so horribly distorted for the six decades after the end of World War II that very few people alive today have any awareness of socialism's role in US history.

For decades, socialists had to hide their views or they were in big trouble. Albert Einstein, the world's most renowned physicist, was a socialist. In 1949 he published "Why Socialism," a thoughtful and impassioned explanation of why society needs to be organized along socialist lines.[1] Einstein thought that the chief problem with capitalism is that it fosters competition rather than cooperation between people. J. Edgar Hoover, the head of the Federal Bureau of Investigation (FBI), ordered agents to carry out a massive spying operation against Einstein. The surveillance of every aspect of his life resulted in an FBI file that was 800 pages long.[2]

Rev. Dr. Martin Luther King Jr. was also a socialist. We celebrate his birthday every year as a result of a long and hard-fought struggle of the civil rights movement. Ironically, it was right-wing Republican president Ronald Reagan who signed the law declaring the third Monday in January a federal holiday. Almost no one in the country knows that Dr. King was a socialist. It is never discussed. "I imagine you already know that I am much more socialistic in my economic theory than capitalistic," a twenty-three-year-old King wrote to his then-girlfriend and later

The radicalism of Rev. Dr. Martin Luther King Jr. and Coretta Scott King has been largely erased. (Photo: Joost Evers)

wife, Coretta Scott King. "And yet I am not so opposed to capitalism that I have failed to see its relative merits. It started out with a noble and high motive, viz, to block the trade monopolies of nobles, but like most human systems it fell victim to the very thing it was revolting against. So today capitalism has outlived its usefulness."[3] King's letter to Coretta was written in July 1952, three years before the Montgomery bus boycott—which he helped lead—launched the modern civil rights movement. In this personal love letter, King continues: "It is probably true that capitalism is on its deathbed, but social systems have a way of developing a long and powerful deathbed breathing capacity. Remember it took feudalism more than 500 years to pass out from its deathbed. Capitalism will be in America quite a few more years my dear." He continues, "Our economic system is going through a radical change, and certainly this change is needed. I would certainly welcome the day to come when there will be a nationalization of industry. Let us continue to hope, work, and pray that in the future we will live to see a warless world, a better distribution of wealth, and a brotherhood that transcends race or color. This is the gospel that I will preach to the world."

King's comments about socialism and the future of capitalism in this letter resulted from his reading of Edward Bellamy's utopian socialist book *Looking Backward*, published in 1887. Coretta gave him the book.

She obviously liked it a great deal, and she wanted to find out his views on socialism. King writes, "At this point, I must thank you a million times for introducing me to such a stimulating book, you are sweet and thoughtful indeed." The letter also indicates that King was familiar with Karl Marx, had read at least some of his works, and agreed with a well-known Marxist theme, ". . . I have learned from reading Marx and books like Bellamy's, and that is that religion [*can?*] so easily become a tool of the middle class to keep the proletariat oppressed."

King's expression of anti-capitalism was more than an effort to impress his pro-socialist girlfriend. Nine years after his 1952 letter to Coretta, he gave a speech to the Negro American Labor Council where he stated, "Call it democracy, or call it democratic socialism, but there must be a better distribution of wealth within this country for all God's children." In April 1968, when Dr. King was assassinated, he was in the middle of organizing the Poor People's March and permanent encampment in Washington, DC. In the months prior to the march, he focused almost entirely on calling for a radical reorganization of the economy. As he said in a speech at the Southern Christian Leadership Conference held in Atlanta on August 16, 1967:

> And one day we must ask the question, 'Why are there forty million poor people in America?' And when you begin to ask that question, you are raising questions about the economic system, about a broader distribution of wealth.' When you ask that question, you begin to question the capitalistic economy. And I'm simply saying that more and more, we've got to begin to ask questions about the whole society . . .[4]

Dr. King had to be very cautious in his comments. The FBI was waging a war against socialism and the civil rights movement. Hoover conflated socialism and communism with the movement for equality for Black Americans. Dr. King, like Einstein, was the victim of a massive spying operation.[5] King knew that if he became too identified as a socialist he would be isolated and perhaps destroyed. That's what had happened to renowned artist and actor Paul Robeson who had been stripped of his passport in 1950. It happened as well to Ben Davis, a member of the Communist Party elected to the New York City Council in 1943. In 1949, Davis was convicted and sent to prison for five years for violating the Smith Act, which criminalized affiliation with any organization that advocated the overthrow of the US government. What was his crime? He was a Marxist and a communist.[6]

Only the Soviet Union escaped the Great Depression during the 1930s. While the major capitalist economies saw tens of millions of workers suddenly lose employment (the unemployment rate in the US was 25 percent in 1932), the planned economy in the USSR experienced massive growth.

'Canceling' Socialism

These days there is a lot of controversy around "cancel culture." Fierce debates rage across both right and left: What is acceptable discourse? Do individuals, groups, and institutions have the right to condemn or silence those they think have crossed a line and said something unacceptable? Can or should the government, publicly funded universities, or social media platforms impose their own restrictions on free expression?

What's been missing from these debates is recognition of the ruling class's long history of censorship and blacklisting. With the onset of the Cold War in 1946, socialism and communism were systematically canceled in US society. While hundreds of millions of people outside the United States embraced socialism, engaged in critiques of this or that trend within socialism, and joined socialist organizations, socialist parties, and socialist-led trade unions, people living in the US were basically barred from participating in socialism's global movement for economic and social justice. The "cancellation" of socialists and communists was universally accepted and enforced by all sectors of the US capitalist establishment—in politics, business, entertainment, culture, sports, education, and especially in the capitalist-owned "free press."

After WWII, the world was divided into two great political camps. Which was the way forward for humanity: socialism or capitalism? No question was more polarizing, more debated. After two consecutive global wars waged by consecutive generations—wars that took the lives of more than one hundred million people—the issue posed by society was how to end the scourge of the regular, intensifying, global conflicts aptly dubbed "world wars." The second of these great wars followed a decade of economic depression that was unlike anything the world has seen. Only the Soviet Union escaped the Great Depression during the 1930s. While the major capitalist economies saw tens of millions of workers suddenly lose employment (the unemployment rate in the US was 25 percent in 1932), the planned economy in the USSR experienced massive growth. There was no unemployment; the biggest problem was a labor shortage. As with the phenomenon of world war, the massive economic depression raised fundamental questions. Were war and depression unavoidable features of capitalism? Was there an alternative system? Could socialism work?

The American people were excluded from this great debate about the future. The irony is that the US government takes pride in guaranteeing free speech as a basic right. Being able to speak one's mind and express one's opinion is taken as fundamental to a free society. The story of free speech is so ingrained as quintessentially American that most people assume it to be true. It's not. It reveals itself as a fairy tale when one considers what happened to people identified as socialists, communists, or Marxists. They were sent to prison, lost their jobs and careers, and endured social demonization and isolation. Actors, directors, and screenwriters were driven from Hollywood.[7] Teachers and educators were either blocked from professional careers or purged from schools and universities. The capitalist class and the government's repressive forces purged the US of one of its most robust social and political movements. People in the US were taught to hate and fear socialism.

This fear and hate drove a modern-day witch hunt. Anti-communism and anti-socialism became a sweeping crusade, practically a national religion. Socialism was bad and communism was worse. Their evilness came to be accepted as an article of faith. Once demonized and shunned by society (usually with ample help from the FBI), the only way socialists could be rehabilitated was if they confessed, renounced their former socialist friends and comrades, and denounced socialism as an evil that they unwittingly subscribed to when they were young and naïve. Individuals applying for jobs had to swear on their application forms that they were not communists. The government confronted leaders of many of the most important labor unions with a stark choice: either renounce your socialist and communist beliefs and hand over the names of socialist coworkers or lose your position in the labor movement. Some suffered the consequences of staying true to their convictions. Many capitulated to the crusade that seemed too big to be defeated by any single individual act of resistance.

America's crusade against socialism was publicly launched by demagogic politicians in Congress. The FBI—as well as state and local police departments in all fifty states—played the role of the secret police. They spied on well-known people such as Einstein, Dr. King, and Helen Keller. And they spied on hundreds of thousands of everyday people suspected of having communist and socialist sympathies, convincing employers to fire them, landlords to evict them, and labor unions to expel them. An army of undercover FBI agents and informants infiltrated socialist groups, civil rights organizations, peace movements, and progressive cultural organizations. Operatives took down the names and license plate numbers of attendees at progressive demonstrations for peace or civil rights. They shared this information with local police departments, employers, landlords, and religious institutions. They kept files and wrecked lives.

Socialism and communism were conflated with the Soviet government in Moscow at a time when the US was actively preparing for war against the Soviet Union. This would be the third world war. The first ended in 1918; more than twenty million people were killed in less than four years. The second ended in 1945, about eighty million having died within just a few years. The third world war would be even worse because the enemy, the "communists in Moscow," had also built thermonuclear weapons. In the coming nuclear confrontation between "communism and democracy," the US would likely suffer mass civilian casualties. School children endured endless drills to prepare for the coming nuclear attack—as if ducking under desks and covering their heads could save them from an atomic blast. Suburban, middle-class families built bomb shelters in their backyards. The country was whipped into a frenzy not only against communists in the Soviet Union but also against socialists and communists in the US. They were portrayed as a domestic "fifth column" ideologically loyal to the communist enemy.

The systematic effort of the capitalist class and the repressive state government expelled the socialist and communist left from US political discourse. Speech associated with socialism became too dangerous to exercise, which meant it wasn't free at all. Socialists learned to self-censor, to camouflage their ideas with vague terms like "progressive" and "social justice." Socialists' own self-censorship rounded out the official suppression of socialist thought in the United States, while the country patted itself on the back for being the bastion of individual rights and free speech.

This long, dismal era of socialist repression and self-repression is coming to an end. A robust exploration of socialism is replacing it. New support for socialist ideas and the creation of an alternative system to US capitalism is emerging across the country. People want to reclaim control of the economy from the billionaires, ultrarich bankers, and corporate capitalists. They want to see an economic system reconstructed with measures that will immediately improve the lives of the vast majority of the people—especially the hard-pressed working class and poor. Socialism is experiencing a revival. Capitalist crises are awakening ever-growing numbers of working people to the need for change.

The Great Recession

When Wall Street banks crashed the economy in 2008, millions of people lost faith in the capitalist system. Without the emergency intervention of the US government, the greed, avarice, theft, and gross criminal conduct of Wall Street that led to the 2008 financial meltdown would have wiped out the US capitalist establishment. The government handed them a $660 billion cash bailout supplemented by an additional $7 trillion in loan guarantees. Absent government intervention, massive bank bankruptcies and the freezing of credit would have destroyed US capitalism as we know it. In the following two years of the "Great Recession," thirty million people lost their jobs. Nine million families were forced into home foreclosure. Personal bankruptcies soared. With no prospects for decent-paying jobs, millions of college graduates faced staggering levels of student debt they might never be able to repay. But there was no bailout for Main Street.

Even before the 2008 crash, the working class was in crisis. Over the previous three decades, huge parts of the country had suffered from factory closings. One major capitalist corporation after another moved millions of jobs to developing countries overseas where they could pay workers a fraction of the wage they paid workers at home. Cities and towns were thrown into catastrophic decline as the US capitalists and the government sang the praise of NAFTA, KTA, CAFTA, TPP, and the other "free trade deals" which facilitated the destruction of the lives and communities of US workers.[8]

The economic crash of 2008–2009 was a defining moment. It led to the unlikely victory of Democrat Barack Obama over Republican conservative millionaire John McCain. In 2007, no one would have expected that the United States was on the verge of electing the first Black president. The conventional wisdom held that the history of racism was too deep for one of the two ruling class parties to risk choosing a Black candidate for president. The capitalist economic crash steamrolled this assumption. The system was discredited. The need for change was obvious—and Obama campaigned on the promise of dramatic change.

On that promise, the Obama campaign generated a wave of national enthusiasm. Support was especially high among young people responsive to Obama's promise to end the war in Iraq and provide health-care coverage to every US citizen. Clearly, the US health-care system needed a drastic overhaul: some fifty million people lacked health insurance. Young people with diminished job prospects welcomed the opportunity to remain on their parents' health insurance plans until they were twenty-six. Obama also promised the millions of people with preexisting health conditions that his new system would bar capitalist-owned health insurance corporations from continuing to prevent the already sick or injured from obtaining coverage. In the midst of the economic carnage of the Great Recession, Obama's campaign appeared as a ray of light. He was different. He was young. He wasn't another rich, white politician from the Washington swamp. The labor movement sent worker volunteers door-to-door campaigning for Obama in the battleground midwestern swing states of the devastated industrial heartland. This included many areas where there was an overwhelming white majority of working-class voters. The message was "We Need Change"—and we need it urgently. "Can we do it?" *"YES! WE CAN!"* was Obama's main campaign slogan and rallying cry. It worked. Obama's victory was shocking. It filled people with hope. Yes, the US can change. Radical change is possible in the United States. That a Black man named Barack Hussein Obama could, in spite of the country's history of extreme racism, ascend to the White House, proved it.

The Law of Unintended Consequences

The revival of socialism could have something to do with what might be called the "law of unintended consequences." In 2009 the right wing of the Republican Party tried to block the passage of Obama's proposed Affordable Care Act (ACA). Condemning "Obamacare" as socialist, they mobilized protests—rifles in hand—at town hall meetings throughout the country. These well-organized, very well-funded, and militant right-wing protests coalesced into the Tea Party movement inside the Republican

The ultra-conservative Tea Party movement waged a fierce campaign against Obama and the ACA and unintendedly popularized socialism. (Photo: Wikimedia)

Party. With "Stop Obama's Socialism" as their mantra, they waged a fierce campaign against the ACA.

The irony is that the ACA was modeled on a Republican super-capitalist plan adopted by conservative Republican Mitt Romney when he was governor of Massachusetts. This plan required everyone, under penalty of fine, to register and pay private capitalist health-insurance companies to qualify for coverage. Although Obama had campaigned on the promise of health-care coverage for fifty million uncovered people, once in office he turned his back on the liberal wing of the Democratic Party and refused to consider a single-payer national health plan (now known as Medicare for All).

The unintended consequence of the fraudulent anti-socialist crusade by the Tea Party is that huge numbers of young, enthusiastic Obama supporters didn't know what "socialism" meant and started to research it. Dictionaries and search engines reported a surge of queries seeking a definition of socialism. Millions of young people concluded that if socialism meant expanding access to affordable health care, and capitalism meant depriving people of the ability to see a doctor when they or their children were sick, then maybe socialism wasn't so bad after all. Socialism wasn't scary; it was rational and humane. By 2012, Merriam-Webster dictionary was reporting that socialism and capitalism were the year's most looked up words.[9]

'We Are the 99%!'—Occupy Wall Street as a Harbinger

After the 2009–2010 anti-socialist crusade against Obamacare, another major political development triggered still more interest in socialism—the Occupy movement. On September 17, 2011, the Occupy Wall Street movement started as a tiny encampment in New York City in lower Manhattan—a few tents in Zuccotti Park erected by a handful of activists under the slogan "We are the 99%!" Initially, the encampment attracted little support. Activists decided to organize a march for the following Saturday, September 24, from Wall Street to an area just south of Union Square. The march was small. It would have gone unnoticed but for the fact that the New York City Police Department, in typical fashion, chose to violently attack it. Images of the police attack circulated in the media, leading other progressive organizers to call for another march on the following Saturday, October 1, to protest police violence. This time thousands of people showed up—and the police attacked again.

The October 1 action resulted in the infamous arrest of more than seven hundred people on the Brooklyn Bridge. Leading the crowd onto the bridge, police high officials and officers walked with their backs to the marchers. Once they reached the middle of the bridge, they turned around and announced that all the marchers were under arrest for "walking on the bridge." Additional police officers established a line at the back of the bridge and threw up a giant orange net to block people from leaving. Confusion and panic swept through the crowd. People had not planned on getting arrested and hauled off to jail. Parents who had to pick up their children were detained; so were people who had to be at work that night or the next day. A large contingent of teachers were on the bridge. Not only were they due in class Monday morning, but every teacher in New York City knows that if they are arrested they can lose their job because of the policies of the board of education. Police had been coordinating and sharing intelligence with Wall Street bankers about Occupy since August 2011—one month before the first tent was set up in Zuccotti Park.[10] The police thought they were doing a big favor for their friends on Wall Street by crushing the October 1 demonstration on the Brooklyn Bridge. Instead, they turned Occupy Wall Street into a nationwide movement.

The surprise attack and arrests on the Brooklyn Bridge became a huge story. Angry young people, many saddled with huge student debt and no job, started occupying spaces in their own cities and towns. Within a couple of weeks Occupy Wall Street encampments were established in almost every major city and hundreds of smaller cities and towns through-

The 2014 mass protests and rebellion in Ferguson, Missouri, opened a new phase of the Black freedom struggle. (Photo: Jamelle Bouie)

out the United States. People were in the streets chanting "We are the 99%!" All over the country, people expressed their outrage at capitalism, inequality, and the vast wealth and power of the 1 percent—the capitalist class, whose greed and avarice had triggered the 2008 financial meltdown and capitalism's biggest economic crisis since the Great Depression of the 1930s. The government bailed out the banks with trillions in aid while thirty million people lost their jobs, nine million family homes were put into foreclosure, and millions of young people were leaving school with staggering levels of student debt and no real jobs available.

The spread of the Occupy movement alarmed the capitalist class. They wanted it shut down. The Obama administration used the FBI—the Fusion Centers created as an intelligence arm to combat terrorism after the September 11, 2001 attacks on the World Trade Center—to create a full spectrum and detailed surveillance and spying operation against the movement. The government set up nationwide conference calls with federal, state, and local officials to share information and to plan.[11] In a nationwide crackdown coordinated by the Obama administration, the FBI, governors, mayors, and local police suppressed the movement. More than seven thousand people were arrested.[12] By the end of 2011, the movement that had erupted like a spontaneous wildfire of political activism had been crushed. But the slogan "We are the 99%" lived on. It had entered the public consciousness and became emblematic of a new generation profoundly discontent with the existing economic and political system. Occupy Wall Street didn't brand itself as socialist or make specific demands on the government or the capitalists. Yet the US government used its enormous repressive force to crush it, just as capital and the state suppressed socialism throughout the twentieth century.

The short-lived Occupy movement was a precursor. It was a harbinger and indicator of what was coming. As another popular slogan declared, "You can't kill an idea whose time has come."

'You Can't Have Capitalism Without Racism'—Malcolm X

On August 9, 2014, three years after the activists who launched Occupy Wall Street held their initial planning meetings, Michael Brown Jr. was shot and killed by police officer Darren Wilson in Ferguson, Missouri. Brown was unarmed. He was eighteen years old. The police left his body in the street for four hours. When the people of Ferguson went out to the streets in protest, they were met with fierce police repression.

Ferguson is located just outside of St. Louis. The police and the courts had oppressed Black people in Ferguson for generations. The oppression was so all-encompassing that it can accurately be described as a police state imposed on the Black community. The murder and demonization of Brown was the last straw. The protests on August 9 evolved into an all-out rebellion that endured for weeks. As the police employed overwhelming violence, including the use of militarized vehicles and other weapons of war, hundreds of thousands of people all over the country took to the streets. A new movement was born. It took its name from the main slogan chanted by people everywhere, Black Lives Matter.

Black Lives Matter was the latest incarnation of the Black freedom struggle in the United States. The Civil War and Reconstruction era were armed struggles of Black people for emancipation. The modern civil rights movement of the 1950s and 1960s continued the struggle against racist and national oppression. The struggle ebbed in the 1970s as a consequence of severe repression against organizations and individuals by the FBI and police departments. This severe repression was coupled with important economic and political concessions by the racist establishment.

In the radically changed political climate of 2014, this same organic movement for equality and freedom came roaring back. What distinguished the politics of the mass spontaneous movement that took shape after the Ferguson rebellion was that its politics were decidedly and explicitly anti-capitalist. It was led by young people who understood that the endless epidemic of racist police killings and abuse was a consequence of capitalism and the capitalist state forces. Routine police violence as well as the expansion of a racist system of mass incarceration in the United States happened after the 1964 Civil Rights Act. The parents and grandparents of the Black Lives Matter activists, the generations who had fought and won the Civil Rights Act and the Voting Rights Act in 1964 and 1965, had hoped that the end of formal apartheid in the US would eliminate the terror imposed on the Black community by the police. Apartheid laws had been struck down, but apartheid conditions and apartheid policing were expanding in the twenty-first century. Millions of young people drew the right conclusion: the problem wasn't a few bad apples in police departments. The problem was the *system* and it had a name—*capitalism*.

You Can't Be Elected President—'You Are a Socialist'

On October 14, 2015, the Democratic Party held its first nationally televised debate on CNN in advance of the primaries that would select the party's nominee for the 2016 presidential campaign. Everyone expected that Hillary Clinton was going to win the nomination; the primary process, including the debates, was just a formality. Vermont Senator Bernie Sanders had been getting surprising levels of support from young people as he spoke around the country about intensifying inequality, the need for a national health plan, and abolishing student debt. The Democratic Party establishment didn't consider Sanders as a serious threat to Clinton's prospects, but they were getting mildly anxious because they wanted Clinton to be effectively crowned early in the process rather than having to endure a potentially bruising primary campaign ahead of the general election.

CNN's Anderson Cooper expected that his very question to Sanders would be the knockout blow that would effectively reduce Sanders to the outer margins of American bourgeois politics.

> COOPER: Senator Sanders. A Gallup poll says half the country would not put a socialist in the White House. You call yourself a democratic socialist. How can any kind of socialist win a general election in the United States?

> SANDERS: Well, we're gonna win because first, we're gonna explain what democratic socialism is. And what democratic socialism is about is saying that it is immoral and wrong that

the top one-tenth of 1 percent in this country own almost 90 percent—almost—own almost as much wealth as the bottom 90 percent. That it is wrong, today, in a rigged economy, that 57 percent of all new income is going to the top 1 percent. That, when you look around the world, you see every other major country providing health care to all people as a right, except the United States. You see every other major country saying to moms that, when you have a baby, we're not gonna separate you from your newborn baby, because we are going to have—we are gonna have medical and family paid leave, like every other country on Earth. Those are some of the principles that I believe in, and I think we should look to countries like Denmark, like Sweden and Norway, and learn from what they have accomplished for their working people.

The hall erupted in applause when Sanders finished speaking. The Sanders campaign reported that their phones and computers lit up with small donations. In the few hours after Cooper pinned the dreaded socialist label on Sanders, the Sanders campaign received more than $3 million in small donations. Nothing like that had ever happened in the history of US presidential debates.

In the 2016 Democratic primary, Sanders won thirteen million votes and 80 percent of younger voters. Democratic National Committee emails released by Wikileaks showed that the Democratic Party establishment violated its own rules to get Clinton the nomination. Republican billionaire candidate Donald Trump beat Clinton by narrow margins in states that traditionally went for the Democrats—Michigan, Wisconsin, and Pennsylvania—thereby winning the presidency. Sanders was far more popular than Clinton in the Rust Belt areas that ultimately broke for Trump, suggesting that he would not have lost those states.

In 2020, history repeated itself with a few added twists. Bernie Sanders was on the verge of securing the Democratic nomination in the Super Tuesday primaries scheduled in fourteen states for March 4, 2020. Polls showed he would win enough delegates so that even the establishment's hand-picked superdelegates would be unable to deprive him of the nomination at the convention in July. On the eve of Super Tuesday, the panicked Democratic Party machine made an all-out, coordinated, last-minute intervention. It convinced a number of the other candidates to end their own campaigns and publicly throw their support to Joe

Biden, despite the fact that Biden was far behind Sanders in the polls and had placed badly in the earlier primary contests. With the establishment forces uniting behind Biden, Sanders won only four of the fourteen state primaries that day. Biden won the other ten. Sanders' prospects for the nomination were crushed once again.

Socialism is Our History—and Our Future!

The Bernie phenomenon was pathbreaking, even mind-blowing, because of the post-WWII witch hunt against socialists and communists. The truth of the matter is that Sanders is part of a long history of socialist politics in the US. Even here, in this capitalist country that seems so far removed from the anti-capitalist revolutionary struggles of most of the world's people, there has been a vital and active movement for socialism.

Before the Cold War-era assaults on communism and socialism, there were hundreds of daily and weekly socialist newspapers across the US. At various times between 1910 and 1916, socialists controlled the municipal governments in Schenectady, New York; Reading, Pennsylvania; Milwaukee, Wisconsin; Dayton and Toledo, Ohio; Granite City, Illinois; Butte, Montana; Berkeley, California, and numerous other cities. The largest state chapter of the one hundred thousand member-strong Socialist Party was in Oklahoma. Eugene Debs, the Socialist Party candidate for President, was sentenced to prison for ten years at hard labor at age sixty-five for giving a speech opposing US entrance into WWI. Debs ran the campaign from his prison cell and won nearly a million votes in the 1920 race.

Socialists were a powerful influence in the labor movement. At least one-third of delegates to the 1911 American Federation of Labor (AFL) convention were socialists by conviction or party membership, and socialists exerted a dominant influence in four of the largest affiliates of the AFL and two of the smaller ones. Outside the AFL, the Amalgamated Clothing Workers of America union, with a membership of 177,000 in 1920, promoted socialism among its members. Even members of the syndicalist Industrial Workers of the World, who expressed antipathy to conventional politics, could be counted on to vote socialist when and where they were eligible to do so.[13]

As noted at the outset of this chapter, some of the most influential people living in the United States were socialists and communists. Among the better known were: Martin Luther King Jr., Coretta Scott King, Paul Robeson, Albert Einstein, Helen Keller, James Baldwin, Lorraine Hansberry, Charlie Chaplin, A. Philip Randolph, Eugene Debs, W.E.B. DuBois,

Socialists in US History

Charlie Chaplin · Jesus Colón · Eugene Debs · W.E.B. DuBois

Albert Einstein · Lorraine Hansberry · Claudia Jones · Mother Jones

Helen Keller · Martin Luther King Jr. · Huey P. Newton · A. Philip Randolph

Paul Robeson · Assata Shakur · Emma Tenayuca · Philip Vera Cruz

Socialism has a rich and diverse history in the US—much of it has been hidden.

Ida B. Wells, John Reed, Huey P. Newton, Kwame Ture, and Bayard Rustin—to name a tiny handful.

Prior to WWII, communists and socialists played the leading role in southern states opposing segregation, lynching, apartheid, and all manifestations of the Jim Crow police state. These same forces led the fight for and won the passage of the Social Security Act in 1935; the establishment of the right to unemployment insurance for workers when they were laid off from their jobs; the right to form labor unions; the desegregation of federal facilities that had barred the participation of African American and Jewish people; the desegregation of Major League Baseball which had barred Black players until 1946; and the desegregation of the US armed forces in 1948.

At the end of WWII, the Communist Party in the US had approximately one hundred thousand members and probably a million active sympathizers. Communists and socialists led the Transport Workers Union of America, United Electrical Workers, International Longshore and Warehouse Union, the Fur and Leather Workers Union, and others. Some of the most famous and respected filmmakers, cultural figures, musicians, and artists during the same period were communists or socialists.

The US has a long socialist tradition extending back into the nineteenth century. Karl Marx died in 1883. He was a German living in exile in London. But the biggest memorial to Marx's contributions to the struggle of working people was not in Europe. It was in New York City where thousands came to Cooper Union to pay tribute.[14] In the middle of the 1800s, the US was the international center for the creation of "utopian socialist" communities. These experimental communities were built in Indiana, Ohio, New York, Iowa, Oregon, and Missouri. They were typically financed by wealthy individuals or progressive Christian groups that attributed society's ills to capitalism. Their "utopian" experiments introduced such notions as "full employment;" the creation of "kindergartens" for young children; "equal rights" for women; and equal pay for everyone living in the community. Ultimately, these "utopian" concepts migrated into public consciousness, changing people's ideas, and becoming accepted as rights.

The Fight to Stop Socialism

Sometimes the best way to measure the strength of an idea is by the ferocity of its opponents. By this measure, socialism is clearly resurgent: all the forces of the capitalist establishment are aligned against it. Just as the

Democratic establishment lined up to prevent Sanders from being nominated for president, so does the Republican Party explicitly orient itself toward defeating socialism. Trump's 2020 reelection campaign proves this point. Trump unofficially began his campaign in his 2019 State of the Union address. His central theme was not actually the state of the union but why he needed to be reelected: if he lost, the United States would become socialist. When Trump defiantly told the audience, "Tonight we renew our resolve that America will never be a socialist country," the members of Congress erupted in applause. Members of Congress jumped to their feet, chanting "USA, USA, USA, USA." And not just Republicans: Trump's supposed archenemies, congressional Democrats like Speaker of the House Nancy Pelosi and Senator Chuck Schumer, joined the ovation. By uttering the magic words, "we renew our resolve that America will never be a socialist country," Trump momentarily united the leaders of both ruling-class parties against their common enemy. They put aside their partisan bickering to genuflect at the altar of anti-socialism. In the current atmosphere of extreme political polarization, rare displays of congressional unity are reserved for pledging allegiance to the flag, massive annual funding for the ever-expanding military budget, spending a trillion dollars to build a new generation of nuclear weapons, maintaining 750 overseas military bases, condoning drone strikes in many countries—and fighting against socialism.

The members of 116th Congress who rose to applaud Trump's invocation against socialism are part of a monopolized political system. They are in one of the two acceptable ruling-class parties in a system devised to prevent any "third" party from effectively challenging their monopoly over political power at the federal or state level. Rather than representing the people or giving voice to new ideas, elections in the US are barriers to democracy. Serving the interests of banks, capitalists, and landowners, they have turned electoral politics into a farce where the best any working-class person can hope for is the lesser of two evils.

These fearsome fighters against socialism have a few other things in common. None of them are wage workers. None of them work in a factory or a mine. None of them are clerical workers. No one there works in retail. There are no janitors or waiters or home-health-care attendants or public-school teachers in Congress. No bus drivers or truck drivers. No taxi drivers. No one drives for Uber. Their job is being in Congress, a senator or representative. Not one of them is poor, living in poverty or near poverty. This is not just because their elected jobs are well paid (substantially better

The ruling class parties find common ground in the fight against their common enemy: the growing movement for socialism in the U S. (Photo: The White H ouse)

than the average worker). Most of the members of the 116th Congress are millionaires, and most of these congressional millionaires don't have a net worth of just $1 million either. They have many millions—tens of millions and even hundreds of millions of dollars. Congress is an elected body but it is not a representative body of most of the United States. Just 3 percent of US households have assets of a million dollars. More than half of US workers make under $35,000 per year, but not a single person from this category (the majority of the population) sits in Congress.[15] Congress is made up of the wealthy, and it represents the wealthy minority of the population. This helps explain their hostility to socialism—a system and a set of principles that puts a premium on human equality.

The millionaires club in the Senate passes itself off as the "world's *greatest* deliberative body." But it is and has always been an empowered body of plutocrats. It was created to block sweeping progressive legislation if the House of Representatives ever passed such laws. As Senator George F. Hoar stated, the very purpose of the Senate is to "resist the hasty, intemperate, passionate desire of the people."[16] This inconvenient truth made headlines when one frustrated member of the Senate expressed his disgust with the breakdown of negotiations over extending unemployment benefits to those who lost their jobs during the COVID-19 lockdowns. Senator Cory Booker complained, "I'm a little frustrated that a body dominated by millionaires—I'm not one of them—is going to focus on just a few hundred extra bucks and try to cut that out from under so many millions of American families."[17] In 2020, millionaire senators from both parties refused to increase the minimum wage a single penny. Under pressure from unions, the Biden White House suggested an increase to fifteen dollars an hour—*over the course of six years* rather than right away, which would be too radical. Millionaire senators from both parties crushed any increase. These super-wealthy plutocrats make decisions that determine the well-being of hundreds of millions of workers and their families.

It's not that hard to figure out why they are the enemies of socialism. They are tied to the capitalist class. That's their real constituency. The bankers and corporations oppose a social system identified with a production and income distribution model that levels the playing field. The wealth of the capitalists and superrich elites is derived from their connection to banks, corporations, and real estate companies, which will become public property under a socialist economic system. The surplus produced by publicly owned enterprises will no longer be a source of profits for wealthy individuals but will be a fund for ensuring the flourishing of people and the planet.

Congress is the enemy of *any* radical change in the system. It is an obstacle, not a vehicle for the transformation society so desperately needs. The Democrats and Republicans have constructed a system that makes it impossible for a nonruling-class third party to compete. We need a new system!

Toward a Third Reconstruction

The premise of this book is that socialism will replace capitalism in the United States. In fact, the United States of America—perhaps the most capitalist of all the capitalist countries—is ideally suited for the application of socialist economic methods and principles. But how will the socialist reconstruction begin? We don't know. We aren't fortune-tellers. What we do know is that revolutions happen—even in the United States. There are moments in history when people rise up against their governments and take power into their own hands.

We can distinguish between political and social revolutions. In political revolutions, governmental power is transferred from one group of people to another. Social revolutions are more profound, changing the fundamental class relations in a society. The English Revolution of 1640–1660 and the French Revolution of 1789 overturned the serfdom of feudal society. The Haitian Revolution of 1791 to 1804 abolished slavery. Enslaved people seized and held power, liberating their country from its colonial subjugation to the French ruling class. In the twentieth century the Russian, Chinese, and Cuban revolutions overturned the existing social class power. The capitalists and big landowners lost control over the factories and the land. The peasants received the land, and the factories were turned into public property; production was oriented away from private profit and toward economic development for public benefit.

The American Revolution was a political revolution, not a social revolution. The enslaved people who constituted the most important part of the working classes in 1776 were still enslaved in 1783. Plantation owners retained control over their lands and their enslaved workforce at the end of the revolutionary war. Some historians argue that the American Revolution was really waged to prevent the abolition of slavery in the thirteen colonies because Britain was embarked on a path of abolishing this evil institution.[18] The US Civil War was more like a real revolution, a social revolution, than the 1776 Revolution. The decisive military factor leading to the defeat of the Confederacy was the belated Emancipation Proclamation signed by President Abraham Lincoln in January 1863 and the subsequent flood of 200,000 free Black people into the northern Army and Navy. The North finally won when the conflict became an armed revolutionary struggle of the Black working class in the southern states. Formerly enslaved people became free people, recognized as citizens with formal rights associated with citizenship and no longer the property of others.

The Reconstruction era (1865–1876) was an attempt to complete the social revolution that ended slavery. But it was defeated by the forces of counterrevolution. During Reconstruction, formerly enslaved Black people were promised land, resources, and political empowerment. None of that would have compensated for 250 years of unpaid labor, but even these promises were broken and drowned in blood.[19] Reconstruction governments in the southern states were initiated but targeted by terrorist violence from the Ku Klux Klan, which had been organized by the defeated slave-owning capitalists. By 1876, different factions of the warring capitalists from the South and the North—overcame their differences, reunited, and reempowered the class of former slave owners at the expense of the rights and aspirations of the formerly enslaved Black people. This was the postwar counterrevolution that made Jim Crow apartheid the law of the land.

In the 1950s and 1960s, many in the civil rights movement saw their new movement as the Second Reconstruction. The political and social achievements of that movement certainly helped reshape the US. Nevertheless, the civil rights movement did not alter the basic class structures in society. It ended apartheid laws, but the predominantly white capitalist ruling class retained control over the banks, corporations, land, and media. Factories belonged to the capitalists, not to the workers who performed the labor that allowed the factories to produce products. Social revolution remains on the historical agenda.

The unfulfilled promises of the First and Second Reconstructions are glaring and persistent injustices in contemporary society. Throughout US history it has been the struggle of the African American people that has been a catalyst for mass movements, radical upheavals, and the expansion of core democratic rights for women, workers, the elderly, and the poor from all sectors of US society.

The Third Reconstruction is premised on socialist control and redistribution of the vast wealth and resources created by the labor of the multinational, multiracial, and multiethnic US working class. Central to its success will be overcoming the centuries of the superexploitation and oppression of the Black working class. The immense fortunes of the capitalist banks and corporations were cemented by the enslavement of a huge part of the US working class and the imposition of a centuries-long system of legal and extra-legal apartheid and enforced segregation. The First Reconstruction promised forty acres of farmable land and a mule to those who had labored but had never been paid. That promise was broken. The Second Reconstruction made only a political promise of equality under the law. The Third Reconstruction, because it will be socialist reconstruction, will finally guarantee both the full economic and political rights for all—with a focus on redressing and overcoming the centuries of super-oppression imposed on Black Americans.

Revolutions don't happen simply because the prevailing system is unjust. They don't occur because society is divided between a minority of elites and a majority whose suffering is getting worse by the day. Revolutions happen when society enters into multiple, cascading, and overlapping crises that the existing power structure is unable or unwilling to solve. Faced with a ruling class unable to continue in the old way, a significant part of the population enters into active politics. The intervention of the people leads to sudden shifts in mass consciousness. Parts of the population that were previously apolitical, and even conservative, enter the fray on the side of progress. State-sponsored repression fails to break them. On the contrary, it makes them more determined and less afraid. The people feel their power, taking the world stage to create a new society.

We are entering a stage in the historical process that will lead to a revolutionary transformation. The last four decades of generally unchecked capitalist expansion have produced a set of systemic existential crises: pending climate catastrophe, great power conflict and the likelihood of major war, and massive automation and job destruction. The US capitalist ruling class and the political system that keeps it in power are unable and unwilling to address the cascading failures rupturing society and threatening the planet. We don't know exactly how this revolutionary transformation will be set in motion. We can't predict which series of events will become the tipping point: mass evictions and homelessness; widespread uprisings against police murder; increasing numbers of infections in a deadly pandemic; food shortages due to droughts, fires, and floods; or frequent and ongoing power and internet outages could all ignite the fire of revolution. What we do know is that what might seem unlikely—and to some impossible—will appear inevitable.

This book sets out a vision for society after the revolution. Socialist reconstruction will solve the problems capitalism creates, ending production for the sake of private profit and replacing it with production based on meeting the needs of people and the planet. Reversing climate damage and moving to a zero-carbon emission economy will proceed at full speed. Redressing centuries of exploitation and oppression will establish an enduring basis for liberation and equality. Revoking the imperialist policies through which the US dominates, destroys, and de-develops countries all over the world will bring an end, finally, to war and threats of war. We don't know exactly when revolution will erupt, but we do know that a socialist system has to be ushered in when it does, because only through socialism will people and the planet flourish.

CHAPTER 2

THE SOCIALIST GOVERNMENT: THE FORM AND FUNCTION OF A NEW DEMOCRACY

A foundational step in the socialist reconstruction of the United States is the creation of a new constitution. This new constitution will differ profoundly from that of the current capitalist state. Socialism revolutionizes the *form* and *function* of government, making it truly democratic for the first time.

Socialism revolutionizes the *form* of government because political power is in the hands of the working class. For the first eighty-seven years of the United States' existence as an independent nation, the slave-owning class dominated governmental power. After 1865, industrial capitalists and Wall Street bankers held it. With the socialist revolution, the working class will control the government and the state. For the first time, majority rule will not be a deceptive slogan masking domination by a clique of capitalist exploiters—majority rule will be real.

Socialism revolutionizes the *function* of government because government's purpose is no longer the preservation of private property and minority power. The central functions of socialist government are 1) meeting the needs of people and the planet and 2) reorganizing the economy to end exploitation in all its forms—the exact opposite of the capitalist or bourgeois government.

These two functions of socialist government are deeply interconnected: meeting the needs of people and the planet and ending exploitation in all its forms require ending reliance on fossil fuels, wage slavery, and market domination. They require as well, and most importantly, the full political participation of all of society in the management of common affairs.

Fulfilling these two core functions thus necessitates a change in the form of government. A society of producers requires a form of political association through which everyone participates. Under capitalism, the productive process involves all of society, but decision-making is controlled by a tiny layer of owners and their political operatives. For a new society, just as production is social, so must government also be social, a matter of the combined efforts of everyone. The affairs of society are too important to be delegated to professional politicians and career specialists and administrators.

Accordingly, under the socialist form of government all positions of political and judicial authority will be based on the elective principle and subject to immediate recall. Holding elected office in any legislative body will not be a full-time job. Professional politicians will be dissolved as a category. Legislators at the federal, state, and local level will earn their primary income from their "regular" jobs. Lifetime judicial appointments will be abolished. Government officials and civil servants at the federal, regional, and municipal levels will be paid the equivalent of the average salary of a skilled worker. Serving in elected office will be carried out by those who are willing to embrace additional responsibilities. Holding office in an elected position will not be a perk or privilege but rather an expression of sacrifice for the greater good.

Socialist democracy, unlike the current republican form of government, will not reduce the role of the citizenry to voting every two or four years for politicians who will supposedly represent them. On the contrary, people will be empowered and integrated into the management of the day-to-day affairs of society. Constitutional and legal recognition of voluntary mass organizations such as unions, tenant organizations, cooperatives, and youth groups is the form of this empowerment.

Building from the form and function of socialist government, this chapter draws out the limits built into the current form of government in the US. We show how those limits protect the rich and prevent anything close to real democracy. This chapter also points to fundamental changes that socialist government can and will bring about to guarantee a better future for all, especially for all who have been historically exploited and oppressed and are entitled to reparations, respect, and a role in shaping their workplaces and communities and all of our common world.

The first step after a successful working-class revolution will be the drafting and adoption of a new constitution. Every major revolution in history has produced a new constitution to reflect the aspirations and gains of that revolution. The successful revolution of the working class in the United States will be no different, producing a constitution to enshrine the expanded rights of the people.

Whatever grassroots political forms are utilized for the drafting, debating and adopting the new constitution—whether it be via constitutional conventions or popular constituent assemblies—this process will unleash the collective creativity of the diverse multinational working class, and it will be far more democratic and participatory than our current system. Thirty-seven million people in the United States lived below the official poverty line in 2020, which is itself a ridiculously inaccurate way to gauge actual poverty; by official measures, someone who made more than $12,760 was considered "not in poverty." A more accurate figure is that 50 percent of the population live either in poverty or near poverty. But not one member of Congress or the judiciary fits into this category. For the working class, the present "democracy" is completely hollow. By contrast, working-class, low-income, and poor people will be guaranteed representation in all the bodies convened for the purpose of drafting and adopting the new constitution, as will young people and communities long denied a voice in the political system.

A New Role for Government

People in the United States are told that they live in the world's greatest democracy. Many believe it. At the same time, they consistently tell pollsters and each other that they actually despise the government. The approval rating for Congress hasn't hit 30 percent in more than a decade. Disapproval of the job Congress is doing normally hovers around the 80 percent mark. This is the state of the legislative branch created by the US Constitution and often held up as a model for "democracy."

To get a sense of the revolutionary change in the form of democracy that socialist government brings about, it helps to contrast it with the core functions of a capitalist government.

The US Constitution establishes the basic form and functions of the US government. Adopted in 1787, the Constitution was amended in 1791 to include the Bill of Rights (the first ten amendments to the Constitution). These rights constrain governmental authority and guarantee certain liberties to the people. Later amendments abolished slavery (except for prisoners), gave women the right to vote, and expanded other democratic rights. At the time the Constitution was adopted, most of the population was prohibited from holding office or even voting. Only white men who owned property could vote until 1828—forty-one years after the adoption of the Constitution. Twelve of the first fifteen presidents owned slaves. Enslaved people—adults and children alike—worked the plantations, making the men who became president rich, well connected, and politically powerful.

Under the US federalist system, the most basic rights and policies vary based on where you live—from abortion access to COVID-19 responses—with conflicting laws and regulations subject to a web of local, state, and federal agencies and courts. (Photo: Liberation News)

The US Constitution sets out a system of government with three branches: the legislative, executive, and judiciary. The legislative branch consists of the two houses of Congress, the Senate and the House of Representatives. The executive branch consists of the president and vice president. The judiciary consists of the Supreme Court and underlying inferior courts. This system upholds the preeminence of private property for those who own capital, regulates commercial trade between the states, and gives Congress the authority to tax the people and to raise an army. More important is what the Constitution does not do: it does not create any social or economic obligations of the government to the people or to society. The federal government can regulate interstate trade, impose taxes, raise an army, and declare war against other nations, but it does not direct, guide, or manage the economy. This means that the Constitution leaves such fundamental matters as food, health, and housing up to the market, that is to say, in the hands of the class of property owners, capitalists, financiers, and landlords.

A socialist government plays a fundamentally different role in society. Recognizing that the collective and social nature of production means that workers should collectively manage society, the socialist constitution establishes a new form of political association. It does so by fulfilling the

28

government's obligation to meet basic needs and by securing mass participation in governance, the economy, and other vital areas of social life.

The Class Character of the Socialist Government

The current US government conceals its bourgeois class character under deceptive labels and its self-branding as a government "of, by and for the people." The new socialist government will openly proclaim that it is a worker's government. All legislative bodies and all governmental agencies and institutions will exercise the political supremacy of the working class for the benefit of people and the planet.

V.I. Lenin highlighted the class oppression at the heart of bourgeois democracy with the term "dictatorship of the bourgeoisie." By calling it a dictatorship, he drew attention to the way that the government was designed to serve the interests of a numerically tiny exploiting minority class. From the legislative, through the executive, to the courts, every institution of bourgeois democracy protects the capitalist system and the capitalist class. The capitalists' central need is to exploit human labor and the Earth's resources in order to accumulate profit. In fact, the exploitation of human labor and nature are the two component sources of capitalist profits. At federal, state, and municipal levels, the current system of government treats exploitation as capital's inviolable right.

In contrast, the socialist government will eliminate the power of big capital and its regime of exploitation by putting under the people's control all the big corporations and productive enterprises. The five hundred biggest companies currently constitute two-thirds of the country's gross domestic product. While expanding rights to free speech, to assemble to redress grievances, and to practice the religion of one's choosing, the socialist constitution will prohibit political parties from advocating for a return to a system based on economic exploitation. Just as serfdom and slavery were banned in earlier epochs, so will socialist reconstruction prevent the return of capitalist rule. Overturning the rule of capitalism will likely include converting many small enterprises into cooperatives; it will not require the nationalization of very small farms and businesses that employ a handful of workers.

A National Unitary System Based on Mass Participation

The new socialist government will transform the words "a government of, by and for the people" from a meaningless platitude into an operational reality. Rather than ceding authority to professional politicians, technical experts, and specialists, it will draw a large part of the population into the affairs of the state and society. At the same time, it will embrace central planning, eliminate market tyranny and wage slavery, and redress centuries of historical wrongs. Centralism will be combined with a widening and expansive grassroots democracy. The masses of people who have been sidelined and excluded will be brought into the governmental apparatus and decision-making process. Centralism and grassroots democracy might seem to be polar opposites. But both are needed if we are to produce the goods and services society requires on an environmentally sustainable basis.

The point of a socialist government is to serve society, to serve the people. But socialist government will not be a system of handouts; it won't treat people as passive recipients of benefits and entitlements. On the contrary, it will actively integrate people into all the "affairs of state." People collectively will engage in meeting the multiple challenges facing contemporary society. Given the looming climate catastrophe, the foremost task before us is the wholesale reconstruction of industrial and agricultural production, housing, transportation, and work. The new socialist government will address the challenge of climate change by democratizing society and democratizing society by addressing climate change.

The existential challenges confronting contemporary society cannot be met piecemeal. They demand centralized economic and social planning on a national scale, the application of the very latest scientific and technological advances, and the mobilization and integration of millions of people into the active management of society. Although socialist society does not cede authority to technical experts and specialists, it values their knowledge, putting it to work in coordination with large-scale, voluntary, mass organizations. The new constitution will mandate that the actions of government agencies be coordinated with mass organizations of labor, women, youth, and others rooted in workplaces, neighborhoods, and schools. These national mass organizations will be designed to serve the people and integrate their members as active participants in political and social life.

More specifically, the socialist form of government will combine a unitary centralized national state empowered to act decisively and with directed purpose over the entire territory of the country with voluntary mass organizations designed to actively involve tens of millions of citizens. This national unitary state will replace the current, fragmented, federalist system. The socialist government will have the same power to act in all parts of the country with respect to matters that are vital to the collective.

The climate crisis, which knows no state borders, shows the need for a united government response. (Photo: Mike McMillan/USFS)

These matters include environmental protection, public-health policy, and the guarantees of social and economic rights. No state will be able to deny any person their basic rights or undermine vitally important national initiatives (such as those addressing climate change).

The Problems with Federalism

It is worth dwelling on the reasons for replacing a federal system of government with a centralist one.

The so-called Founding Fathers were a tiny handful of capitalists and landowners who created a form of government that secured their narrow and so-called inalienable rights to secure and profit from their private ownership of land, enslaved people, and commercial capitalist enterprises. They designed a form of government that was a limited, tortured form of democracy, a form of democracy that only existed to protect their political supremacy in "their territory" and for "their commercial enterprise."

The federal system they designed makes it impossible for us to deal with the existential crisis we face today: a looming global climate catastrophe that threatens the existence of humans and other living things. This system even prevents us from responding to the extreme weather events and rising sea levels that are happening right now. A wildfire that starts in California can make it hard to breathe in Oregon and Nevada. Smoke and soot don't take state boundaries into account. Michigan approved a nuclear power plant on the shores of Lake Superior. If this plant—built by capitalists prioritizing the money in their pockets—melts down, the released radioactive waste can contaminate the Great Lakes, which contain 25 percent of the planet's fresh-water supply. The catastrophic impact extends far beyond the boundaries of Michigan.

The federal system also blocks the kind of collective and public-minded action necessary for confronting pandemics. COVID-19 is the latest but certainly not the last pandemic. As the whole world knows, COVID-19 casualties in the United States are the highest in the world. Each state—and even different cities and towns in a given state—adopted its own rules, regulations, and health policy protocols in response to a virus that infects you whether you live in Texas, New York, or anywhere else in the country. The federal system wastes state resources—which are produced through the labor of working people; it uses them ineffectively and at counter purpose to the cascading, multiple crises.

Most of us think of people in the US as sharing the same set of constitutionally guaranteed rights. The problem with the federal system is that it creates a patchwork of rights. The state you live in has a big impact on the rights you have. A woman living in New York State can schedule an abortion any time during her pregnancy at any one of hundreds of medical facilities. As of early 2022, a woman living in Texas has just six weeks after conception to schedule an abortion—and many women don't know they're pregnant for months! Although the laws are changing rapidly as Republican legislatures wage war on women's reproductive freedom, in approximately thirty states, women must receive state-directed counseling designed to discourage abortion before their procedure. Twenty-six states require an additional waiting period before the procedure, typically twenty-four hours, which requires a second trip to the facility. To top off this nightmare, in June 2022, the unelected US Supreme Court overturned *Roe v. Wade*, eviscerating abortion rights and freeing states to further their attacks on reproduction and sexual freedom.

Workers' rights are another example of how the federal system is a weapon designed to limit democracy and democratic rights. If a worker gets laid off from their job in Montana, they can receive up to $552 as a weekly benefit and collect unemployment benefits for twenty-eight weeks. But if a worker gets laid off in Florida, they can receive no more than $275 per week and their benefits run out after just twelve weeks. Likewise, each state provides different benefits, requirements, and rights when it comes to health-care access for low-income workers and their families.

The Affordable Care Act (ACA), or Obamacare, expanded eligibility for Medicaid (the government-paid health-care insurance available to very poor people). The expansion meant that people who made up to 138 percent of the federal poverty level could receive government-paid health-care services. In 2010 (before Obamacare), the federal poverty level for a single person was defined as $10,830. This meant that if you made $11,000 per year you weren't officially poor and so too rich to qualify for Medicaid. Obamacare tried to change that by expanding Medicaid eligibility so that more people would qualify. Individuals with income up to $14,484 and families of four with income up to $29,726 would receive Medicaid coverage. But in 2012, the Supreme Court ruled that states could opt out of the Medicaid expansion even though the federal government was paying 90 percent of any additional cost. Ten years later—and even while those states were being ravaged by COVID-19—there were still twelve state legislatures that wouldn't permit the Medicaid expansion for the poor people in their state. Those twelve states are some of the biggest in the country. Texas, Florida, and Georgia—three of the twelve—are the second-, third-, and eighth-most populous states in the country with an aggregate population of over sixty million people. Texas, Florida, and Georgia are also the top three states of residence for the Black population in the US—constituting nearly 25 percent of the African American population.

As devastating as the federalist system is for the social, economic, and political rights of hundreds of millions of people in the US, it has also been a primary driver of the corporate capitalist destruction of the environment, pollution, and environmental racism. For example, on August 1, 2020, a law took effect in Louisiana barring locally elected governments from banning or interfering with natural gas utility services. At the time the law went into effect, no local city council or any other local governing body in Louisiana had ever taken such an action. Soon thereafter, Oklahoma, Tennessee, and Arizona adopted similar measures. Why did these states pass these laws? Because capitalist oil and gas corporations exert a lot of power in those states. The capitalists were scared that they risked losing profit. And why were they scared? Because the city council in Berkeley, California had voted to make their city the first in the nation to ban natural gas hookups in new buildings. The Berkeley City Council knew that natural gas, especially methane, exerts potent heating effects in the atmosphere and has to be phased out in order to prevent catastrophic global heating. The capitalist fossil fuel corporations responded to the actions of one city council in a distant state by manipulating lawmakers in other states to pass laws expressly designed to prevent necessary action on climate change. The federal system benefits big oil and gas while harming people and the planet. The effects of the necessary actions taken by some local governments are canceled out by states that do the bidding of their fossil fuel overlords. This is a road to ruin.

Ending the use of fossil fuels is the key to survival of humans and other species. It requires urgent action. It also requires full spectrum planning so that the transfer to other energy sources can happen quickly and effectively, as we set out in chapter 3. Only nationwide planning and large-scale reconstruction of the entire economic system can mitigate the economic disruption energy conversion will cause. This has far-reaching consequences for supply chains, methods of production and distribution of industrially produced goods, agricultural production, travel in and between cities and towns, and myriad other areas of economic and social life. Because the federal system prevents adequate, necessary, and centralized action, it has to be abolished and replaced. The supposed benefits of federalism—local empowerment and the protection of "minority rights"—are a sham and in fact can be more substantively fulfilled in a new socialist government, as we describe below.

The Form of Socialist Government

Although we know that the socialist government must be centralized rather than federated, we cannot—and would not want to—determine in advance its precise institutional structure. After all, the governmental structure of the United States evolved over two hundred years. It has not been set in stone but changed and amended over time, sometimes as a result of engaged popular struggle. New political forms will emerge in the struggle for socialism as people respond to expected and unexpected challenges. So we cannot establish the exact form the new socialist government will take, but we can identify its core functions: securing basic political, social, and economic rights for all; managing the economy with an eye to mitigating the climate catastrophe; and guaranteeing the flourishing of people and the planet. These core functions can't be achieved through the form of government we've inherited from capitalism, as our discussion of the problems of federalism demonstrates. We thus encounter the dilemma of needing a new form but not being able to say exactly what it will be. The actual form the socialist government will take has to be determined through the application of revolutionary and democratic processes at the start of the socialist project. In full recognition of the fact that revolutionary struggle will itself produce new governmental forms, we offer here a sketch of what such a socialist form might include. We don't include all the familiar features of bourgeois constitutions, such as the judiciary and a presidency, which will be worked out at a constituent assembly, the body that will write the new constitution. We base this sketch on the functions and presuppositions of socialist government.

Rational Administrative Units

The new socialist government will be more socially, demographically and geographically representative of the population than the current one. More than 80 percent of the US population live in urban areas. But urban populations are widely underrepresented in federal and state bodies. Urban representation is undemocratically diminished in proportion to less populated rural and small-town areas in the way the president, US Senate, House of Representatives, and state legislatures are chosen.

When citizens vote for the president of the United States, they are actually choosing electors who will cast votes in the Electoral College. The Electoral College significantly underrepresents the areas where the bulk of the population lives. It follows that we have to abolish the Electoral College. We likewise have to abolish the Senate. Four states—California, Texas, Florida, and New York—have a combined population of more than 110 million people. Together they elect eight members of the US Senate. Another four states—Wyoming, Vermont, Alaska, and North Dakota—have a total population of 2.8 million people. Those four states also have a total of eight seats in the US Senate. That is obviously not equal representation. Basic democracy entails that the form of socialist government is not compatible with the continued existence of the Senate.

Neither is socialist government compatible with the antiquated divisions of states, counties, and municipalities. Large urban areas have vastly different needs than smaller cities and towns. New York State has a population of 19.5 million people; nearly half of them—8.5 million—live in New York City. The issues facing New York City residents differ significantly from those in western or upstate New York. But the votes of New York City's representatives in the state assembly are essentially canceled out by the votes of those who come from smaller areas with their own distinct issues and needs. The current federalist form of government that was created more than two centuries ago—when the majority of the population earned its income from agriculture—is clearly unsuited to be a democratic form. Why should New York or any state be a distinct unit of governance?

The new socialist government will reflect modern realities. More and more people are moving into urban areas, but the antiquated form of government disempowers them relative to the much smaller non-urban population.[20] Instead of fragmented into separate states, New York City, Newark, Jersey City, and parts of Connecticut—with a combined population of twenty million people—may be grouped into an administrative unit equivalent to what is now a state. Similar reorganizations throughout the country will lay the administrative groundwork for a rational and representative socialist government. Local government jurisdictions that unnecessarily divide large, contiguous, urban metropolitan regions with artificial and outdated city limits will also be replaced. Again, New York City and parts of nearby New Jersey and Connecticut are a good example insofar as they clearly constitute a recognized urban regional area. In the interests of furthering democracy and facilitating planning, socialist reconstruction will institute more rational administrative units.

National Representative Assemblies

Socialist government has to ensure that decisions impacting the entire country are taken and overseen by bodies with representation from the entire country. To this end, we envision a central socialist government that, like the current US government, also has two chambers. For legislation to become law it will need to pass both chambers. Unlike the current government, the socialist one will be designed to be truly representative.

The first chamber will be the National People's Assembly. Conforming loosely to the current House of Representatives, the National People's Assembly will consist of delegates elected from local election districts and from mass organizations representing various sectors in society—labor unions, women's organization, youth, etc. It will need to be numerically much larger than the current 435-member House of Representatives in order to guarantee adequate representation from all urban regions, smaller towns, and rural areas. Currently, there is about one representative in Congress for every 750,000 citizens in the country. This an absurdly small number for a democracy. For instance, in Cuba there is one member of parliament for every twenty thousand citizens. In addition to expanding the number of representatives, socialist reconstruction will establish guidelines guaranteeing the working-class character of the National People's Assembly and requiring women make up at least half of the elected delegates. The redrawn administrative units discussed in the preceding section will ensure that the National People's Assembly is representative of the multinational working class. No longer will the 83 percent of the country who live in urban areas be dominated by the interests of those living in low-populated, primarily white districts. None of the delegates will be full-time politicians.

The second chamber will be the Assembly of Oppressed Nations. The Assembly of Oppressed Nations will replace the US Senate—the US version of Britain's House of Lords. For the last 440 years, the US capitalist class has secured its wealth and domination over society by the theft of the lands of the Indigenous peoples and nations of North America and by the enslavement and subsequent super-oppression and exploitation of African Americans. Institutions of racism were constructed to enforce this system and ensure the ongoing disenfranchisement and marginalization of tens of millions of people. To correct this historic injustice and to guarantee the full unity of the working class on the basis of genuine equality, the Assembly of Oppressed Nations will function as a second chamber. It will consist of delegates from oppressed nationalities and peoples. To become law, proposed legislation will need to secure a majority vote in both the National People's Assembly and the Assembly of Oppressed Nations.

Regional and local affairs will be managed by either a Regional People's Assembly, for larger urbanized regions, or a Local People's Assembly for smaller cities, towns, and rural areas. Unlike the undemocratic and ineffective federal system, in the centralized socialist system laws will be universally applied throughout the country.

Collective Executive Power

Currently the US Congress has the ability to pass laws, levy and raise taxes, approve a federal budget, declare war, approve judicial nominees for the federal courts, and impeach the president and federal judges. Before it becomes law, every resolution requires passage in both the Senate and the House of Representatives and then must be signed by the president. In addition to serving as head of state and commander in chief of the armed forces, the president is responsible for implementing the laws written by Congress and appointing the heads of the fifteen different federal agencies that execute government policies in different areas.

As capitalism has transformed into monopoly capitalism over the past century, the executive branch has accrued substantially more power at the expense of the legislative branch. This growing centralized power in the executive branch corresponds to the centralism in the economy whereby a handful of megacorporations and banks exert overwhelming control. In fact, the most important agencies in the executive branch are organized to serve the interests of capitalist-owned corporations. The Departments of Treasury and Commerce serve the banks and biggest corporations. The Department of Agriculture is the servant of the enormous conglomerates of agribusiness. The Department of Defense is basically a mechanism for handing $750 billion every year to the capitalist weapons manufacturers. The socialist government will break the capitalist class's hold on government by nationalizing the corporations. Government will exist not to enrich the few but to serve the people—to meet the needs of the working class and to protect the environment and mitigate the damage to the planet wrought by climate change.

The new constitution will identify the socialist government's legally binding obligations to society and to every individual: to maintain an environmentally sustainable economic system that ends reliance on fossil fuels; to abolish economic exploitation and wage slavery; and to guarantee free or affordable housing, health care, lifetime education, child care, access to participatory sports and other physical activities, regular and free access to cultural and art activities, and meaningful work of different forms. A new set of central government agencies will manage the institutions and enterprises necessary for meeting these obligations. Every agency will be supplemented by national, regional, and local mass organizations. Instead of delegating executive actions to professional civil servants, tens of millions of volunteers will be mobilized to intervene directly into the affairs of society.

Specific examples help depict what this collective arrangement of executive power will look like. Consider banking (explored in more detail in chapter 4). The new socialist government will take possession of all the existing capitalist banks and create one People's Development Bank. The People's Development Bank will exist as a public utility charged with assessing and administering the financial resources necessary for national-level projects. One of its immediate tasks will be directing credit and investment as part of a nationwide economic plan for socialist reconstruction on the basis of ending the use of fossil fuels and transitioning to renewable energy. Another example is the Central Economic Agency. The Central Economic Agency is the administrative body that will exercise oversight over all the newly nationalized, formerly capitalist, core enterprises for the purpose of economic planning. It will establish an Executive Authority that is responsible for establishing five-year, ten-year, and twenty-year national economic plans designed to meet the needs of society while ending the use of fossil fuels. A third example is the People's Health Administration (described in chapter 7). The People's Health Administration will operate all hospitals, medical facilities, pharmaceutical companies, and medical equipment manufacturers in accordance with the constitutional requirement of providing free health care for every person. Private health-care insurance companies will be dissolved. Similar central agencies will be responsible for housing, transportation, agriculture, education, culture, international affairs, and public safety. What is crucial is that a mass organization that enlists large numbers of the citizenry on a volunteer basis will accompany every major federal, regional, and local agency, as subsequent chapters make clear. These mass organizations will have legal status for input, decision making, and implementation of government policy.

The mass organizations are the most vital element of socialist governance. In a sense, the executive power of socialist society is in the people's hands; we carry out the decisions that we make. Without organization, the power of the people is lost. Real democracy requires full participation in making and implementing the decisions that affect everyone's lives.

One hundred and forty million people go to work every day in the US. For a big part of the working class, about half our waking hours are spent on the job during five or six of each seven days. But in today's capitalist society almost all decisions in the workplace are made by employers and the managers they hire. Even though unions have no say in what is produced and how it's distributed, they at least give employees a seat at the table when it comes to decisions about wages, benefits, and working conditions. But only 6 percent of US workers are organized into labor unions. It used to be higher, but the anti-union offensive of the capitalists since the 1970's has reduced the percentage of unionized workplaces. Thus, most workplaces operate as a dictatorship of the employers. Whether someone is even able to keep their job is a decision left to the employer.

The constitution forming the new socialist government will include a provision that every workplace be unionized so workers have a direct say in how work is organized, and to provide protection for workers' rights in the event of mismanagement or abuse on the job. Core decisions regarding how work is organized can only be taken after consultation and consent from the union. Unions will become mass organizations representing and including workers from every workplace in the country. This will enable them to serve as powerful forces for grassroots organizing.

All the major enterprises will be publicly owned. They will belong to the people, to the working class. The government will hold title to the enterprise, but the employees will be directly involved in all the relevant decisions. Our direct involvement will help guarantee that labor is organized to fulfill the needs and socialist obligations of government as outlined by the constitution.

Additionally, the inclusion of workers in workplace management will increase the capacity of government agencies to meet the challenges that arise at local, regional, and national levels.

We have focused on unions, but mass organizations of any sort that contribute to the development of socialist consciousness and environmental and collective well-being will be encouraged. Sports and cultural clubs, women's, LGBTQ, and youth groups, historical societies, and neighborhood and environmental associations are just a few of the various kinds of mass organizations that will be provided material support.

The Central Role of Mass Organizations

The socialist reconstruction of society will require the mobilization of great masses of people. While the exact form of socialist government cannot be determined prior to a constitutional convention, we know for certain that it must be anchored in an immense expansion of democracy and participation. This is especially true given the existential crisis of climate change. Mass organizations of the people—especially at the local level—will be key to meeting the needs of people and the planet in the face of extreme weather events, global health emergencies, and similar such disasters.

No currently existing government is "the model" for the best way of involving masses of people in problem solving. Nevertheless, there are lessons from those that exist now. One of the most important is how China managed the COVID-19 pandemic. The Chinese success with the coronavirus pandemic was not the government's alone. The voluntary, mass organizations of the people were essential.

China, with a population four times the size of the US, had fewer than five thousand COVID-19 deaths at the time of this writing. In contrast, the death toll in the US was over eight hundred thousand as of January 2022. China is still a poor country compared to the United States. Why did China's system of governance succeed while the US failed so miserably? The answer is that in China the central government called on governmental institutions and civil society to wage war against the coronavirus. Not only government institutions like the health ministry, but all of civil society including mass organizations of young people, business groups, and others swung into action.

Because the mass organization model is unfamiliar to people in the United States and because China has been so demonized in the US media, many think a positive description of anything coming from China should be dismissed as "pro-China propaganda." This is important context for reading the Washington, DC-based Brookings Institution's description of how the Chinese people managed COVID-19:

> One of the first item [sic] of order was mobilizing teams of medical personnel, including doctors, nurses, and community leaders, who became frontline foot soldiers. The first batch of emergency medical teams arrived in the embattled city [Wuhan] just one day after the lockdown started on January 24. Also that day, the National Health Commission dispatched teams from multiple hospitals in Guangdong, which each had temporary branches of the Communist Party embedded in them. Shortly afterwards, the Communist Youth League of Wuhan issued a public notice online and recruited over 7,000 volunteers in less than 12 hours. Donning red vests and matching armbands . . . volunteers got to work in neighborhoods and communities, delivering groceries and essential supplies. These volunteers often worked in concert with the state-led neighborhood committees and community grid management teams to knock on residents' doors, checking each person's temperature, registering returnees from Hubei province, and handing out educational pamphlets. These were the most visible of "volunteers" at the grassroots level.[21]

Wuhan, a city of twelve million people, was locked down on January 23, 2020. No one lost their job. No one was evicted from their home. Government institutions and mass organizations of the people provided the necessary logistical support. Everyone who was quarantined received food deliveries to their home from volunteers from the mass organizations. Health-care professionals and volunteers went to the home of every family to check on them. This system succeeded. On April 8, 2020 the Wuhan lockdown was lifted. The Associated Press reported, "Residents celebrate their freedom after 76 days with riverside parties while the city puts on a sound-and-light show emphasizing its resilience and the courage and sacrifice of first responders."

Of course, the new socialist form of government in the United States will be based on what is needed in this country—and how we choose to relate to the rest of humanity. The US differs from other countries in many ways. But we can learn from others as well as from the study of our own conditions and circumstances. China is still a poor country—it is much poorer than the US—although it is a rapidly developing country. China has many defects as well as positive attributes. The point is not to make China or any country "the model" for the US or the rest of the world. But we, the people in the US, need to learn from the experiences of other countries. Health care is free in many parts of the world. Child care is free or affordable in other advanced industrial economies. Vacations elsewhere are much longer than they are here. Women have full access to abortion rights in a number of other countries. Education at the university level is free in a number of countries. Many of these important advances have even taken place in countries that still have capitalist-dominated economies and governments.

The new socialist government needs to be based on the accumulated experiences from inside and outside the United States. We can't predict and won't prescribe every aspect of the new form of socialist government. But we premise our proposal on a vision of a new, more inclusive democracy that vastly expands the integration of millions of people into the day-to-day management of the affairs of society. That is the key.

The new socialist constitution will legally empower many mass organizations of the people. This is essential to democracy and effective governance. Instead of acting as spectators while a handful of career politicians, professional administrators, and governmental staffs and specialists make all the decisions, a socialist government will draw in millions of citizens to initiate, manage and maintain all the myriad affairs of state and society.

CHAPTER 3

AN ENERGY FUTURE FOR PEOPLE AND THE PLANET

*T*he climate crisis is here. From record heat waves and raging fires to intensified hurricanes, blizzards, droughts, and floods, the catastrophic impact of global warming on land, air, and water disrupts the basic conditions of life for all the Earth's species. Capitalism can't provide a solution to the climate crisis because capitalism is the crisis: capitalist production always and necessarily places profit over people and the planet.

Capitalism can't provide a solution to the climate crisis because capitalism is the crisis: capitalist production always and necessarily places profit over people and the planet.

Capitalism has a contradictory attitude toward climate change. On the one hand, it acts as if the environment is outside its control. Driven to accumulate, capitalism pretends that markets provide the mechanisms for dealing with the climate catastrophe, when markets are really a way of redistributing negative effects of global heating onto racialized and colonized people. On the other hand, capitalism puts forward dangerous, experimental, high-tech geoengineering solutions like spraying sulfur dioxide into the stratosphere to create sulfuric acid clouds to reflect solar radiation. Maintaining the imperialist world order and the capitalist system, that is, making sure that the billionaire class and most privileged sectors of society don't have to change how they produce and consume energy, is prioritized over the risk of even more extreme and unpredictable ecological damage. This chapter demonstrates how a socialist reconstruction of energy—in response to the climate crisis and in contrast to capitalism's contradictions—lays the basis for redressing histories of exploitation, colonialism, extractivism, and imperialism. We can regenerate damaged environments and develop new knowledge, skills, and capacities for cooperation and collectivity.

As we note in the introduction, Karl Marx describes the Paris Commune as the political form through which the working class works out its emancipation. Climate change, species loss, ecological devastation, and environmental racism remind us daily that how we get free has ecological dimensions. Liberation—especially on a warming planet—depends on how we manage our relation to our environment. Responding to climate change provides an extraordinary opportunity for mass mobilization around rebuilding infrastructure, revitalizing underserved communities, and restoring ecosystems. It also gives us the opening to develop new socialist habits and collective ways of being.

In this and subsequent chapters, we don't tell people exactly what to do and how to live. Socialism is about equal freedom, coordination, and planning, not command. We describe some of the frameworks through which we might nurture and regenerate the planet while deepening everyone's engagement in meeting human and nonhuman needs. A primary component of the socialist reconstruction of the economy involves addressing climate change by transforming the production and consumption of energy.

Energy has to be decommodified; it can no longer be treated as a commodity produced for the sake of exchange and profit but must be collectively managed for the common good. Energy must also be decolonized. This means that it can no longer be used as a means for maintaining the power and privilege of wealthy countries while billions struggle under increasingly harsh conditions. Energy must be decarbonized. The US especially has to end its dependence on fossil fuels, decreasing its overall energy consumption while increasing its reliance on renewable sources such as solar, wind, and water. In sum, energy must be decommodified, decolonized, and decarbonized. This chapter outlines how we do it.

Decommodifying Energy

A socialist approach to the climate crisis begins with the abolition of private ownership of the means of production and capitalist energy markets. We assume from the start the expropriation of the privatized wealth of banks and corporations and the elimination of capitalist control over production and distribution. We will replace capitalist private prop-

Carbon Emissions Embodied in Goods Consumed, Per Capita (kg per capita, thousands)

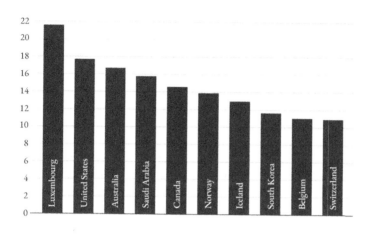

Source: Organisation For Economic Co-operation and Development

erty with collectively owned social property. Production and distribution will be democratically planned and coordinated.

Ending the profit motive in energy production—the essence of decommodification—can happen nearly instantaneously. As soon as we socialize ownership and production, we claim all energy-producing enterprises and corporations for the people and transform them into public utilities. In one sweep, we replace production for the sake of profit with production based on need. This fundamental transformation has remarkable effects: many of the so-called "challenges" to addressing climate change under capitalism immediately vanish. For example, we won't have to worry about oil and gas companies' "stranded assets" (the oil fields and gas reserves propping up the stock valuations of corporations like Chevron and ExxonMobil). Complicated cap and trade schemes—mechanisms for distributing carbon credits—will not be necessary because there won't be a market in energy. Instead of a commodity, energy will be a common resource, the production and distribution of which state and democratic mechanisms will plan and coordinate. Such a system will treat heat and electricity as basic rights.

In contrast with decommodification, decolonizing and decarbonizing energy will not happen overnight—but must happen quickly. As we detach from fossil fuels and shift to renewable energy sources, we will prioritize benefiting those countries and communities imperialism exploited for its own enrichment.

Decolonizing Energy

The global movement for climate justice has worked to bring the inequalities of the climate crisis to the attention of the imperialist powers. Undeveloped, exploited, and oppressed countries are the ones experiencing the most substantial initial impact from the rising temperatures. Rich northern countries industrialized at the expense of colonized countries. The industrial development of these northern countries is responsible for the dramatic increase of carbon in the atmosphere. And yet it is the smaller, less industrially and technologically developed countries, especially in the Global South, that already confront the destabilizing effects of climate change—famine, war, mass migration, and social upheaval. Our commitment to decolonizing energy follows their lead.

In 2010, over thirty-five thousand delegates from social movements in 140 countries participated in the World People's Conference on Climate Change and the Rights of Mother Earth held in Cochabamba, Bolivia. The People's Agreement arising out of this meeting noted the massive "climate debt" that the developed countries owe to the rest of the world.[22] This powerful concept of the "climate debt" is at the basis of our socialist reconstruction of energy production and use. We highlight five aspects of the United States' climate debt to colonized and Indigenous people.

First, we acknowledge the historical responsibility of the US capitalist class for genocide, settler colonialism, and imperialism. The prosperity of the capitalist, landlord, and financial class in the US was purchased at the cost of hundreds of millions of lives across the world. US capitalists got rich through industries and practices that devastated environments, habitats, and the ways of life of exploited and racialized people.

Second, recognizing the climate debt inherited from the US capitalist class in practice means the US is accountable for the tens of millions of people forced to migrate because of climate change. The new socialist government will have to assist in their relocation, including ending harsh immigration restrictions against those forced to leave their countries because of searing heat, droughts, floods, and failed harvests.

Third, because of our climate debt, we are obliged to help other countries adapt to the changing climate. We will share with them the technological and financial resources they need for development, enabling them to shift from fossil fuels to renewables like wind, solar, and water. Abolishing capitalism's exclusive and proprietary orientation to intellectual property and recognizing both our climate debt and our common world, we will dissolve patents and pool our knowledge. Practices of co-education, co-development, and co-production will drive adaptation and innovation.

Fourth, and relatedly, we will learn from Indigenous people, agricultural workers, and small farmers around the world. As we replace environmentally destructive industrial agriculture with regenerative and labor-intensive farming practices, we will benefit from their knowledge and experience. We will study Indigenous practices of water, soil, and forest conservation. Sharing knowledge for replenishing the Earth will strengthen social ties, orienting us away from competition and exploitation and toward mutual regeneration.

Fifth, we recognize the imperative of reforming the much-vaunted "American way of life." US practices of overconsumption do not provide a social model for the rest of the world: five Earths would be needed if everyone on the planet consumed as much as the average American.[23] The environmental footprint of the capitalist class is especially damaging: "The overconsumption of a wealthy minority is fueling the climate crisis yet it is poor communities and young people who are paying the price."[24] As we detail below, this means the US—particularly its middle and upper classes—has to make unilateral changes to its way of life to eliminate wasteful practices and certain excessive habits. We have to transform our energy consumption without demanding similar changes from other countries.

Decolonizing energy has a domestic component. Fossil fuel developers consistently undermine Native Americans' tribal sovereignty, failing to respect Indigenous land rights and violating sacred spaces.[25] Native Americans have been exposed to nuclear radiation from uranium mines and nuclear waste. Here decolonization can be carried out quickly through the immediate recognition of the sovereignty of Indigenous people and the reaffirmation of their right of self-determination. Accompanying this recognition will be reparations and restoration assistance as needed.

Highly polluting fossil fuels like coal, oil, and gas don't just cause global heating, and they don't just pollute our rivers, streams, and ecosystems. They pollute communities. Under capitalism, fossil fuel infrastructure has been invariably built close to Black, Indigenous, and linguistically diverse working-class communities, reducing people's homes, schools, and parks to "sacrifice zones." Emerging out of struggles against white supremacy, the term "environmental racism" describes this "deliberate targeting of communities of color for toxic waste facilities."[26] It is no accident that Black communities routinely face "the life-threatening presence of poisons and pollutants." Discriminatory housing policies trap Black people in lead- and arsenic-ridden houses and schools, in neighborhoods with poisoned water and polluted air. Few real estate developers place high-income housing in close proximity to toxic waste dumps, power stations, refineries, freeways, mines, or landfills. The result of capitalist development has been premature death as Black people in particular are exposed to chemicals, carcinogens, and particulate matter that lead to increased rates of asthma, cancer, and heart and lung disease.[27] Decolonizing energy demands decolonizing the Black community, nothing less.

Acknowledging the climate debt is indispensable to creating the conditions of trust and solidarity necessary for responding to climate change. If we are to avoid endless war, disruptive mass migration, and widespread social dislocation, the US has to restore what it has destroyed and repay what it has stolen. As an unearned benefit, the US, too, will gain from the knowledge and experience of the people and cultures it has historically sought to dominate.

Decarbonizing Energy

According to the International Panel on Climate Change, the world has less than ten years to respond to the climate crisis if we are to avoid more than 1.5°C of global warming. This means we need a swift and democratic plan for decarbonization. We have to keep fossil fuels in the ground. The "Cap and Adapt Plan" put forward by climate scholars Larry Edwards and Stan Cox establishes the basic features of a plan that can be immediately put into place.[28] The plan has three parts: a limit or "cap" on fossil fuel extraction and imports, the transition to renewable energy, and a plan to respond to any energy shortages that arise during the transition.

The first part, the cap, limits how much fossil fuel can be produced and imported. Each year, the cap grows tighter, and the amount of fossil fuel produced and imported decreases. For example, a ten-year plan to eliminate fossil fuels requires a 10 percent decrease the first year, a 20 percent decrease the second year, and so on until fossil fuel production is eliminated entirely in the tenth year. One benefit of this supply-side or production-oriented plan is that it does not rely on the fundamentally inequitable carbon-budget based approach underpinning many current policy recommendations (which are inequitable in part because the US artificially reduces its emissions count by off-loading production onto other countries). Another benefit of the cap plan is the rapid and guaranteed decline in greenhouse gases. Because we know fossil fuels release the largest amount of the gases responsible for global warming, we know decreasing and then ending their production will result in significant reductions in the amount of carbon released into the atmosphere. Still another benefit is that the ten-year plan enables the industries going off-line to retrain and redeploy their workforces as they reconfigure and repurpose the means of production.

This steady decrease in fossil fuel production leads to the second part of the "Cap and Adapt" plan, adaptation. The managed phasing in of wind, hydro, and solar power occurs at the same time as the managed phasing out of oil, coal, gas, and nuclear power. The massive scale necessary for this conversion of the economy suggests that the "Cap and Adapt Plan" should really be called the "Cap and Convert Plan," which is what we will do as we redirect the entire society to respond to the climate emergency. Millions of workers will be trained and employed to clean up the sites of former mines, oil wells, pipelines, and oil refineries. Many will retrofit buildings and build a continent-wide electrical grid nourished by community-managed microgrids. Millions more will figure out and implement the transition from car-centered private transportation to electric public transportation. And still millions more will participate in the exciting project of reactivating local and regional manufacturing to meet needs for material goods in responsive and regenerative ways.

Finally, the third part of the (renamed) Cap and Convert Plan is a backup plan for handling energy shortfalls that could arise as fossil fuels are phased out and renewables are phased in. In contrast to a market-based approach to shortages—which really means price gouging and hoarding by the rich—a socialist one meets basic needs and prioritizes historically oppressed and disadvantaged people. A crucial element of the response plan is the "energy inventory" it will undertake. As energy needs and expenditures are assessed, we will gain insights into usage patterns and develop more responsible habits of energy consumption.

How will we carry out Cap and Convert? Four agencies reporting to and under the general guidance of the Central Economic Agency will oversee the creation of boards and councils at community, industry, and regional levels to implement, monitor, and educate the people about the decarbonization effort. These agencies will meet regularly to share information and harmonize their work.

The Fossil Fuel Cap Agency will take charge of the process by which fossil fuel production is steadily decreased.[29] To this end, it will produce, coordinate, and enforce production expectations; develop means for assessing compliance; and plan and manage the distribution of declining supplies of fossil fuels in accordance with socialist principles of meeting social needs and prioritizing the historically disadvantaged. For example, this agency will ensure that homes of formerly oppressed national minorities are heated before the swimming pools of the remaining upper class. It will also oversee the decommissioning of nuclear power plants and the dismantling of the weapons, armament, and any related industries determined to no longer be energy-eligible. This agency will include unionized workers from all relevant sectors, scientists, environmentalists, and community leaders. It will cultivate approaches to assessment, compliance, and distribution that will be useful in managing the post-carbon economy as unions, community groups, and local enterprises take on new responsibilities and acquire new capacities for energy conservation and management.

The Climate Mobilization Agency will work closely with unions to organize the massive transformation of production required to shift to renewable energy sources. This transformation includes the expansion of wind, solar, and hydro power; the development of efficient, ecologically sound batteries and energy-storage capacities; and the construction of a continent-wide electric grid. It will require fundamental changes throughout the industrial, manufacturing, and construction sectors. The Climate Mobilization Agency will supervise and centralize data-gathering processes to monitor energy consumption and use. It will also take charge of worker retraining, collaborating with the Department of Education in coordinating vocational education to ensure that workers from dismantled sectors and people from historically disadvantaged groups are provided a full range of opportunities to use and develop their capacities to assist and benefit the overall conversion effort. It, too, will be composed of unionized workers, scientists, technicians, engineers, and educators.

The Fair Response Agency will develop and implement the plan for responding to any energy shortages that arise during the transition. It will begin with an inventory of energy needs and priorities, working directly with community boards and unions in an energy audit. This agency will distribute energy and water meters to every household and workplace, integrating them into a publicly accessible energy-consumption information network. Anyone, anywhere will be able to see how much energy is being consumed, where, when, by whom, and for what. The agency will use this knowledge to guide their response to energy shortages. As a parent agency to community and union response boards, it will work with communities and workplaces to develop culturally- and location-responsive plans for dealing with shortages. Members of the Fair Response Agency will primarily come from fields such as logistics, social services, energy, and information science.

The Research and Education Agency will coordinate climate and energy-related education and research. Under its purview will be popular education projects, scientific and technological development, and large-scale adaptation and mitigation experiments. The Research and Education Agency will coordinate the sharing and dissemination of multiple forms of knowledge about climate change, the environment, and the ecological impacts of social choices. The members of this agency will come from a wide range of fields, including education, culture, climate science, urban planning, and soil conservation. It is essential that members include Indigenous people with knowledge of nonindustrial modes of production. Drawing on the experience and expertise of associations of peasants and small farmers from around the world, the Research and Education Agency will support and learn from such popular organizations, spreading their knowledge and enhancing their cooperative networks.

The socialist reconstruction of energy will be guided by a commitment to making reparations for genocide and slavery, while fully aware that reparations can never wipe out the stain of these historic crimes. Decarbonization thus begins by rebuilding the infrastructures and meeting the needs of historically oppressed, exploited, and disadvantaged working-class communities. Members of these communities will lead the reconstruction effort, determining what it will look like and how it will be implemented. Each of the four agencies will develop corresponding networks of popular organizations (councils, unions, committees, and assemblies) to participate in planning, developing, and carrying out their respective tasks.

Reconstruction of the 'American Way of Life'

Cap and Convert will rapidly decarbonize the US energy supply, but to live within ecological limits we need to go further and decrease our overall energy consumption. The challenge here is that the new socialist government will inherit the country's existing layout of housing and physical infrastructure, not to mention the consumer habits cultivated over generations. On the one hand, the socialist government will not take away individuals' cars or homes; contrary to anti-communist propaganda, these will be recognized as personal property. On the other hand, the country's existing housing and automobile stock is unsustainable and will need to be adapted. The US can no longer hold out its idealized vision of success: private ownership of large houses, spread out in the suburbs, with SUVs parked in the garage. Such a vision has never been within reach of the majority of people in this country, much less the world—and for good reason: it's ecologically out of reach and environmentally disastrous.

The US is one of the world's largest consumers of energy. In 2019, the country consumed a massive 79,897 kilowatt hours of energy (kWh) per capita. For comparison, the citizens of other high energy-consuming countries such as Germany and France consume a little more than half of this at 43,703 kWh and 41,281 kWh respectively. Residents of all three countries consume much more than the global average. Despite manufacturing many of the US and Europe's consumer goods, China's per capita energy consumption was just 27,452 kWh in 2019. Brazil's was 16,325 kWh, Russia's 56,756 kWh, and India's a little over 7,000 kWh. These are the BRIC or developing countries. In the global periphery, consumption is considerably lower. Our smartphones, laptops, and televisions are built with raw materials such as cobalt, which is mined under brutal labor conditions in the Democratic Republic of Congo (DRC). Per capita consumption in the DRC was just 849 kWh in 2019. Our coffee is produced in countries like Kenya (1,906 kWh), Ethiopia (777 kWh), and Colombia (10,618 kWh), and many of our clothes are hand-stitched by super-exploited labor in Bangladesh (2,995 kWh).[30]

Reducing the formerly imperialist core's energy consumption is thus an integral part of building a world of human and nonhuman flourishing. At the same time, many countries in the Global South will need to increase their energy consumption to ensure a good quality of life for all. Thankfully, the world's entire population can flourish on much less energy than the US currently uses. A recent study found that global energy consumption in 2050 could be reduced to the levels of the 1960s while still providing what it describes as a "decent" life for all, despite a global population in 2050 that is estimated to be three times larger than that of the 1960s.[31]

At a certain point the social returns on per capita energy consumption start to decline.[32] Energy stops being used to satisfy human and ecological needs and starts contributing almost exclusively to the accumulation of profits or the conspicuous consumption of the wealthy. The previously referenced study calculates that combining energy efficient technologies with changes in demand-side consumption will reduce global energy needs up to

US Greenhouse Gas Emissions in 2020

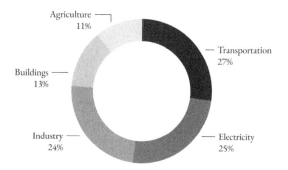

Agriculture 11%

Transportation 27%

Buildings 13%

Industry 24%

Electricity 25%

Transportation
Cars, pickup trucks, and minivans: 57%
Freight trucks: 25%
Planes: 8%
Trains: 2%
Ships, boats, buses, and other vehicles: 7%

A STRONG INVESTMENT IN PUBLIC TRANSIT COULD DRASTICALLY REDUCE THIS NUMBER!

Electricity
Coal generation: 54%
Natural gas generation: 43%
Petroleum generation: 1%
Other: 3%

COAL PRODUCES THE MAJORITY OF GREENHOUSE GASES FROM ELECTRICITY IN THE US DESPITE ONLY PRODUCING 20% OF THE ELECTRICITY!

Industry
Chemical production: 20%
Oil and gas drilling and transportation: 16%
Production and use of hydrofluorocarbons (HFCs): 10%
Metal production: 10%
Coal mining: 3%
Other: 44%

Buildings (not including electricity)
Offices and other commercial buildings: 54%
Homes and other residential buildings: 46%

RETURNING TO EARTH-FRIENDLY METHODS OF FOOD PRODUCTION COULD GREATLY REDUCE THE AMOUNT OF FERTILIZER USED!

Agriculture
Fertilizer use and poor soil management practices: 53%

Livestock: 30%
Manure: 13%
Rice cultivation: 3%
Other: 2%

Sources: United States Environmental Protection Agency, Rhodium

60 percent while still providing a decent standard of living for all. In high consuming countries like the US, cuts of as much as 95 percent are possible, especially once the excess consumption of the very rich is eliminated.[33]

A world with high-quality, low-energy housing, public transportation, and healthy food is clearly within reach. We can meet everyone's basic needs and more, securing the background conditions in which we can collectively thrive.

What is a "decent" standard of living? The study defines it as meeting essential human needs and maintaining overall well-being. A decent standard of living obviously requires physical health and safety, clean air and water, and sufficient nutritious food. But it also includes social and political engagement, education, communication and information sharing, and the time and space for play, creativity, friends and family, and other forms of self-actualization. In the US, capitalism undermines the quality of life for the majority of the working class. As the rich have gotten richer, elements of the good life within the reach of workers with a high school diploma—good union jobs, regular vacations, affordable housing, public schools that make college education a real possibility, and reliable pensions—have been taken away. What an earlier generation expected as basic rights—the fruits of organized working-class struggle—has vanished, transformed into privileges available only to the upper class.

A world with high-quality, low-energy housing, public transportation, and healthy food is clearly within reach.[34] We can meet everyone's basic needs and more, securing the background conditions in which we can collectively thrive. In subsequent chapters, we outline specific changes in agricultural production, housing, and infrastructure designed to decrease energy consumption. Some changes are realizable within the first decade of socialism. A more fundamental transformation of our housing and transportation infrastructure and redesign of our urban and suburban landscapes is a much longer-term project, one that requires large-scale democratic planning.

Conclusion

We conclude this chapter by emphasizing why socialist reconstruction is necessary for people and the planet to flourish.

As long as production is oriented towards profit, capitalists and corporations will put the needs of their stockholders first. Green capitalism is a myth—unless "green" refers to money. By replacing profit-oriented production with production based on meeting the needs of people and the planet—that is to say, by shifting from the demands of the market to democratically determined plans—we can already expect a significant decrease in our energy demands. Why? Because most of us prefer not to spend our lives working for the enrichment of the few at the cost of our futures. Given the choice, we will decide to diminish the amount of social labor spent producing—and importing—goods that are unnecessary, quickly obsolete, and destined for landfill. When we understand our impact on the environment and plan our production accordingly, we will collectively acquire the habits of conserving and cherishing the resources that go into the goods we make and the resources these goods command after they are made. When production is based on need, our focus will not be export-oriented and dependent on long supply chains and fossil fuels.

The twentieth-century myth of the American way of life (always modeled on the upper-middle class, white, patriarchal family) has never been the only vision of how to live in the United States. Throughout US history there have been experiments in communal living—religious communities, multiple generations, extended families, and families of choice living together—as well as people who choose to live alone or keep moving. When the labor movement was strong, it was able to force concessions from the capitalist class that included immense investments in public services and infrastructure. At specific points, women have been able to push employers to provide free on-site child care (although these wins haven't spread or endured the way they should). Socialist reconstruction will expand public services in improved, sustainable, and ecologically responsible ways; such services have briefly been part of US life and already accepted as crucial to a decent life in all developed (and many developing) countries around the world. Through the universal provision of basic services, we can exercise collective responsibility for the essential elements of our common life.[35] Such services include child care, education, health and medicine, libraries and science, public parks and green spaces, sports and recreation facilities, infrastructure maintenance, management of common affairs, emergency preparedness and response, culture, housing, transportation, water, communications, the postal service, and electricity. Pooling our efforts on its own eliminates some inefficiencies in energy use, and reframing aspects of our common life as universal basic services (UBS), rather than items of individual consumption, shifts our practices and habits. As one UBS advocate observes, "the UBS framework can help to constrain excessive consumption by changing incentives and redirecting resources."[36] People's expectations of what it means to live well, of what a decent quality of life looks like, will change, especially insofar as they are involved in deciding on and providing these basic services.

Involving everyone who is able in meaningful work planning and providing for the collective meeting of basic needs guarantees a decrease in the amount of time any individual has to work. This will take shape with a decrease in working hours and working days, and an increase in vacation time, family time, free time, and time to do with what we will. Reductions in working time will decrease overall energy consumption (and carbon emissions). Under capitalism, reduced working time is either the privilege of the wealthy or a burden placed on the unemployed. Under socialism, it will be our common right and benefit, one of the ways that the planet benefits as the people get free.

CHAPTER 4

ENDING THE STRANGLEHOLD OF DEBT AND FINANCE CAPITAL

*I*n a *New York Times* editorial published on July 2, 2021, filmmaker Astra Taylor observes, "Whereas the American dream used to be owning a home with a white picket fence, now it is getting out of debt." For many of us, even this seems unlikely. Whether we have medical bills, student loans, criminal justice fees, credit card debt, car payments, back rent, or mortgage payments, we are saddled with debts designed to keep us down, keep us dependent on meaningless jobs, and keep us poor. The capitalist economy needs a low-wage labor force willing to work long hours at multiple miserable jobs. Debt is one of the ways it produces this labor force.

At the same time that debt keeps some of us dependent and poor, it makes others rich. Financial institutions treat debt as a commodity, something that can be purchased and sold. Wealthy people buy and sell debt as a way to enrich themselves.

In 2008, the big banks' commodification and manipulation of debt led to a massive financial crisis. The result was the Great Recession and a dramatic increase in wealth inequality in the United States. What happened is the banks issued mortgages not primarily for the purpose of enabling people to buy houses, but so that the mortgages could be resold and bundled into financial instruments, "mortgage-backed securities." These securities were then grouped together, carved up into wildly esoteric financial instruments, and sold to investors to bet on. The purpose of the original mortgages was not to make housing more affordable; it was to use some people's debts to enrich other people.

Provisions in the US tax code enable the wealthy to use debt to avoid paying taxes. Written by the wealthy for the wealthy—and defended by armies of lawyers—these provisions let the superrich avoid spending their investment income. Instead, they hold onto it, borrow money at low-interest rates to fund their consumption, write off the debt as a loss, and set up trusts in ways that let their children avoid inheritance tax. When rich people go into debt, they are considered smart investors. When poor people go into debt, we are demonized and sometimes even criminalized.

These same patterns whereby debt is used to enrich the few and impoverish the many appear at national and international levels. In exchange for elaborate tax breaks, corporations agree to locate their operations in the cities and states that offer them the best deal. Often the corporations promise to improve or upgrade their facilities in order to get governments to extend tax breaks, but few mechanisms exist to hold companies accountable when they fail to deliver.

Imperialist debt policies have hit African countries especially hard, coercing these countries into cutting public services and repaying banks exorbitant amounts before taking care of their own citizens. On average, African countries spend more paying interest on their debts than they do on much-needed doctors and clinics.

The very tax breaks that benefit corporations and rich investors seriously damage communities. Cash-strapped municipalities cut back on services. Some cities use tickets, fees, and fines to make up budget shortfalls. For example, the uprising following the police murder of Michael Brown drew attention to Ferguson, Missouri's use of such measures. The city's court and police "openly extracted millions of dollars from its low-income African-American population."[37]

All over the world, debt is used to extort political and economic concessions from susceptible countries. Whether the concessions are disadvantageous trade agreements, privatization, or economic restructuring, they uniformly benefit capitalist institutions like the World Bank and the International Monetary Fund while further immiserating the people of the indebted country. In recent years, we've seen German banks pressure the

European Union to force Greece to undertake massive, crippling austerity measures. Imperialist debt policies have hit African countries especially hard, coercing these countries into cutting public services and repaying banks exorbitant amounts before taking care of their own citizens. On average, African countries spend more paying interest on their debts than they do on much-needed doctors and clinics.[38]

Anthropologist David Graeber writes, "the whole financial sector is a scam of sorts." He continues, "The overwhelming bulk of its profits come from colluding with government to create, and then trade and manipulate, various forms of debt."[39] Under capitalism, debt is a weapon of class warfare, a means by which the rich get richer by making the poor poorer, a way that the wealthy are freed from taxes and work while the poor are entrapped in increasingly serf-like conditions. Risk is socialized and reward is privatized. Debt is also a symptom of the problems created by the use of debt as a weapon—lack of income and inadequate financing of public goods. It's no surprise then, that people's movements consistently demand debt abolition. Socialist reconstruction requires nothing less.

This chapter outlines a socialist approach to abolishing debt and ending the despotism of finance capital. The underlying premise is that working people have taken power and constitutionally transformed private property into the common property of the collective people. We now democratically manage our common property for the good of people and the planet.

What is property? Although it might seem to contradict our common sense, "property" is not just land or stuff. As we know from trademarks and brands, the term refers to more than material things. "Property" is a legal designation used to determine who can do what with a particular asset (who can use or sell it, for example). In the early twenty-first century, much of what is considered property is intangible, like financial "securities" and "intellectual property," that is, things like stocks and bonds or patents and copyrights. Billionaires like Jeff Bezos and Mark Zuckerberg are billionaires because of the value of their stocks, intangible financial assets. Because so much property in the twenty-first century takes financial form, socializing the means of production—transforming our economy from one that is based on private profit to one that is oriented to the public good—necessitates overturning the entire financial system.

Two basic steps comprise our approach to ending the despotism of finance capital: abolition and reconstruction. In the first step, we abolish most current debts and the institutions that create, sell, and profit from debt. In the second step, we reconstruct the credit system to fund and support social priorities at local, regional, national, and international levels. This approach is rooted in the idea that debt abolition can function as the mechanism for overturning private property, de-financializing the economy, and ending the stranglehold of banks and finance capital over people's lives and futures. By abolishing the debts that hold people and communities back and by eliminating the institutions that enrich the few and create class inequality, we establish the basis for a socialist economy capable of meeting the needs of people and the planet.

We should be clear. Abolishing debt and eliminating private property and finance capital means eliminating markets in stocks, bonds, and other financial commodities. Although no one can say for sure how revolution in the US will unfold, the premise of this chapter is that even before the working class comes to power, capitalism's economic and political crises will lead to crashes in the global financial system. The goal of capitalists would be to "save the banks," which is just what they did in 2008 when the subprime lending crisis erased some $19 trillion of household wealth. In contrast, the socialist goal will be to save the people, to use the inevitable crisis to establish a strong basis for the new socialist society.

The Marxist economic analyst Doug Henwood explains that the one thing that financial markets do well is concentrate wealth. Henwood gives the example of government debt, issued as bonds. "Instead of taxing rich people, governments borrow from them, and pay for the privilege."[40] In this way, the capitalist government helps the rich get richer when it could very easily tax them and redistribute the wealth into social services. So after the revolution, after the working class has come to power, we won't try to restore the capitalist financial system and prop up the banks and markets that serve the rich. In fact, since under socialism all the major industries are collectivized—state-owned—speculative capitalist markets are unnecessary, especially once we recognize that under capitalism their principal purpose is creating wealth for the ruling class.

Eliminating finance capital—the primary way assets are rendered private property in late-stage capitalism—likewise requires eliminating hedge funds, venture capital, private equity, and all the complex financial machinations operating behind our backs to expropriate our work, time, and futures. And this means outlawing speculation, usury, payday loans, and predatory lending in all their forms. In place of these devices for maintaining class inequality, the socialist economy will employ a common credit union and centralized planning to allocate resources in accordance with social needs and values.

Two Sides of Finance

Given the dominance of the financial system, eliminating finance capital might seem like a daunting task. But it's not as challenging as one might think. As Karl Marx and V.I. Lenin pointed out long ago, capitalism's own processes create the conditions for their overcoming. Capitalism itself has developed the tools we need for replacing it with socialism. This is the case even with something as capitalist as finance. Finance contains not only the familiar predatory capitalist aspect associated with speculation and debt but also a socialist planning aspect.

For well over a century, finance capital—and a small group of big banks in particular—has played the determinant role in the capitalist system. Every major capitalist enterprise, whether engaged in the production of goods, services, infrastructure, or housing, is reliant on the banks for financing and credit. The same is true even of city and state government initiatives; their budgets are ultimately beholden to their standing with the big banks. The agents of finance capital in corporate boardrooms serve as the most powerful centralizers of the modern economy. Whether they are securing short-term profits or affecting long-term restructuring, gutting some industries and building up others, these financiers choose where and how capital gets used. They routinely make decisions that affect how billions of people will live, all for the purpose of securing private profits.

Standing behind and propping up the big banks is the United States Federal Reserve, popularly called the "Fed." The Fed is the central banking system that controls US monetary policy, primarily by controlling the flow of money. The Fed has enormous power to determine the economy's winners and losers.[41] It uses this power to redistribute wealth upward to the owners of capital. For example, the measures the Fed took during the crisis of 2008 benefited the stock market much more than the overall economy, a clear win for investors. Likewise, the Fed's policies during the COVID-19 pandemic led to a $10 trillion windfall to the top 1 percent.[42] Because the Fed is a capitalist institution, its decisions generally favor capitalists as a class.

What's important to keep in mind is the role the state plays in the economy even under capitalism. The state engages in all sorts of planning—plans for taking from the many and giving to the few. Socialist planning will replace this predation on the workers with an economy oriented toward meeting social needs.

More specifically, on the one hand, finance creates and maintains the wealth of the capitalist class. Debt is a powerful financial weapon in the capitalist arsenal because it gives creditors the right to make claims on debtors' future revenue. This provides creditors with a degree of control over debtors, especially when creditors' rights are enforced by the power of the state. Given the variety of debt instruments (mortgages, credit cards, car loans, student loans, court fees, medical bills, and so on) and the many needs that capitalism insists be addressed through markets rather than collectively (housing, food and other necessities, transportation, education, legal representation, health care, and so on), most of us find ourselves caught in a web of debt. The interest alone can be so steep that we can barely pay it, much less the principal, that is, the amount of the initial loan. Unlike the wealthy capitalist elite, who have lawyers, accountants, and politicians working for them, we are at the mercy of the market—and the market shows no mercy.

On the other hand, as we see with the Fed, "the financial system is also where conscious planning takes its most fully developed form under capitalism."[43] Through finance, the state gives shape to markets, putting in place the structures, agreements, and expectations through which market transactions occur. The state is also deeply involved in finance in ways that exceed the Fed: regulations, laws, and policies impact borrowing decisions from the individual to the international level. For example, the so-called free market didn't decide that student loans were ineligible for bankruptcy protection but business loans are. That was a political decision, a matter of law. Likewise, making mortgage interest but not rent tax-deductible is a political choice. These dimensions of the system through which certain activities are financed are institutional decisions, not market determinations.

According to J. W. Mason:

> The development of finance reveals the progressive displacement of market coordination by planning. Capitalism means production for profit; but in concrete reality profit criteria are always subordinate to financial criteria. The judgment of the market has force only insofar as it is executed by finance. The world is full of businesses whose revenues exceed their costs, but are forced to scale back or shut down because of the financial claims against them. The world is also full of businesses that operate for years, or indefinitely, with costs in excess of their revenues, thanks to their access to finance. And the institutions that make these financing decisions do so based on their own subjective

judgment, constrained ultimately not by some objective criteria of value, but by the terms set by the central bank.[44]

In other words, finance capital involves planning, deciding which activities and enterprises should be supported and how risks should be managed. Some companies receive billions of investment dollars and never make a profit. Other companies operate successfully, but then are purchased by aggressive corporate raiders in leveraged buyouts that use debt to restructure and ultimately dismantle them according to obscene but legal investment strategies. Our point is that even the most capitalist of decisions are not determined by markets. They are made in and by institutions according to institutional priorities, and their priorities are capitalist investors and wealth managers, not working people. Planning is carried out with predatory aims as the wealthy prey on everyone else.

The forms of debt that impact most working people can be understood in terms of these predatory and planning aspects. Attention to the predatory capitalist aspect alerts us to the problems that debt pretends to address but actually deepens. Attention to the socialist planning aspect alerts us to tasks that socialist organization can and will solve. The problems debt pretends to address, like access to housing and education, are better handled collectively. Cooperative solutions and public services will meet social needs in ways that promote equal flourishing rather than private gain.

The Debt System

Specific examples of different forms of debt bring out these aspects of predation and planning. Here we consider debts related to housing, education, everyday purchases, transportation, and health care. All these forms of debt are the result of political choices to support private property and capitalist profit rather than the common good and meeting social needs.

Mortgages are loans that enable people to buy houses. The American system of long-term (twenty or thirty years) housing loans emerged during the Great Depression. In the nineteenth century, "Terminating Building Societies" (TBSs) financed the construction of private houses. These societies consisted of small groups of people who pooled their savings to pay for the building of each other's houses. TBS members generally made contributions twice a year. Once the houses of everyone in the group were completed, the TBS was terminated. According to a report from the US Department of Housing and Urban Development, these societies were a "communal solution" to housing provision.[45]

Over the years, these communal forms evolved into "Permanent Building Societies" and then into savings and loans and mortgage banks as holders of capital came to treat mortgages as investment instruments. The boom-and-bust cycle of the capitalist economy made mortgages risky investments. People who lost their jobs when the economy tanked couldn't repay their loans. As the Great Depression set in after the 1929 stock market crash, hundreds of thousands of people lost their homes. Roughly half of all mortgages went into default. New housing construction and building repairs came to a virtual standstill. The US government responded by focusing on the banks, on the financial institutions, rather than on the people who were unhoused or at risk of eviction. The government's measures included creating mortgage insurance companies—designed to protect lenders, that is, creditors—and establishing long-term mortgages and other incentives that would stimulate the market in mortgages. So instead of backing communal housing associations oriented toward meeting real housing needs, the US government decided to support lenders and banks, to incentivize investment, and to generate more markets in mortgages, mortgage-backed securities, and mortgage insurance.

As of 2020, the overall amount of mortgage debt in the US was over $14 trillion.[46] The average consumer's mortgage is their single largest source of debt. Mortgages are also hefty sources of profits for lenders. In 2020, mortgage banks made $4,202 per loan they originated, a staggering 285 percent more than they made per loan in 2019.[47]

The second largest source of debt in the US is student loan debt. Growing faster than any other source of individual debt, student loan debt doubled between 2008 and 2020.[48] By February 2021, it totaled $1.7 trillion.[49] Women owe more student debt than men by about $3,000 on average. The student loan debt of Black people is 50 percent larger than that of white people, a $13,000 difference on average.[50] Most of the forty-five million people with student loan debt owe it to the US government, not private banks. The vast majority of these debtors, over 68 percent, are over the age of twenty-five.[51] Students and their families have this debt because the capitalist United States has determined that education is a private rather than a public concern. The country needs scientists, mathematicians, engineers, physicians, nurses, teachers, social workers, architects, and other experts. Education provides people with historical, political, and cultural knowledge that helps make them informed citizens. Nevertheless, the US treats higher education as a private good that individuals purchase on the market.

A number of capitalist countries recognize that higher education is a public good. Denmark, Finland, Germany, Sweden, and Turkey have public institutions that don't require students to pay tuition. Their high school graduates are not deterred from further study by the fear of crippling debt. Their college graduates don't begin their professional lives saddled with debts that will take decades to pay. Even in the US, there have been instances where college tuition was free. The University of Florida didn't charge residents tuition until the 1970s. Parts of the City University of New York were free until the 1970s. California made college tuition-free to residents until the 1970s.

Why did states stop investing in their citizens and future workforces? One explanation is a reaction to the student protests against the Vietnam War. Conservatives sought to punish students for exercising the basic right to protest. Another explanation is the tax revolt of the late seventies. Unwilling to pay its fair share, the capitalist ruling class fought to reverse the gains working people had won through popular struggle. And yet another explanation is racism. Some white people resented the progress made during the civil rights movement. They rejected desegregation and equal access to educational opportunities and became unwilling to support public institutions. Actually, this is not completely accurate. The public institutions these elite white people were willing to support were prisons. At the same time that funding for public education was cut, funding for more prisons increased.

In addition to mortgages and student loans, most households in the US have credit card debt (around $6,000 on average) and an auto loan (totaling $1.4 trillion).[52] The interest rates on these debts vary, with rates on credit cards generally being substantially higher. A high-quality public transportation system will eventually end people's dependence on private cars. Better wages and an orientation away from consumer goods (sped up with the abolition of constant advertising) will lessen people's dependence on credit cards, breaking the grip these companies have over our future earnings.

Abolishing the fees and interest rates that card companies charge to users will transform credit cards into how they were initially imagined. The utopian socialist Edward Bellamy first used the term "credit card" in 1887 in his best-selling novel *Looking Back*. Bellamy depicts residents of a socialist United States using credit cards as the means for spending their "citizen's dividend," the pay they receive from the government. No one profits from the cards. The cards are not ways for capital to make claims on workers' future earnings or subject them to discipline. On the contrary, the cards are ways people spend their portion of the collectively produced social surplus.

For roughly a third of cardholders in the US, the largest component of credit card debt is medical expenses. They use their credit cards to pay their medical bills because they have no other way to pay them. One in six people in the US has outstanding medical debt on their credit report—$81 billion nationwide.[53] So in addition to having to find a way to pay the inexcusably high costs of medical care, they end up having to pay interest on their outstanding balance, frequently getting stuck with extra fees when they can't pay. For some people, medical debt becomes a debt they will never be able to repay, a debt that—because of the high interest rates charged by credit card companies—can lead them to be unable to pay their rent and get evicted as well as to bankruptcy. Medical bills are the main cause of people being harassed by aggressive and predatory collection agencies.[54] This problem won't arise when the US has a fully funded public health-care system.

Abolishing these debts—mortgage, student loan, credit card, auto, and medical—is an important step toward socializing our economy. It's a way for the working class to retake what is already ours. Some workers may complain of unfairness on the individual level—someone who has been paying a mortgage for one year will have their debt abolished just like the one who has been paying for thirty years, for instance—but that is a short-term issue. The larger result is that all workers win by freeing themselves from the shackles of debt one way or another. The bankers, credit card companies, and financiers will complain that they aren't getting what they are owed. But we owe them nothing. And when they say, "but this will destroy the entire basis of private property," we will smile and nod, "Precisely!"

Corporations Owe Us Everything

The two sides of finance—predation and planning—provide guidance for socializing the economy. They tell us what to eliminate and what to accentuate as we focus on people and the planet and end private accumulation by billionaires and corporations. Public social solutions replace private profit-oriented market solutions.

What about municipal debts, the bonds that cities issue in order to raise funds and that investors purchase in order to avoid taxes? And what about corporate debts, the bonds issued by companies?

Debt abolition is the means through which we will socialize the economy. Under socialism, all large-scale industries, corporations, services, and enterprises will belong to the collective people, not to specific individuals, families, or shareholders. When we take these for the people, for the working class, we won't pay for them—these industries, corporations, services, and enterprises should have been ours from the beginning since they are the products of our labor.

The dissolution of stocks and bonds—and the markets in stocks and bonds—entails an enormous demolition of the paper wealth held by shareholders—tens of trillions of dollars. For the working class, this is a most miraculous development—we had almost none of that money to begin with. For the capitalists, this will be a disaster; everything that separates them from the rest of us—everything that lets them buy multiple houses and airplanes and yachts and drive up housing prices and treat the rest of us like their personal servants—will disintegrate.

What will remain are material structures (the fixed capital of buildings, plants, and machinery), people, knowledge, and land—the real sources of wealth which capitalism distorts with its specific form of value. These structures, people, knowledge, and land will become the basis for the socialist economy. Instead of being arranged via a financial system oriented toward capital accumulation, they will be arranged in the interest of the flourishing of people and the planet.

A fact of late-stage capitalism is that successful companies may not make any profit (at the time of this writing Uber is a prime example), may rely heavily on tax breaks (Amazon), and may receive substantial government subsidies (Boeing, General Motors). The US government pours tax dollars into the pharmaceutical industry, enriching shareholders and executives when it could be treating the entire industry as a branch of government. Despite the fairy tales capitalists like to tell, the profit motive and competitive markets have not been fundamental features of the capitalist economy for a long time. As the economic historian Robert Brenner argues, what's going on instead is the politically driven upward redistribution of wealth. Protected by the police and the military, the rich use the state apparatus to expropriate wealth from the rest of us.

Some might raise concerns that without financial markets, what will guarantee a dignified retirement going forward and give people confidence that their children will be economically secure?

When answering these questions, we have to remember two things. First, the new socialist society will guarantee everyone food, housing,

Companies like Amazon rely heavily on tax breaks and may not make a true profit within the structures of late-stage capitalism. (Photo: Joe Andrucyk)

health care, education, dignified retirement, and other necessities of life as basic rights. No one will ever need to worry about foreclosure, eviction, starvation, or astronomical medical expenses. Many families currently count on cashing out their retirements, selling their houses, or taking out equity loans so as to have enough money to retire, pay for medical bills, elder care, or their children's college tuition. All of these most common economic anxieties will be permanently eliminated. While capitalism has left Social Security in serious danger—primarily because legislators in Washington, DC refuse to make the tax adjustments that will let this popular program flourish—the new socialist government will transform the program into a fully functioning retirement system for all, for the first time.

Second, under capitalism, the financialization of retirements and savings is not a workable system for the vast majority of people. Our savings can never be secure. We can't count on the money we save being there when we need it. Companies go bankrupt, and retirees lose their benefits. For example, when the energy corporation Enron went bankrupt in 2001, its collapse wiped out $2 billion in pensions. Most companies eliminated defined-benefit pension plans long ago. Whatever retirement benefits employees receive are tied to the markets and so are at risk when markets crash or retirement funds are squandered in speculative invest-ments. For public sector workers like teachers, there are striking gaps between the benefits states are slated to pay and the revenue that states expect to generate.

The capitalist system has ensured that a quarter of the US population have no savings at all. Capitalism's continued reproduction depends on the existence of a large reserve of unemployed people and on people who have to sell their labor in order to survive. Structural racism features heavily in this absence of savings: on average white people have larger savings than Black people because white people have had access to better paying jobs and inheritances. The bottom line is that under capitalism, none of us is secure. People fortunate enough to have employment with retirement benefits are ultimately in the same boat as the millions of low-wage and precarious workers who have never had an income large enough to make ends meet, much less save for the future.

Socialism will change the system. Instead of being dependent on risky markets that benefit the rich, it will guarantee full social and economic support for all.

A New System for a New Society

The elimination of debt, finance capital, and paper wealth clears the way for socialist reconstruction. This reconstruction entails establishing an interconnected set of planning agencies with the capacity to determine and implement wages, prices, and rents according to a broad set of priorities: reparations and redress, valuing essential work, meeting social needs, and stewarding the planet to ensure its flourishing for future generations. These agencies will be the forms of association through which the working class organizes life and work.

Some debts can never be repaid—the debts to Indigenous people and African Americans are undeniable examples. The United States built itself through genocide and slavery and nothing can ever fully redress those crimes. What we can do, however, is recognize and support rights to self-determination, politically and economically empowering oppressed nationalities to ensure their liberation, equality, and prosperity. In this way, we take a step toward paying long-owed reparations.

The core or "engine room" of the new system will be the Bureau of Wages, Prices, and Rents. This bureau will synthesize information from across the country to establish the range for fair wages, prices, and rents. It will use this range as a mechanism for setting priorities and coordinating production and distribution. Access to the means of survival—food, shelter, clothing, and health care—will not depend on work. Everyone is guaranteed basic subsistence. Through the Bureau of Wages, Prices, and Rents, the working class will generate and administer the plans that enable us to collectively account for what we have, what we need, and what we will create together. It's an organizational means for ensuring the flourishing of each and all.

Housing for All

As chapter 6 addresses in detail, socialist reconstruction treats housing as a social good and basic right. Recognizing housing as a social good means that society, all of us together, have an interest in clean, safe, attractive, and environmentally responsible modes of housing. The flourishing of people and the planet is a primary value that impacts the sorts of housing we will maintain and develop. Recognizing housing as a basic right means that everyone is entitled to safe and secure housing. No one will ever live in fear of being kicked out on the street because they can't afford to pay for housing. In practice, housing as a basic right entails the abolition of landlords, landlordism, and the market in housing. As previously explained, it also requires the abolition of mortgages: your house is your house, not the bank's. When you and your household no longer need it, the house or apartment will return to the community who will find its next set of residents.

Capitalism has distributed housing in vastly unequal ways. A primary task of the new socialist government will be redressing the inequalities we inherit from capitalism. Some people will have been living for years in overcrowded apartments. Other people will have vastly more space than they need, houses that are more like palaces with screening rooms and fitness centers and more bathrooms than most public schools. Why should a wealthy couple get all this space when a large working-class family doesn't have room to breathe? This problem is not solved simply by abolishing debt and declaring that everyone owns their houses free and clear. Capitalist development has also been grossly uneven across the country. Some cities are overcrowded while other areas have been depopulated. There are communities no longer able to provide basic services; the nearest medical facilities and grocery stores are miles away, requiring long drives. Blocks of houses are empty and abandoned—houses that can be restored, bringing the community back to life.

Added to this legacy of inequality and unevenness is the reality that people have different needs and desires. Not everyone wants to live in the same way. Some want to live in mountain cabins so that they can have opportunities for rock climbing and hiking. Others want to live in urban apartments where they can enjoy views of the city skyline and the noise and variety of city life. Still others want to live in old houses in need of loving restoration. Socialism will enable this diversity to flourish and expand. Because housing won't be constrained by the capitalist market, people will be free to cultivate diverse ways of living. But how will this work?

People doing the hardest and most essential jobs—teaching our children; caring for the sick, elderly, and disabled; cleaning and maintaining buildings and grounds; producing goods in factories; producing and preparing the foods we eat; facilitating the storage and delivery of goods, and so on—tend to receive the lowest pay.

Resolving these issues will be the combined task of the Bureau of Wages, Prices, and Rents and the National Housing Association, working closely with local and regional councils and popular housing associations. Rent is one mechanism for carrying out this work. By "rent" we do not mean a fee that landlords charge tenants. On the contrary, landlordism will have been eliminated. Housing belongs to the community for the community. That people "own" their houses or apartments doesn't mean they own them in the old capitalist sense that they can sell them, rent them, demolish them, or turn them into nightclubs. It means that people cannot be kicked out of their homes. They have the security of knowing there is a place where they belong. But what if they want to move? And what if communities with a lot of empty housing want to attract new residents? Or what if a young person is ready to leave home or school and start out on their own? This is where rent comes in. Rent designates the extra or additional cost for housing above the guaranteed minimum for a person or household.

An example can clarify the idea. Let's say that in large, crowded cities a family of four is generally guaranteed a two- or three-bedroom house or apartment for which they pay very minimal costs. If the family wants something larger or more desirable, they will have to pay the difference, what we are calling "rent." This rent will not be charged in order to make money for a landlord. It will be charged as a mechanism for distributing housing and generating funds for ongoing maintenance, building, and improvements. Similarly, communities seeking more residents will likely make larger houses or houses with more amenities available below the rent typical for those houses in other places. Here, the decrease in the differential cost will create an incentive for people to come to this community.

The Bureau of Wages, Prices, and Rents will focus on coordinating rent in relation to wages and prices. The National Housing Association will focus on coordinating rent with respect to available housing inventories and needs. Together they will work closely with popular councils to ensure that everyone has the safe, secure, and reliable housing that will enable them to flourish.

Socializing Work

As everybody knows, there is nothing fair about compensation under capitalism. Jobs that most of us don't understand, usually with lofty titles like West Coast Benefits and Services Advisor or Regional Vice President for Digital Advertising, come with generous compensation packages. People doing the hardest and most essential jobs—teaching our children; caring for the sick, elderly, and disabled; cleaning and maintaining buildings and grounds; producing goods in factories; producing and preparing the foods we eat; facilitating the storage and delivery of goods, and so on—tend to receive the lowest pay. These essential but low-paid and unnecessary but highly paid jobs are distributed unevenly by race and gender, with Black and Brown women most likely to be relegated to care work while white men get more of the white-collar positions.

The capitalist market is terrible at one of its primary roles—distributing labor. As COVID-19 made clear for many people who had to work remotely, much of the time we spend at work is unnecessary. Most of our tasks don't require forty hours a week; nonstop email and trivial meetings feel like work but are really just time sinks. While at work, some of us wait around for something to do while others of us are managed by algorithms that track our every move, docking us for tending to basic needs like going to the bathroom. Some of our workplaces are terribly understaffed as the bosses try to get everything they can out of us. Other workplaces overflow with extra administrators who try to justify their position by loading the rest of us with busywork. In some areas of the country, there are not enough people for all the jobs that need doing, while in others there are hundreds of applicants for every job. These are not insurmountable problems. Both large capitalist employers and the US public sector regularly allocate their workforces according to thoughtful plans based on goals and needs. The problem is that the goals and needs don't put people and the planet first. They prioritize profits and protecting the interests of the ruling class.

Socialist planning will let us reconfigure our approach to work. Jobs important to the capitalist economy in financial services, health insurance, and advertising will no longer be necessary. This frees up between six and seven million people for more meaningful and productive work rebuilding our material infrastructure; engaging in energy-efficient and sustainable manufacturing; regenerating forests, grasslands, and wetlands; and providing essential health, education, and public services. The infusion of these six-million-plus workers will allow us to provide dramatically more attentive and personalized health care. It will let our education system better meet student needs. It will mean that no one will get stuck in some computerized purgatory, endlessly prevented from speaking to an actual person. And best of all, because "many hands make light work," we will all gain more free time.

Instead of following the typical capitalist approach of purchasing workers' labor time, socialist society will allocate work according to criteria that match specific needs and requirements. Work will be classified into three broad categories: professional expertise, socially necessary tasks and shared responsibilities. These categories often overlap; much work falls along a spectrum rather than clearly within one category or another. Nevertheless, by treating work in terms of social needs and requirements instead of a market in labor time, we will be able to generate solutions where everyone is engaged in meaningful work and has more free time.

Figuring out the details of this arrangement will be an immediate task of the Bureau of Wages, Prices, and Rents, but here is a sketch of the basic idea. Occupations in some fields require a great deal of education and training, for example, neurosurgery, climate science, artificial intelligence, and astrophysics. People who go into these and similar areas generally devote their entire working lives to them; they have a passion for their fields. Other occupations require less specialized education, making them attractive options for larger numbers of people. Training is still necessary, and the work may take a number of years to master. The point, though, is that doing the job well does not require a lifetime commitment. People may change their areas of work and pursue different paths during their active working life. Most socially necessary work falls into this category. Examples include working on power grids and electrical lines, primary school teaching, construction, physical therapy, and graphic design. Finally, there is a wide array of tasks that are the responsibility of nearly everyone for most of our lives (although for millennia ruling classes have forced these tasks onto slaves and servants). This category of work involves caring for one's own well-being and living environment and includes cooking, cleaning, laundry, procuring necessities, maintaining one's personal property, and, often, tending to children. Under capitalism, this labor of "social reproduction" has typically been unwaged and assigned to women. Households with disposable income often hire women from oppressed racial and national minorities facing barriers to better jobs to do this domestic work. By approaching the distribution of labor in terms of social needs and requirements and recognizing these three kinds of work—specialized, trained, and shared—we will be able to jettison capitalism's preoccupation with jobs and careers distributed in a labor market and focus instead on the tasks and services our society needs to flourish.

Socialist planning will guarantee that we have a workforce with the skills and talents necessary for the tasks at hand. Gathering data from communities, enterprises, unions, and agencies from across the country, the Bureau of Wages, Prices, and Rents will compile a massive database of the kinds of expertise and knowledge necessary for achieving local, regional, and national short- and long-term goals. It will coordinate with the relevant education and training institutions to set and reach output targets—ten thousand people with advanced skills in accounting, twenty thousand optometrists, three hundred thousand general contractors, and so on. People will not choose occupations just "for the money," as they do under capitalism. They will make choices based on their interests, skills, and general social need.

Local offices of the Bureau of Wages, Prices, and Rents will engage communities, enterprises, and unions in developing systems for the distribution of necessary tasks. Tasks like attending to young children; trash removal; the maintenance of parks, yards, and green spaces; and weeding and harvesting common gardens will likely be collectivized, with everyone expected to pitch in. Some people might elect to pitch in a few hours every week. Other people might choose to do their part of this work for months at a time in order to secure for themselves larger continuous blocks of free time. Communities will use delivery apps like Instacart and Deliveroo to pool food distribution tasks. Instead of a person "being" a driver or delivery person, instead of delivering goods being their occupation, a person will sign up for a specific number of tasks per week, depending on their interests and the needs of the community. Bureau offices will look for ways to incentivize people to take on challenging tasks. There may be instances where the bureau determines that an increase in pay is necessary to convince enough people to take on seriously difficult work (such as hazardous waste disposal or roofing). Coordinating with national and regional offices, local ones will decide whether especially attractive housing is needed to induce people to move to their communities. Generally, though, incentives will take the form of increased amounts of free time, funding for new activities and ventures, and participation in more rewarding and challenging opportunities.

Unions will play an important role in the bureau's work in setting wages and prices. They will guarantee workers' voice in any plan, insuring the fair alignment of costs and compensation.

Postal Banking: People's Development Banks

Banks serve important functions even in a socialist economy. Once predatory fees and practices are eliminated, banks will concentrate on the useful tasks of maintaining accounts and facilitating payments. They will also be institutional sites to organize saving, lending, and borrowing, for pooling people's savings and directing state-provided funds to long-term projects.

Postal banking, a system where the post office provides basic banking services, is one popular model of an inclusive, non-predatory approach to finance. Used in over a hundred countries around the world, postal banking was part of the US system from 1911–1967. In contrast to extortionate banking practices that prey on poor people, charging exorbitant interest rates on payday loans and overloading people with multiple fees, postal banking services are typically low cost. Under socialism they will be free. People will no longer pay a fee for every "service" because banks won't be oriented toward making profits for stockholders and paying executives enormous salaries.

The new socialist system will expand postal banks into a network of people's development banks. Taking on the planning aspect of finance, its role in allocating social wealth to specific projects, these banks will help communities determine how to prioritize and what to support. If a new school is built, will repairs on the water treatment plant need to be put off for another year? How much will music and theater groups be granted for their artist development programs? Regional branches of the people's development banks will assess the decision-making processes of the local banks: were they inclusive, how did they redress historic patterns of oppression and discrimination, what needs were being met, how is the work meaningful, and what is the environmental impact? The very process of allocation will be an opportunity to strengthen social ties and produce new cooperative arrangements.

Eliminating the profit motive lets planning move to the fore. Instead of preying on people's vulnerabilities, banking will become a means through which people develop new socialist habits and orientations. At the national level, the Central People's Development Bank will exist as a public utility. Its tasks include oversight of the financial requirements of all national-level projects, most importantly the allocation of funds necessary for ending reliance on fossil fuels and transitioning to renewable energy sources.

People's development banks will provide an infrastructure for paying reparations and building equality. Regions in the United States are impacted differently by the changing climate. Clean water, reliable electricity, and generous shade trees are not equally available to everyone. Oppressed national minorities are more likely to live in contaminated areas and areas overly exposed to fire, floods, and other consequences of global heating. At the regional and national scale, the people's development banks will provide a form for putting resources where they belong most. These banks will work with communities and enterprises to support the retrofitting and renovation of factories. Factories shut down in the first decade of the twenty-first century will be brought back online, reconfigured in environmentally responsible ways, and placed under workers' control.

People's development banks will also be expanded as institutions for international cooperation. Again, instead of acting in a predatory, profit-focused way, socialist banking will function as an organizational infrastructure for allocating funds that can meet social needs. Based on the abolition of all international debts, these banks will provide a starting point for creating the mutual trust and goodwill necessary for responding to the climate crisis and redressing the consequences of centuries of US imperialism.

Conclusion

This chapter has shown how debt abolition provides the mechanism for de-financializing the economy and establishing a basis for socialist planning. The capitalist system likes to blame and shame poor and working-class people when we go into debt. But the system is at fault: the capitalist system uses debt to redistribute wealth to the upper class, and it makes private individuals responsible for meeting needs that should be met socially and collectively. Housing, education, health care, and transportation are too important to be left to the market. They are basic rights necessary for all and should be provided to all. Through proper planning they will be.

We can't predict the multiple exciting ways people with the power to reconstruct society will choose to employ their talent and creativity. Freed from the servitude in which finance capital and endless debt have enchained us, what skills will we teach ourselves and our children? What will we learn about the world around us and how we, and it, can adapt to the changing climate? What new relations will we cultivate with one another and the plants and animals of our planet? We don't know the answers to these questions, although we expect they will be wonderful and surprising. What we do know is that only through socialist reconstruction and the abolition of debt and financial capitalism will we have a future in which all working people can join in answering them.

CHAPTER 5

RECONSTRUCTING AGRICULTURE

We all have to eat to live. Some of us live to eat. We dream of barbecue, mac and cheese, tacos, pizza, sushi, falafel, ramen, hamburgers, and chocolate chip cookies, foods that remind us of home and foods that open us up to new people and experiences. We live our cultures through food, marking special occasions with feasts and large gatherings where we sit and eat with others. But under capitalism, food and the land it grows on are commodities. Food is produced not for our nourishment and community life but for the private profit of the few.

The week before Christmas 2020, a year when the world was ravaged by the COVID-19 pandemic, one out of every four people lacked reliable access to nutritious food. That's eighty-one million people in one of the richest countries on the planet.

The capitalist system controls food production in the interest of private wealth accumulation. A striking symbol of this control is the largest owner of agricultural land in the US: billionaire Bill Gates. Although no one would mistake the founder of the Microsoft Corporation for a farmer, Gates owns close to 270,000 acres of farmland in nineteen states. Through his Alliance for a Green Revolution in Africa, Gates is pushing reliance on chemicals and commercial seeds onto African farmers.[55] Agricultural production under capitalism isn't organized to care for humans, animals, communities, or the environment. It's dominated by enormous multinational corporations that traffic in bioengineered seeds, pesticides, and machinery. The focus is always on the bottom line—making money for investors and corporate CEOs.

This focus on profit installs a fundamental contradiction in the food system: starvation amidst abundance. For example, even in the United States, some people don't get enough to eat. The week before Christmas 2020, a year when the world was ravaged by the COVID-19 pandemic, one out of every four people lacked reliable access to nutritious food. That's eighty-one million people in one of the richest countries on the planet.[56] At the same time as some people are going hungry, over 40 percent of Americans suffer from health conditions related to the poor quality of the food we eat; our diets are awash in sugars, fats, chemicals, and processed foods.[57] That's because capitalist agriculture relies on and pushes overproduction, putting profit ahead of healthy food and a healthy planet.

Food production in the US is high-yield, low-nutrient, carbon-intensive, and ecologically damaging. The agricultural sector is organized so that "food giants" control the entire chain of production from "farm to fork."[58] They dictate the composition of crops; genetic engineering of seeds; composition and use of fertilizers and pesticides; technologies for harvest and slaughter; as well as the branding, marketing, packing, and distribution of food. Seventy-five percent of global ecological damage, as well as 40 percent of greenhouse gas emissions, stem from industrial agriculture.[59] The four hundred aquatic dead zones worldwide are the consequence of industrial fertilizer and pesticide runoff into waterways.[60]

The devastating impact of US corporate agriculture extends beyond the borders of the United States. It's a weapon in the arsenal of US imperialism. Because agriculture is heavily subsidized—and because its environmental and health costs are excluded from pricing—the US can undercut the prices of most other agricultural producers around the world. This drives farmers in the Global South out of business and often to suicide, decimating communities. Decreases in local food production render countries more dependent on imports and less able to negotiate trade agreements as equals. The US overproduces food in order to bring other countries to their knees.

Poor management of land and poor production of food lie at the heart of the US capitalist economy. Socialism will transform both. The socialist reconstruction of agriculture will replace capitalism's profit motive with care for people and the planet. Food will be a basic right that we as a society guarantee to all who live here. Land will be nationalized, held in common by the collective people. Farmwork and workers will be respected, with more people learning and teaching the techniques of agroecology that will reinvigorate the soil and diminish animal suffering. We will grow food and other agricultural products to nourish and flourish, not exploit and oppress. By nationalizing the land, adopting socialist planning, engaging more people in food production, and ensuring that those who are working on the land control how it is worked, we will regenerate damaged environments and reinvigorate devastated communities.

The Cancer of Overproduction

As the world's largest exporter of food, the US likes to tell a happy story of capitalist success. In this story, American technological know-how solves the world's hunger problem. Replacing old-fashioned farming methods with science and machinery, US industrial agriculture has dramatically increased productivity. Large sections of the workforce have been released from the drudgery of farm labor. Everyone's diet has improved. Like any fairy tale, this one isn't true. It's a big lie.

In 1910, Black farmers owned between sixteen and nineteen million acres of land. Over the next hundred years, anti-Black discrimination and capitalist predation expropriated 90 percent of it.

The story of American technological know-how erases the history of industrial agriculture in colonialism and slavery. Historians emphasize the importance of cotton in the development of capitalism in the US. Cotton became a major export crop after white settlers exterminated the native population, expropriated their land, and brought in a workforce of captured and enslaved African people. These same enslaved workers had knowledge of food production that their settler captors lacked. Eric Holt-Gimenez explains that "West Africans were experts at sophisticated forms of floodplain and tidal irrigation and adept at the difficult and arduous process of hand milling. Rice-producing slaves were initially able to exchange knowledge of rice cultivation for land."[61] Once the plantation owners learned the techniques, this exchange came to an end. The knowledge plantation owners gained from enslaved workers became a basis for their enslavement of others. Similarly erased from the fairy tale of American farming is the systematic oppression of free Black farmers. In 1910, Black farmers owned between sixteen and nineteen million acres of land.

Over the next hundred years, anti-Black discrimination and capitalist predation expropriated 90 percent of it.[62]

Abundant food production has not meant an end to hunger and starvation. Because food is produced as commodities to be sold on the market, people have to have money to pay for it. If people can't afford to pay, then farmers are stuck with the excess product. The economics of farming is such that if prices decline dramatically, farmers are motivated to increase production in order to cover the difference from what they've lost. Bringing more food onto the market makes prices decline still further, trapping farmers in a no-win situation. This happened during the Great Depression. "Farmers dumped milk on highways, slaughtered sheep in the fields, and plowed crops into the ground, desperately trying to cut their losses and bring up prices. Long breadlines of hungry and destitute people wound through the nation's cities even as grain rotted in silos across the country."[63] Today, the US government pays farmers *not* to produce crops in an effort to keep prices high enough for farms to stay afloat.[64]

The "brutal market logic of overproduction within a highly productive food regime," as Holt-Gimenez rightly terms it, benefits powerful corporations and landowners and drives small farmers out of business.[65] The US consistently takes advantage of this brutal market logic for its own imperialist ends. After World War II, industrial farming took off in the US. As the economy reconverted from its wartime mobilization, chemical production shifted over to fertilizers and pesticides; the manufacturing of tractors and other agricultural equipment took over for some of the production of jeeps and tanks. Large companies that had profited off death and destruction during the war rebranded and converted explosives and war chemical manufacturing into fertilizer and pesticide factories. Most of the pesticides used today contain the same nerve poisons that were used in Nazi gas chambers.[66] After the war, easy credit allowed farmers to take out loans, buy more land, and expand. For a while, the resulting surplus went to Europe as food aid. Then the fertilizers, pesticides, and machinery were sold to European countries, which created their own food surpluses. Instead of producing less, the US dumped the surplus onto countries in the Global South, driving prices down, destroying domestic markets, and eliminating these countries' capacities to feed themselves. Proceeding as if this de-development were indicative of Third World underdevelopment or backwardness, the US (and other countries in the Global North) convinced countries in the Global South to take out loans to buy farming equipment, patented seeds, fertilizers, and pesticides as the means for

The domination of agribusiness monopolies has wiped out small farmers, ecosystems, and biodiversity. (Photo: Lindsay Eynik)

"solving" the food problem that overproduction in the North had created. Production in the Global South increased, which, again, led to declining prices, which, again, made it hard for farmers to repay their loans. Many small farms went under, forced to sell to their larger and more prosperous competitors. Formerly self-sufficient peasants migrated to cities in a massive wave of urbanization. What the Global North marketed as a Green Revolution "produced as many hungry people as it saved."[67]

The big lie of capitalist agriculture also covers up the environmental havoc wrought by industrial farming methods. The high-yield hybrid grains of the Green Revolution wiped out some 90 percent of local agrobiodiversity.[68] Concentrating on single crops for exports—monocropping—not only forces farmers to purchase food on the market that they had previously grown themselves, but also quickly degrades the soil. Whereas previous farming methods had been able to nourish the soil by growing different plants at the same time, monocropping strips the soil of nutrients. Growers are then compelled to undertake more intensive irrigation and use more fertilizers and pesticides, thereby making agriculture a major polluter and emitter of greenhouse gases. In many parts of the world, in order to keep up with their debt payments under conditions of falling grain prices, farmers have cleared more and more land, burning millions of acres of forests, grasslands, and wetlands. Because forests absorb carbon from the atmosphere and are a critical part of the Earth's water cycle, diminishing the world's forests contributes to the increase of carbon and thus to global heating. Likewise, large-scale farming's reliance on extensive irrigation makes agriculture a major user of the planet's freshwater.

One further example of the environmental havoc caused by the capitalist food system is industrial meat production. It releases more heating gases than transportation. It has also become excessively grim with the development of "Concentrated Animal Farming Operations" (CAFO). These operations cram thousands of animals into tight rows where the animals can barely move. Some animals are injected with hormones to make them produce more milk or get fatter faster. Feeding is automated, administered by computerized systems overseen by someone at a distant terminal. More likely to get sick because of the overcrowding, the animals are pumped full of antibiotics. The confined living conditions, increased tolerance to antibiotics, and genetic similarity of animals reared in CAFOs make them ideal hosts for new and potentially lethal diseases. As biologist Rob Wallace says, "agribusiness is so focused on profits that selecting for a virus that might kill a billion people is treated as a worthy risk."[69]

The COVID-19 pandemic made the global effects of US industrial agriculture clear. Corporate agribusiness's land grabs and deforestation release pathogens from their former isolation into the human food supply chain. As the climate warms and habitats are further encroached upon, ecosystems are stressed. More diseases arise in species, increasing the likelihood of pandemics occurring in a business-as-usual future. Market-driven overproduction, economic immiseration, megacities, slums, degenerate health care, and the global movement of people and products turn viruses into pandemics. COVID-19 was not the first pandemic. If our food system remains dominated by the dictates of capitalism, it will be neither the last nor the worst.

Industrialized agricultural production does not prioritize healthy food. The commodification of food prioritizes yield per acre over nutrition per acre. A "Health Per Acre" report, conducted by the Navdanya organization cofounded by Vandana Shiva, found that crops grown using agroecological methods contained up to 5,174 percent more vitamins than those grown using industrial methods.[70] Because of the degraded quality of the soil, the foods that are produced lack nutritional quality. Not surprisingly given this degradation, the largest crops grown in the US, corn and soybeans, are used primarily for animal feed and fuel. Treated as a commodity and broken down into industrial inputs, the food in the US that is fit for human consumption is highly processed. Preservatives make industrial foods better suited for transport and give them longer shelf lives. Additives make them tasty and addictive. The health effects are significant: increased rates of diabetes, cancer, obesity, and cardiovascular disease.

The overproduction of cheap, processed, unhealthy food has significant class effects: people with more money can afford higher quality, fresher, and more nutritious food. The working class is stuffed with junk food. Tony Weis writes, "Many of the same small farmers in the developing world who cannot earn a decent livelihood on the land can now find a can of Coke, a tin of Nestlé Milo or a bag of Doritos in their rural shops."[71] Children who don't get adequate nutrition can suffer from cognitive and developmental impairment. People of all ages who are deprived of sufficient nutrients are more susceptible to disease. Their ability to combat disease is further compromised because the widespread use of antibiotics in industrial meat production is making antibiotics less effective.

The impact of industrial food production on health extends beyond the food we eat. In the US, air pollution from farms causes over seventeen thousand preventable deaths a year.[72] "Gases associated with manure and animal feed produce small, lung-irritating particles capable of drifting hundreds of miles. These emissions now account for more annual deaths than pollution from coal power plants."[73] Farmworkers, at least half of whom in the US are undocumented, face exposure to toxic chemicals. The World Health Organization reports that globally 222,000 people die each year from pesticide poisoning.

During the pandemic, meat and poultry processing plants were COVID-19 hotspots, primarily due to overcrowded working conditions and inadequate personal protective equipment. Across the United States, workers staged walkouts, bringing attention both to corporations' failure to provide even minimal protections to essential workers and to the broader conditions in the industry. Workers in meat and poultry processing plants have had to endure dangerous speedups on fast-moving production lines, floors slippery with blood and fluids, and being forced to work past exhaustion with minimal breaks. To use a more specific example: in 2017, Tyson Foods, the largest chicken processing company in the world, decided to stop feeding chickens antibiotics. Did this lead Tyson to cut back a bit on production and provide better conditions for their workers and for the chickens, perhaps ones that would make them less likely to get sick? No. It led to a worsening of the already bad conditions for poultry processing plant workers, most of whom are immigrant women from Central and South America. Tyson decided the chicken carcasses would be sprayed with peracetic acid. The impact on the workers in the processing plant has been headaches, sore throats, eye irritation, sinus conditions, and asthma.[74]

Industrial food production destroys communities. In the midwestern US, the rise of CAFOs pushed thousands of small- and medium-sized farms out of business. As overproduction drives down prices and increases farmer debt, farmers are forced to sell their land to more powerful corporations. Tim Gibbons with the Missouri Rural Crisis Center explains what happens when multinational corporations come to exert monopoly control over livestock production:

> They are vertically integrated, from animal genetics to grocery stores. What they charge isn't based upon what it costs to produce, and it's not based on supply and demand, because they know what they need to make a profit. What they have done, through government support and taxpayer support, is to intentionally overproduce so that the price stays low, sometimes below the cost of production. That kicks their competition out of the market. Then they become the only player in town.

> Over time, it has extracted wealth and power from communities. We can see how that has impacted rural main streets. You can see the boarded-up storefronts. You can see the lack of economic opportunity.[75]

When farmers leave, the stores that supported them go out of business. Demand shrinks. People move away, diminishing the community's tax base. Services are cut. And the corporations rake in profits.

The nightmare reality of industrial farming is the truth of capitalist agriculture. But it's not the whole truth: overproduction is not only a story of capitalist markets. It's also a story of state intervention. State policy has played a major role in the design and implementation of the food system for hundreds of years. US agricultural policy generally serves the interests of landowners, capitalists, and imperialists, not people and the planet. One partial exception was the New Deal, passed because of the pressure that a growing workers' movement in the 1930s put on the government. Policies were enacted to support farmers and break with destructive competition and overproduction by establishing a floor under which market prices could not sink. The government also built up "grain reserves to avoid food shortages and food price spikes."[76] In practice, not

all farmers were supported. Southern Democrats ensured that sharecroppers were excluded from the policy. Unions of tenant farmers struggled to get their fair share of the payments. Hunger still stalked the land. But even the basic framework for assisting growers and workers didn't last. Capitalist power was too strong, and the Supreme Court ruled that the policy was unconstitutional.

The state has the capacity to create a just food system, one that respects growers, supplies everyone with nutritious food, and cares for nature. But so long as the state is a dictatorship of capitalists and landowners, we are doomed by overproduction. Capitalism cannot resolve the contradictions of capitalist agriculture.

Land Nationalization

Socialism will solve the problems of capitalist agriculture. It will decommodify food production by eliminating private property, competition, and market dependence. It will abolish imperialist suppression of food independence. And it will restore ecosystems, water resources, and soil health—even drawing down carbon—by producing food in ways that work with, rather than against, biophysical processes.

In 1872, Karl Marx said in an address to the Manchester Section of the International Working Men's Association: "The nationalization of land will work a complete change in the relations between labor and capital, and finally, do away with the capitalist form of production, whether industrial or rural. Then class distinctions and privileges will disappear together with the economical basis upon which they rest."[77] The socialist reconstruction of agriculture will begin by nationalizing multinational and large-scale producers and distributors in the US: Monsanto, Archer Daniels Midland Company, DowDuPont, Cargill, Tyson Foods, Walmart, and others. Their land and infrastructure will be held in common by the collective people and arranged into collective farms and cooperatives. Production will be managed according to plans made by growers and communities in consultation with a new Department of Food Production. The corporations' affiliated research facilities will be transformed into public research centers dedicated to improving agroecological farming practices and repairing the damage of agribusiness. Knowledge of best practices will be shared internationally and no longer hidden behind patents, which will also be dissolved. This is an essential step in the US effort to repay the accumulated imperialist debt to the lands and laborers of the Global South. CAFOs will be abolished, and the animals will be redistributed to farming collectives with an eye to redressing historical and ecological wrongs.

In the first decade of socialism, smaller-scale capitalist producers will not be forced to give up their old ways. Rather they will be shown the benefits of socialism and incentivized to transition voluntarily. Working with rural communities and work groups, the state will support improvements such as water management systems, reforestation and grassland restoration initiatives, and increased flood defenses that are beyond the means of small-scale capitalist or socialist cooperative farms to deliver. Farms running along socialist lines will have access to state-financed seasonal labor squads, seed banks, food services, and tool sheds from which agricultural equipment can be used freely. Those still seeking personal profit in the transitional period will be required to purchase these services on an ever-shrinking capitalist market. They will come to see from their own experience that producing for people and the planet creates a better life than producing for individual gain.

Agroecological Farming

When Marx was writing the first volume of *Capital*, it was already clear to anyone who cared to see that capitalist agriculture would devastate the world's soils and ecological cycles. As Marx wrote:

> All progress in capitalist agriculture is a progress in the art, not only of robbing the worker, but of robbing the soil; all progress in increasing the fertility of the soil for a given time is progress towards ruining the more long-lasting sources of that fertility . . . Capitalist production, therefore, only develops the technique and degree of combination of the social process of production by simultaneously undermining the original sources of all wealth— the soil and the worker.[78]

A legacy of capitalist agriculture's destruction of the natural environment is that socialist agriculture cannot simply seize hold of capitalist agricultural methods and put them to socialist ends. Even if modern industrialized farming was decarbonized—its polluting chemical fertilizers and pesticides replaced with organic alternatives—agro-industrial farming would still rob the soil and workers, just as Marx describes.

Capitalist agriculture's monocrops dramatically simplify ecosystems, reducing natural habitats for wildlife.[79] Habitat destruction and fragmentation—largely due to clearing land for crops and livestock—are key causes of global biodiversity loss and the sixth mass extinction currently underway. The species of corn, rice, wheat, and vegetables we are accustomed to eating are favored for their quick growing times and speedy realization of profits, despite their relative lack of nutrients compared to slower-growing varieties.[80] And modern approaches to livestock management, which keep livestock, agriculture, and woodlands apart, use land in ecologically inefficient ways. Beyond these ecological concerns, modern agriculture is a lonely endeavor. Labor-saving machinery drives down labor costs, but leaves off-season farms to be managed by a few isolated individuals. Underreporting makes attaining accurate data difficult, but studies suggest that suicide rates are 3.5 times higher among US farmers than the general population.[81] This is to say nothing of modern agriculture's seasonal reliance on super-exploited and unfree immigrant labor or the dangers of industrialized meat processing plants.[82]

Capitalist agriculture kills people and the planet so that capital can live. Socialist agriculture will flip this on its head. Capitalism will die so that people and the planet can live. This transformation demands the complete overhaul of how, where, and by whom food is produced. We will achieve it by implementing agroecological farming on a planetary scale.

The term "agroecological" is interpreted in many ways today. Defined loosely it means incorporating environmentally and socially responsible farming techniques into agricultural systems. This includes the implementation of cover crops, wildflower borders, managed grazing systems, field rotations, organic fertilizers, and natural pest reduction strategies. Understood in this loose sense, agroecology is fully compatible with capitalist social relations and development programs. In recent years, capitalist international organizations such as the Food and Agriculture Organization of the United Nations have been doing all they can to make this the dominant interpretation of agroecology.[83]

Scholar Susanna Hecht provides a more expansive sense of agroecology, one where agroecology includes political, social, and normative prescriptions incompatible with capitalist social relations and the profit motive.[84] According to this definition, agroecology involves significant decreases in off-farm inputs like chemical pesticides, fertilizers, and diesel fuel (although of course it does not presume the complete elimination of machinery). Agroecological systems also involve working with local communities to ensure that food is produced in fair and sustainable ways that tend to be more labor intensive than industrialized labor-saving systems, relying instead on increased human care and attention. Agroecology in this sense is about empowering local food producers and surrounding communities to manage landscapes in ways that work with, rather than against, natural nutrient cycles, ecosystems, and cultures. This is something that capital's subordination of the soil and the worker to accumulation at all costs cannot accept.

Capitalist agriculture kills people and the planet so that capital can live. Socialist agriculture will flip this on its head. Capitalism will die so that people and the planet can live.

Agroecological farming puts social and ecological justice front and center. It builds on the knowledge practices of those Indigenous and Black communities in the US who have historically practiced and recently revitalized agroecological techniques including perennial crop production, intercropping, silvopasture (the incorporation of trees in livestock systems), natural pest management systems, and the development of locally adapted varieties of staple crops.[85] Agroecology is, by definition, responsive to climatic changes, creative, and experimental. It incorporates conservation, forestry, and coastal and wetland management into food systems, and it brings food production into urban centers. These qualities make agroecology uniquely suited to our age of planetary warming. Capitalist agriculture is water-intensive and favors large-scale monocultural production, rendering it susceptible to droughts, heat waves, and pest infestations. By contrast, as Miguel Altieri and his coauthors argue, agroecology's diversification of agroecosystems and careful management of soil and water systems support a climate-resilient food system.[86]

The transformations that agroecological farming will involve are so extensive that it may be better not to think of socialist agriculture as agriculture at all. It's a way of managing complex ecosystems that can deliver a variety of social and ecological benefits, one of which is nutritious and plentiful food for everyone. Studies show that small farms using agroecological methods can obtain yields per hectare sufficient to feed between fifteen and twenty people a year.[87] Well-designed urban agroecological farms can be hugely productive. For example, in Cuba, where agroecological farming is the norm, an intensively managed urban plot of ten square meters can yield up to 200 kilograms of produce per year, potentially meeting the annual vegetable needs of a family of five.[88] Researcher Max Ajl points out that the US has more than enough land to provide for its population's food needs.[89] The UN estimates that agroecology can feed the world.[90] Beyond providing food enough for everyone, agroecological farming can repair damaged soils, improve biodiversity, and produce fibers and building materials such as bamboo, hardwoods, and some sustainable biofuels.[91] To repair the damage done by centuries of capitalist extraction and exploitation, we will need to combine these practices with other kinds of landscape management. Reforestation will improve flood defenses. Rewilding and conservation will return useful and beautiful plants and animals to US landscapes. In their book *Nature's Matrix*, Ivette Perfecto, John Vandermeer, and Angus Wright view these practices as best delivered by transforming the landscape into a patchwork of forests, pasturelands, and agroecological farms.[92]

The combination of agroecology, reforestation, rewilding, and conservation will contribute significantly to drawing down carbon, restoring water resources, cooling the planet, and potentially enabling temperatures to return to pre-industrial levels. Project Drawdown presents a decarbonization strategy that withdraws or sequesters 1,576 tons of carbon between 2020 and 2050, which would put the world just above the 1.5°C increase agreed at the 2015 COP21 climate change conference in Paris. Project Drawdown's strategy leans heavily on land-use changes and agroecological farming methods including silvopasture, peatland protection and rewetting, tropical forest reforestation, the spread of perennial staple crops, managed grazing, and regenerative annual cropping.[93] Another recent study found that global cropland soils could sequester 5.5 billion tons of carbon a year, just under the US's current annual emissions. These figures will decline as soils reach carbon saturation. Nevertheless, when combined with the elimination of fossil fuels, such carbon sequestration strategies will play a big part in helping to cool down the planet and averting runaway climate catastrophe.[94]

Agroecology isn't preferred by capital for two reasons. First, because agroecology reduces off-farm inputs like fertilizer and heavy machinery, it reduces opportunities to profit from food production. Corporations specializing in the production of chemicals and farm equipment lose their markets. Second, because agroecology is more labor-intensive than fossil-fuel guzzling and labor-saving industrialized agriculture, the labor costs are higher. More workers have to be paid. Higher labor costs increase the cost of food production, inflating the price of labor across all sectors, and cutting into corporate profit margins. Under socialism, these issues will no longer be a concern. Our goal is meeting needs not making profits.

Critics will argue that agroecology's higher use of manual labor makes it undesirable. Implying that all forms of machinery will be abandoned and all work will be done by hand, they describe the labor of farming as the kind of backbreaking drudgery people will do anything to avoid.[95] Even with advanced equipment, preparing soils, harvesting crops, and caring for and butchering livestock are all hard work, as anyone who has tended a community garden or farm will tell you. What the critics omit is that this work is also hugely rewarding. Working in collectives will reduce loneliness and lead to a richer social and cultural life in the countryside. Since labor no longer needs to be saved to drive down the costs of production, farmwork will be shared among as many people as want to participate. Rather than spending full days in the field week in and week out, food production and land management will become part of our daily routine, something we do for the fulfillment of providing for ourselves, our friends, family and community. Already, many young people across the US are doing just this, joining Community Supported Agriculture initiatives, and managing small farms run according to agroecological methods. Reductions in labor time will be achieved as people experiment with agroecological practices. Outside of pathbreaking countries like Cuba, agroecology has not received the huge sums of money that have flowed into agro-industrial research on livestock hormones, genetically modified plants, and fossil fuel reliant fertilizers and pesticides. Under socialism, agroecological research centers and local community experiments will refine our food systems, securing a nutritious diet for all and maximizing carbon sequestration.

Many of these changes can be introduced only at the pace of the larger social consciousness and insofar as the conditions of rural life have been improved to attract much larger numbers of workers. Because agroecology has yet to be instituted on a mass scale at anything near the size of the United States, it will have to be rolled out step by step. Model farms and communities will experiment with crops, technologies, and techniques, demonstrating in practice their wider applicability. No overhaul will be undertaken that will jeopardize the existence of adequate food supplies. The transformation of agricultural production will also not be permitted to cause any harm to countries that have become reliant on US food imports. On the contrary, creating more cooperative and solidary relations within the global food system is crucial to realizing the environmental and climate goals.

Planning: The Central Land Bureau

Premised on nationalizing the land and reorganizing the food production system according to the agroecological farming techniques necessary for addressing climate change, the socialist reconstruction of agriculture will replace market dynamics with coordinated planning.

Land nationalization is a matter of ownership. It establishes who has the right to a certain area of land and under what conditions. When socialists nationalize the land, we will take it away from capitalists who use it for their own profit and claim it for the people to use for common benefit. The fact that states, borders, and jurisdictions are political matters rather than attributes of nature reminds us that, really, no one can own the land. We are here to inhabit, enjoy, and steward it, responsible for ensuring that it will be as beautiful and bountiful for future generations if not more so. This is where planning comes in. To prevent market-driven, profit-seeking behavior from destroying environments and communities, we will plan what we will grow, where, under what conditions, how the work will be done, by whom, and so on. That's a matter of integrating the needs and knowledge of farmers and communities. Currently, we hear a lot about eating local: eating food that is grown nearby, rather than food that has to be imported long distances and that leaves a large carbon footprint. But not every locality has the capacity to meet local needs. Not every community can grow all that its members need to survive and flourish. Negotiated planning and coordinated production and distribution will solve this problem.

The Central Land Bureau will be the umbrella agency for coordinating food production, forest and grassland regeneration, coastal and wetland protection, and watersheds and water-use oversight. Each of these four areas will constitute a department within the bureau. Each department will establish a network of local and regional councils charged with monitoring, assessing, and communicating needs and capacities. They will also be the key loci for developing and executing production and regeneration plans. Given the agricultural focus of this chapter, we outline only the work of the Department of Food Production. It provides a model for the other three departments.

As its name suggests, the Department of Food Production will take responsibility for ensuring the production of nutritious food in environmentally responsible ways. Instead of dividing up food production along the lines of poultry, beef, pork, dairy, grains, fisheries, and fruits and vegetables, that is to say, instead of thinking of food first as commodities, the Department of Food Production will recognize the interrelation between food sources. It will organize growers and producers regionally, guiding farm collectives in the process of determining what they can reasonably produce in a given season and guiding community cooperatives in the process of estimating their food needs. This department will integrate these expectations into a central plan capable of accounting for climate, soil, and water differences across the country. It will encourage and support new growers' cooperatives, aiming toward the rapid expansion of community gardens and food production on urban as well as rural land. Here the Department of Food Production will incorporate insights from the wide array of farming initiatives already undertaken in Detroit as well as from the existing cooperative movement. Finally, the Department of Food Production will work with growers and communities to coordinate the participation and training of more people in farming, in the work not of necessarily becoming full-time farmers—unless they want to—but of taking turns cultivating and caring for crops, animals, and land.

Orienting food production toward the needs of people and the planet will have numerous benefits. Knowledge and practice will be integrated rather than divided between experts and workers. Farming collectives will become accustomed to pooling information and resources. Growers will gain more control over their working conditions, no longer compelled by the market to contribute to harmful practices. They will be respected for their understanding of the complex interrelations between food, environment, people, and animals. Planning will eliminate excess and waste. Farmers won't be forced to slaughter thousands of surplus animals and burn piles of grain. Consumers will appreciate the work that goes into growing food. They will learn more about the composition of healthy diets. Political advantages will include the dissolution of the sharp divide between town and country as society itself administers the production of food instead of trying to dominate and control the producers. The social advantages will be beyond measure. As people reengage with nature and other people, as we participate in feeding and building communities, we will acquire a new sense that our work and lives are meaningful. We will see, feel, smell, and taste what we cocreate together. The labor of social reproduction won't be assigned to people on the basis of class, race, or gender. It will be shared. Each will be free as all will be free.

Global Agriculture

Socialist agriculture will be anti-imperialist agriculture. It will abolish the overproduction behind the aggressive dumping of surplus staple crops onto the Global South. In place of this imperialist practice, it will work with producers in the Global South to restore the techniques necessary for national food sovereignty. The scourge of harmful monocropping will be overcome and the growing of diverse crops encouraged. Research networks that learn from and share indigenous and local knowledge—especially of plants, their habitats, and interrelations—will be developed. Trade relations will be reconstructed on cooperative rather than market grounds to determine which foods are best produced where and to institute the mechanisms and institutions for global planning. Quotas will be established to meet the needs of farmers and consumers. Until food sovereignty is achieved worldwide, US agriculture has a role to play in reducing global hunger and freeing oppressed nations from the struggle for basic survival.

Much of socialism will build from the achievements of capitalism. In agriculture, social reconstruction will also build from noncapitalist achievements, from practices and forms of knowledge that capitalism has generally expropriated, exploited, and eliminated. Climate change as well as the soil depleting and soul-destroying effects of capitalist agriculture require us to dismantle the imperialist agricultural-industrial complex and replace capitalism's profit motive with care for people and the planet. We have a world to win.

CHAPTER 6

INFRASTRUCTURAL RENEWAL: HOUSING AND TRANSPORTATION

*T*he spaces where we live, work, farm, play, travel, and learn are products of the cooperation of millions of people. Workers construct buildings and pave streets, drive buses, clean office buildings, staff day-care centers, and produce public art. Our cities and towns are socially produced by people, but under capitalism, these built environments are designed, controlled, and accessed to serve the interests of private capital—to make money for the few, rather than meet the needs of the many.

For example, every year in the United States 3.5 million people experience a period of houselessness. About half of them are children. According to the US Census Bureau, there are currently seventeen million empty housing units across the country. The working class built these housing units but doesn't own them. Banks, developers, and landlords own them. Capitalism uses markets to determine the building and distribution of housing. Instead of giving a house or apartment to everyone who needs one, capitalist society allows housing units to be sold or rented as a source of private profit. The millions of human beings who cannot afford housing are left to face indignity, hardship, and insecurity.

The issue of transportation also exposes the contradictions of capitalism. Modern society requires an enormous amount of transportation: the daily movement of workers from home to workplace and back, the shipment of products to houses and distribution centers, etc. Today our cities are chaotic, tangled networks of interstates and high-speed roadways, hot and noisy from the traffic of millions of automobiles and miles of reflective concrete pavement. The physical infrastructure of our country is such that for many people, it is literally impossible to get around without access to a private car—and the costs, headaches, and dangers that come with it. The destructive impact of this system of mass personalized transportation is widely recognized—from the unnecessary deaths associated with car crashes, to the damage to communities as houses are demolished to make way for highways, to the catastrophic impact of carbon emissions on the environment.

A robust public transportation infrastructure in every city, with reliable bus and train service, tree-lined bike paths and accessible sidewalks, safe roadways, and beautiful places for recreation would clearly be more efficient, safe, and pleasant for our society than what we have under capitalism. Transportation would be treated like the necessary social good it is. Yet, rather than make people-centered investments in our cities, capitalist government has worked with the automobile, oil, and construction industries to create urban environments that revolve around the private automobile, the transportation model at the basis of these industries' profits.

Since the end of the twentieth century, the imbalance between rich cities and declining cities in the US has increased dramatically. Alec MacGillis documents how whole sectors of the economy have consolidated and become concentrated in certain companies. Profits and growth opportunities once spread across the whole country flow to places where dominant companies are located (MacGillis uses Amazon as an example.) Large parts of the US are left behind as wealth concentrates in a handful of cities, making life increasingly difficult for working-class and low-income people even in the rich cities. In 1980, almost every part of the country had mean incomes within 20 percent of the national average. By 2013, a stark pattern emerged such that virtually the entire northeast corridor from Boston to Washington, DC and the coast of northern California had incomes more than 20 percent above average, while the vast majority of the country's interior—the rural South and Southwest, Midwest, and Great Plains—had incomes more than 20 percent below average. Within cities, moreover, inequality also intensified. Over 20 percent of the population of Atlanta, for example, live in poverty. In Washington, DC, 15 percent of the population lives in extreme poverty. As MacGillis writes, "With a winner-take-all economy came winner-take-all places."[96]

Capital, constantly moving and redirecting toward the places and spaces where the opportunity for profit is highest, endlessly disrupts the lives and social conditions of the human beings in its path. The remorseless, churning search for profit that characterizes capitalism has left a trail of destruction in its wake. Socialist reconstruction of our cities and towns—our places, the ones we call home—will resolve the fundamental contradiction of the capitalist system and remake our communities according to the needs of people and the planet. As geographer and housing policy analyst Samuel Stein writes, "The City must belong to those who build it, not who buy it."[97] In this chapter, we present a new vision for cities and towns—based on local, regional, and national planning—that is truly by and for the people.

Rethinking planning

Planning (or urban planning at the local level) is critical for the operation of basic services like water, housing, parks, and transportation. Under the US's current system, large federal agencies like the Federal Highway Administration and the Department of Housing and Urban Development set policy and direct funding streams from Congress to local agencies to carry out planning. Although the United States touts itself as democratic, a look at its planning process reveals that it is anything but. Lobbying from corporate interests, large donations to political campaigns, and pre-written legislation garner enormous profits for developers and infrastructure giants but mean poor outcomes for the majority of people. Banks and investors direct the flow of money locally and determine which projects get a share of society's resources.[98] Environmental concerns are tossed to the wayside as developments use enormous amounts of energy and resources and disrupt ecosystems. It is true that many communities have development offices with business bureaus that work to attract companies to their areas. In practice, this means helping to broker deals that let companies avoid paying taxes. Instead of improving communities, these companies leech off them, relying on community services and infrastructure for which they don't help to pay.

The planning institutions created under capitalism were designed to facilitate the expansion and movement of capital with a minimum of public outcry. These institutions were never meant to serve the people. The socialist reorganization of society requires rethinking what planning can do for us and for the planet. Rather than the top-down model of planning we have today, where capitalist interests work behind the scenes to produce plans, rules, and regulations, we propose a model of networked, responsive planning which is both "top-down" and "bottom-up," flexible and dialogic.

New national transportation and housing agencies will be created and vested with the power to set policy and guide implementation in consultation with corresponding networks of popular organizations (cooperatives, assemblies, unions, and councils). High-level planning will deal with broadly shared concerns: for example, a river monitoring body that spans the entire length of a river, from origin to egress, or a high-speed rail network that links communities across the country. At the same time, each locality and region will have its own specific history, capacities, conditions, and needs. The new socialist government will combine high-level planning with local popular control, retaining the flexibility to intervene "from above or below" if plans go awry or somehow conflict with the people's collective interest in redressing past harms and promoting the common good. In the sections that follow, we consider how this type of socialist planning will transform the infrastructure of US cities in the areas of housing and transportation.

Housing as a Social Good

Everyone needs a home, but in the US there is no guarantee everyone will get one. For those of us in the working class, with no source of income other than our job, whether and how we are housed depends on our wage. This makes housing extremely precarious for most of us, an endless source of stress and anxiety. Rents are too high and wages are too low.

Half of all renters in the US are "housing insecure," meaning that an unsustainably high amount of our income goes toward housing costs. Gentrification drives up rents as developers build luxury apartments, and the availability of decent and affordable apartments declines. For the 65 percent of people in the US who "own" our homes, two-thirds of those homes are mortgaged. We have to regularly pay money to the bank or risk foreclosure. Until our mortgage is fully repaid, it's really the bank that owns our house. When the economy crashes, as it regularly does under capitalism, large sections of the working class lose our jobs and can no longer afford to pay our rent or mortgage. The result is mass evictions and foreclosures.

For many working-class people, especially people of color and LGBTQ people facing harassment and discrimination, the housing that is affordable is often inadequate and unhealthy. It may be situated near busy roadways or toxic industrial sites, resulting in asthma, cancer, and other health issues. As is well known, lead pipes threaten the drinking water of millions of people in low-income and segregated neighborhoods. Necessary resources like grocery stores, job centers, public transit, health care, walkable streets, and parks are absent from many neighborhoods and rural towns. Seniors and disabled people face housing challenges related to isolation, affordability, physical accessibility, and access to medical and other services.

An encampment in Oakland, California: in the current system, access to housing isn't a given nor a right, leading to housing crises and mass homelessness. (Photo: Grendelkhan)

Even six decades after the civil rights revolution, housing in the United States remains extremely segregated, a reflection of the racist character of US capitalism. Four out of ten Black people live in "racially isolated" neighborhoods; three out of every four white people live in virtually all-white neighborhoods.[99] Segregation in housing is the deliberate outcome of decades of racist policies exacerbating inequality and depriving oppressed communities of services and resources to which they are entitled.

Disparities in housing are also regional, a reflection of the "winner-take-all" economy mentioned previously. In those neighborhoods, towns, and cities from which capital has fled—places like Cincinnati and Detroit—populations have declined and abandoned buildings and neighborhoods are left to deteriorate. In places where capital is concentrating, like Seattle and New York, the problem is gentrification. Developers in search of profits push poor and oppressed residents out of their homes and communities, purchasing and redeveloping buildings to attract people able to pay higher rents and more costly mortgages.

Far from accidental, the shortage of affordable housing in every US city and the stark segregation and inequality from neighborhood to neighborhood are "according to plan"—this is what structural racism looks like. As housing costs have risen and workers' incomes have remained the same or declined, the government has reduced the housing assistance available to bridge the gap. Permanent, federally funded, low-cost housing first came into being in the 1930s as part of the New Deal. This was a concession by the capitalist state during an era of widespread and militant working-class struggle, and a way to manage the mass migrations from the countryside to the city that accompanied agricultural monopolization, mass industrial production, and two world wars. In the three decades after World War II, the federal government built more public housing while it subsidized suburban homeownership with implicit or explicit racist guidelines. The government simultaneously subsidized the destruction of many housing projects and poor neighborhoods under the guise of "urban renewal"—or "Negro removal," as James Baldwin more accurately termed it—making way for interstate highways and high-rise apartment buildings deliberately cut off from the city. Millions of Americans, especially people of color, lost their homes and communities.

Over the next decades, already inadequate federal investment in affordable housing programs continued to decline. More and more public housing units were destroyed or privatized. Clinton-era "welfare reform" even included a law capping the total number of public housing units at 1999 levels. Housing assistance moved away from public housing and became based on insufficient and hard-to-access vouchers to low-income tenants while developers received tax credits for building affordable housing. The trick is that the tax credits have a time line: once they expire, the owner can convert the affordable housing units to market-rate units. Today, when developers present their plans to "renew" communities, they point with pride to the number of affordable housing units that will be created, but disguise the number of affordable housing units they are destroying. There is no federal legal requirement for the one-to-one replacement of demolished affordable housing. And though some local planning authorities require a certain amount of affordable housing in their plans, they routinely offer exemptions that allow developers to pay their way out of the mandate.

The core issue underlying all of these problems is that housing is distributed via markets for the purpose of private capital accumulation. In contrast, socialism treats housing as a human right and social good. In the words of Gianpaolo Baiocchi and H. Jacob Carlson, housing is the "linchpin of human flourishing and community stability."[100] They highlight promising models of social housing already present under capitalism: community land trusts, tenant cooperatives, mission-driven nonprofits, and well-functioning public housing. These exciting experiments in social housing can inspire a housing framework for the future.[101] They point to an array of different options communities can employ as they work collectively to make sure that everyone has the safe and reliable housing that meets their needs.

Under present-day US capitalism, public or social housing has been defunded and degraded to the point that it is largely looked down upon as an option. Owning a private house appears to be the ticket for economic security—a source of equity for a family to pay off tuition, medical, or elder care bills or to pass on to one's children. Socialist reconstruction will not take away families' private houses—quite the opposite, the private homes people live in will belong to them—but we will quickly build a new model for housing. There is no reason public housing has to be inferior.

In Vienna, Austria, for example, 62 percent of citizens live in public housing projects that are affordable, highly attractive, sustainably designed, and in which tenants' rights are protected from the whims of the market.[102] Residents describe these social housing estates as not only highly desirable places to live, but also as places where people get to know each other and become comfortable living next to others with different backgrounds. Recreation, socializing, and community engagement increase when home dwellers are not crushed by the burden of rent. If this is already a reality in the capital city of Austria, a capitalist country, one can easily imagine what is possible in a socialist society where the working class is in charge!

Social housing will not only decommodify housing; it will rebuild communities. "Social housing requires imagining a kind of housing whose production, distribution, and management is guided by deeply democratic principles, a logic of intentional inclusion, and an ethos of care and environmental stewardship. For this reason, while social housing needs to be publicly backed to function at scale, it also has an indispensable bottom-up element that renders it incompatible with exclusively top-down statist directives."[103]

In that spirit, the new socialist government will create a National Housing Agency to set broad housing policy, administer publicly owned housing, and oversee the creation and implementation of a democratically decided national housing plan. The National Housing Agency will initiate the formation of a network of popular organizations in every city and town, including tenant cooperatives, apartment boards, neighborhood assemblies, and regional councils. These organizations will represent local popular control and will be responsive to individual residents, neighboring organizations, and higher bodies such as the National Housing

Agency. The local and regional organizations will participate in the design and implementation of the national housing plan, as well as their respective local and regional housing plans. Rather than placing exclusive emphasis on formal education and technocratic expertise, planning and decision-making will integrate different forms of knowledge and will value local experiences.

Comprehensive housing plans will be developed to ensure the abolition of structural racism. These plans will focus on eliminating segregation; environmental racism; energy and water insufficiency; sprawl; the absence of shade trees, parks, and green spaces; and other pressing problems.

Working with the popular organizations, the National Housing Agency will initiate a regular, comprehensive inventory of housing units and survey of people's individual housing needs, including proximity to work, access to services like child care and elder care, availability of parks and recreation, building accessibility, and other important aspects of housing. It will enlist neighborhood and building-level organizations to help gather this information and relay data to local agencies and planning bodies. Depending on the type of need, local agencies will provide services directly or provide resources to residents' and workers' councils to address the needs. Local, regional, and national planning bodies will use the national survey and inventory to organize the development of new public housing units as needed. There is no "one size fits all" housing arrangement—from single people to large groups, people who like to move around and those who prefer to stay in the same place, there must be a wide array of available housing possibilities. The inventory and survey process will bring planning directly to the people, demystifying resource allocation.

The National Housing Agency's immediate priority will be to end houselessness and housing insecurity. It will take immediate steps to address overcrowding, inaccessibility, and unhealthy or unsafe housing, with priority given to specially oppressed communities and individuals. To this end, it will direct the seizure and nationalization of vacant housing units which will be redeveloped and administered as public housing. Working together with the Bureau of Wages, Prices, and Rents (see chapter 4), the National Housing Agency will immediately reduce rents to a nominal cost and give renters the option to own their homes. As detailed in chapter 4, the new socialist government will unilaterally forgive all mortgage debt. No workers need to fear that their houses will be snatched out from under their feet. On the contrary, only the banks, landlords, and mortgage brokers need to be afraid. With the market in housing abolished, they will no longer be able to capitalize on people's need for housing. Of course, no person will be allowed to own more than two houses, and those with vacation homes will be encouraged to make them available for others to enjoy. People occupying substandard housing will be given opportunities—along with anyone who wants to join them—to learn plumbing, electrical, and carpentry skills so that they can participate in renovating, repairing, and restoring theirs and others' houses. This training will provide the basis for communities' ability to collectively maintain and develop their housing stock. Young people and others looking for new work will be encouraged to get trained themselves, adding to the number of people with skills in building, plumbing, carpentry, painting, masonry, roofing, and electrical work and thereby providing for the long-term maintenance of quality housing.

Once these first steps have been taken, comprehensive housing plans will be developed to ensure the abolition of structural racism. These plans will focus on eliminating segregation; environmental racism; energy and water insufficiency; sprawl; the absence of shade trees, parks and green spaces; and other pressing problems. After so many decades of redlining and deprivation of resources, there is an urgent need for reparations with regard to the built environment. These reparations are a central feature of socialist reconstruction.

Long-term issues connected with climate change and regarding land use, urbanization, and suburbanization will also be confronted. The capitalist class can't take on these questions. Since its only motive is profit, it has no interest in or capacity for the large-scale participatory planning necessary for an adequate response to the climate crisis. Under socialism, the people will have the power to address these problems themselves.

Consider some of the basic issues that climate change poses for housing. In the US, about 21 percent of all energy use comes from

An Amtrak train in 1978—there has been little investment in mass transit in decades.
(Photo: Drew Jacksich)

housing. Much of the private housing in the US was built before 1980 and so not designed, constructed, or maintained with energy efficiency in mind. Retrofitting these buildings will generate enormous energy savings, but under capitalism these urgently needed improvements are left to the initiative and budgets of individual homeowners and profit-minded landlords. Even relatively "low-tech" improvements like insulation; air sealing; LED lighting; and new heating, ventilation, and air conditioning systems will immediately and significantly lower greenhouse gas emissions. The National Housing Agency will oversee a massive free retrofitting program as part of the "Cap and Convert Plan" (see chapter 3), as well as a program to install solar arrays and other distributed generation systems on houses and apartment buildings. In addition, all new buildings will be built to be "net zero" (consuming less energy than they produce). Given that the US is the world's largest carbon emitter, we have an obligation to the world to make these changes to our housing stock. Since lawns are one of the largest irrigated and most heavily fertilized crops in the US, the National Housing Agency will guide their transformation into communal recreation areas and native-plant gardens that improve biodiversity and soil health while aiding water retention and surface-area cooling.

The advanced labor force and productive capacities that currently exist in the United States already make it possible to provide everyone an affordable, environmentally sustainable, safe, clean, spacious, and beautiful home in a neighborhood that meets their needs. Under socialism, workers will be organized to build and cultivate housing that improves the quality of life for all, while reversing the decades of neglect and devastation brought upon poor and oppressed communities.

Transportation Under Capitalism

Transportation is a challenge for most working people. We have long been forced to make hard trade-offs—between cost, time, and safety—in order to get where we need to go. Basic tasks like getting to and from work at the same time that we have to get our kids to and from school and do the grocery shopping that puts food on our tables present enormous challenges because of capitalism's inability to plan for and provide safe, reliable, and convenient public transportation. We end up working hours from where we live, while the rich speculate and profit from technological pipe dreams such as high-speed transportation hyperloops that benefit the few and create new harms for the working many. Necessary transportation for everyday living, such as accessible sidewalks, regular and reliable bus service, safe roadways, and places for recreation are missing from most working-class communities, urban and rural.

With the fiscal crises of the 1970s, cities were forced to privatize and disinvest from social services. Funding for passenger rail (Amtrak),

Parking & Housing

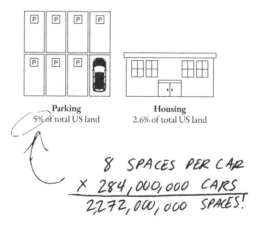

Parking
5% of total US land

Housing
2.6% of total US land

8 SPACES PER CAR
X 284,000,000 CARS
2,272,000,000 SPACES!

Sources: NRDC, Statista, Strong Towns, National Association of Home Builders

109

intercity bus travel, and city bus systems was and continues to be slashed. These services were forced to operate not as public goods but as profit-seeking businesses. Financial professionals and management consultants try to fix our ailing transit systems, but instead of doing the very thing that would turn ridership around—increasing the frequency and reliability of service—they cut services to reduce costs, which only spirals the system into further disuse and disrepair. Despite the fact that buses are used almost as frequently as rail, that millions of working-class people depend on them for basic transportation is often overlooked. In 2019, the national share of trips occurring by bus and rail was nearly identical, (47 percent and 48 percent, respectively).[104] Cuts to bus routes severely impact workers' lives and livelihood. As a general rule, the US prioritizes major road building over mass transit. For instance, the fiscal year 2021 transportation bill allocated only $18.9 billion to the Federal Transit Administration but $62.9 billion to the Federal Highway Administration.[105] These political choices affect how we move and how we live.

Under capitalism public space is not for everyone. The police, as agents of the state, serve propertied interests and enforce who can safely and comfortably traverse or enjoy space. The police regularly murder and harass Black and Brown people who are simply driving, bicycling, or walking. Even the idea that someone could call the police introduces fear into places like parks that people typically associate with peace. For example, in 2021, a white woman called the police after a Black man engaging in leisurely bird-watching asked her to leash her dog. Cities invest public dollars in amenities like rail lines, bike lanes, parks, and walkable commercial corridors in order to attract capital. The benefits of these investments accrue primarily to the private real estate sector by means of higher rents and property values, while poor and marginalized people are pushed out.

In the nation's largest cities, cars account for about a third of greenhouse gas emissions. Transporting people and goods accounts for approximately 70 percent of all US oil use.[106] Control over oil markets as a strategic resource has long been a driving force of US imperialism: Harvard's Kennedy School estimates that one-quarter to one-half of all wars between nations since 1973 have been due to oil.[107] Relentless US imperialism has killed and injured millions of working-class people worldwide. Its crazed pursuit of oil dominance shows few signs of abating.

In areas where transit service is insufficient and there are no safe ways to bike or walk, workers are forced into private car ownership and the personal and social costs that accompany it. According to the American

Public Transit Association, "The average household spends sixteen cents of every dollar on transportation, and 93 percent of this goes to buying, maintaining, and operating cars, the largest expenditure after housing."[108] Parking occupies more land than housing.[109] There are an estimated eight parking spots per car in the US (Des Moines, Iowa, has 19.4 spaces per household!).[110] Automobile dependency was not accidental. It was a product of state action and inaction, as crucial transportation and infrastructure decisions were subordinated to the interests of the big capitalists of the auto industry. The result of this coordinated campaign is not only fossil fuel dependence, pollution, high rates of carbon emissions, and the massive waste of space (parking); it's also the theft of our time. Commuters in the most congested cities lose up to a week a year stuck in traffic, time they could spend with friends and families, doing what they will.[111]

Capitalism configured our transportation system through racist disinvestment, imperialist greed for oil, profit-seeking highway building, and gentrification. The new socialist government will replace this system with just and sustainable public transportation. We will build a future where people—and the goods we need to survive—move through space safely and with dignity without relying on fossil fuels. The socialist reconstruction of our transportation system will rectify the harms of the past and produce a mobility future where people and the planet come first. The goal is to reorganize the physical environments of where we live and work and thereby rapidly reduce reliance on expensive, carbon-emitting, private cars. And no one will have to travel long distances for work, school, health care, food, or basic recreation.

Transportation Under Socialism

Social philosopher André Gorz writes, "Above all, never make transportation an issue by itself. Always connect it to the problem of the city, of the social division of labor, and to the way this compartmentalizes the many dimensions of life."[112]

Everyone who has encountered the detours and delays of road repair projects knows that reconstructing an entire transportation system cannot happen overnight. It takes time and planning. As we've said, the vision we outline in this book is of socialism's beginning, not its mature form. From the beginning, though, socialism will improve the lives of working people all over the country. Moving from profit to planning and private gain to public interest will produce a transportation system able to meet basic needs while transitioning away from fossil fuels.

The new socialist government will create a new Department of Transportation to set broad transportation policy and administer regional and national transportation including municipal, county, and interstate roads and highways. Freight, air, buses, and rail will be nationalized and placed under Department of Transportation direction. The department will form and mobilize local and regional transportation councils to tackle issues of local delivery and household travel. It will also inventory the types of transportation that best serve communities. Local public transit will immediately be made free. Instead of being oriented toward private profit and the interests of the rich and the white, transportation will be recognized as a fundamental social good, a basic service necessary for the well-being of all.

Coordinating with local and regional communities, the Department of Transportation will produce plans for schedules and routes that meet working-class needs. It will work with the Department of Education to train operators, dispatchers, mechanics, and systems engineers. Together with the various branches of the Fossil Fuel Cap Agency, the Department of Transportation will take the necessary steps toward reducing transportation system emissions to zero as quickly as possible. As we outline in chapter 3, the production and importation of fossil fuels will be slowed and eliminated for the sake of the planet. The Department of Transportation will also work with transportation unions to identify and transform fuel consumption patterns while implementing improvements in public transit and land use.

As the agency through which the working class attends to the common need for reliable transportation, the Department of Transportation will prioritize public transportation services and easily accessible routes between workplaces, housing, schools, health-care centers, and food sources. These services and routes will be marked first for upgrades and repairs. Hybrid and electric buses and vans will be built and supplied for short routes. The Department of Transportation will also repair the country's long-neglected and decaying bridges. At the same time these necessary improvements to our vital national infrastructure are being made, regional transportation agencies will begin coordinating plans for building high-speed, electrified rail networks between major population centers.

Police forces that have long operated like occupation armies in Black, Brown, and impoverished communities will be immediately disbanded and replaced with new public safety organizations built from the ground up. Now that power is in the hands of the multinational working class, we will make our shared recreational spaces available for free use by all people.

Community councils and local groups will work together to increase public safety concerns not already alleviated through solutions like social housing. To eliminate problems that capitalism and racism embed in our material infrastructures, the Department of Transportation will require communities to plan and implement safe street designs which make transportation much less dangerous for all users regardless of whether they are driving, riding, or walking.[113] Safe designs slow down cars and provide wider sidewalks and more convenient and visible crosswalks for cyclists and pedestrians. Traffic enforcement will be oriented towards keeping people safe rather than revenue collection and racist intimidation.

Local public transit will immediately be made free. Instead of being oriented toward private profit and the interests of the rich and the white, transportation will be recognized as a fundamental social good, a basic service necessary for the well-being of all.

Local transportation councils will complete audits of sidewalks, bike infrastructure, and transit systems to note accessibility and design problems. Under capitalism, most communities in the US already have planning boards that address these issues. The problem is that their decisions are generally made for the benefit of private property and capital; that is, with an eye to the interests of business rather than the needs of the people. As part of the socialist reconstruction of infrastructure, local councils will ensure the general accessibility of all sidewalks, building entrances, and transit systems to those using mobility devices, strollers, and wheelchairs. Working with housing councils and workplaces, local transportation councils will determine and coordinate needs for bicycles, bicycle storage, bus stop amenities, and more. As automobile usage declines, cooperation will play a crucial role in the redesign of roadways for quick, convenient, and safe travel by foot, bikes, and modes of public transportation like moving sidewalks and electric streetcars. People need travel options beyond private automobiles. Local transportation councils will play crucial roles in developing them.

Ending mass reliance on private cars will open up paths for improving our social world. Land used for parking can be turned into housing, schools, hospitals, community centers, and parks—as determined by the local councils. Councils might decide to offer buybacks for private vehicles and make some acquired vehicles publicly shared and operated—whether at the workplace, neighborhood, or building-level, according to the transportation requirements in that community. For-profit private models for such options already exist (Zipcar, Free2move) and can be appropriated and expanded. Reducing the private car industry does not need to mean the end of family vacations—not at all. The automobile industry—nationalized and placed in the hands of the workers along with all other industries—can be reengineered toward production of electric vehicles and smaller vehicles for urban deliveries such as electric-assist cargo bicycles ("e-cargo bikes") which have the same capacity as trucks and are more nimble, safe, and environmentally friendly.[114]

Land use—the pattern of different uses such as residential, industrial, commercial, and agricultural—will shift as we reorient the economy toward meeting people's needs. Coordinating jobs and housing and aligning resource distribution with resource creation will ensure that people and goods do not have to travel long distances. We will change "buying local" from the niche matter of bourgeois taste it is today into an obvious, convenient, and practical way of living for everyone. People in the US have long complained about the alienation and isolation of suburban life where houses on large lots are cut off from the vitality of community interactions. Rather than remaining trapped in lonely and environmentally damaging subdivisions, communities will adopt patterns of land use that allow for easy walking, biking, and public transit for most everyday activities,

Fifty years ago, Gorz imagined socialist cities after the revolution. He envisioned cities surrounded by greenbelts where everyone spends several hours a week growing food for their communities. He dreamed of municipal bicycles, driverless electric taxis, and communally shared automobiles. "The car would no longer be a necessity. Everything will have changed: the world, life, people. And this will not have come about all by itself."[115] We agree. This people- and planet-friendly version of the future is possible now—but it won't happen by itself. It will happen when the working class has the power to make it happen. It will happen under socialism.

CHAPTER 7

MEDICINE FOR THE PEOPLE!

When this chapter was being written, more than nine hundred thousand people had died in the US from COVID-19. Two years into the epidemic, we still had no functioning public health-care system. By capitalist standards, public health isn't profitable. Frontline workers, people of color, and our elders have borne the most severe impacts of the coronavirus pandemic. Many have paid the ultimate price. As always happens under capitalism, working-class, poor, and vulnerable people are the first to die. Meanwhile, capitalist media and politicians from both mainstream political parties downplay the unnecessary suffering, lack of support, and economic hardship we've had to endure.

Other epidemics predate the coronavirus pandemic. Most are less dramatic but nevertheless life-threatening. They include chronic diseases like hypertension, diabetes, heart disease, and obesity. These conditions directly correlate with increased stress, lack of safe housing, poor diet, financial insecurity, and insufficient exercise. Medical and public-health experts refer to these factors as "social determinants of health." With this crucial concept, mainstream medicine recognizes that health inequities are primary causes of chronic disease. It admits that capitalism is the problem. Capitalism makes people sick. Capitalism kills.

We can't wait for public-health policymakers to develop a coherent plan for health care. They are unwilling and unable to challenge the capitalist system, even though they know it's at the root of the health-care crisis in the United States. In the wealthiest country in the world, people suffer from unnecessary diseases and die unnecessary deaths as the system causing them generates profits for corporations, banks, and landlords. Life expectancy in the US is falling. Our lives depend on abolishing the deadly capitalist system and building a socialist one.

This chapter shows how socialist society will produce healthier people and better health care for all. It's not a detailed blueprint or roadmap. During the revolutionary period, people will generate new solutions to problems as they arise, creatively responding to the health-care needs of

Life Expectancy Change in Months (2019 - 2022)

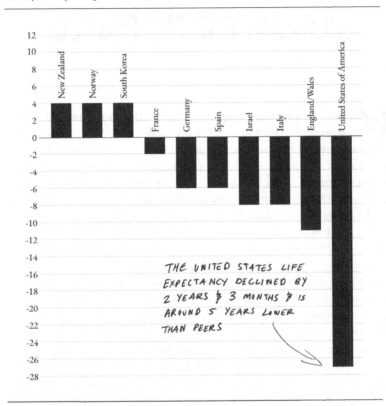

Source: medRxiv

the moment. Nevertheless, this chapter is a starting point for envisioning the health-care system and future we will create under socialism.

Abolish the Medical-Industrial Complex

The fundamental problem with health care in the United States is that it is generally organized as a market. Instead of recognizing that securing people's health and longevity is a fundamental social responsibility and governmental obligation as most countries do, the US treats health care as a commodity, as something individuals purchase from others who seek to make a profit. This market approach to what is a fundamental right and public good makes health a privilege of those with the money to pay for it. It fails to acknowledge systemic causes of poor health, such as exposure to environmental toxins and lack of nutritious food. It undermines the sense of collective responsibility crucial for generating popular support for public-health measures in times of crisis, as the tragedy of the US response to COVID-19 has taught us. For these reasons, the socialist government will immediately disband the for-profit health-care model.

We said that health care in the US is "generally" organized as a market because even in this profit-oriented system there are forms of socialized medicine. In some instances, the US government recognizes that health care is a social good and governmental responsibility. All members of the US military, military retirees, and their dependents receive free health care from the Military Health System. For the most part, though, even in its publicly funded programs like the Federal Employees Health Benefits Program (for government workers), Medicare (for senior citizens and people with specific disabilities), Medicaid (for low-income people), and the Children's Health Insurance Program (CHIP, a program that provides federal matching funds to states to help provide health insurance to families who may not qualify for Medicaid), the US relies on insurance rather than a national health-care system. Some insurance is government provided and some is private, that is, sold by corporations to customers for a profit.

This system is costly, confusing, and cumbersome. It's also grossly unequal. In addition to the economic inequalities built into a system that uses the market to deliver health care, there are significant disparities across the United States. Because the states administer Medicaid and CHIP, they can and do enact different eligibility requirements and provide different kinds of coverage. The state in which a person lives makes a big difference in the sort of health care they receive, especially if they are working-class.

Consider abortion. The Hyde Amendment (implemented in 1977) outlaws the use of federal funds for abortion except in cases of rape, incest, and danger to the mother's life. Some states also cover abortion in the case of fetal abnormalities. Additionally, some states use their state funds to pay for almost any medically necessary abortion, whether they provide this coverage voluntarily or by court order. Wealthy women who don't need Medicaid aren't affected by these different and confusing laws. Poor and working-class women are—and where they live determines the medical treatment they can receive.

The new socialist government will replace this unfair and inefficient combination of expensive private insurance and uneven government programs with a single People's Health Administration. No longer needed, the private insurance companies will be dissolved—along with their billing and copays. Health care will be completely free. The advocacy organization Physicians for a National Health Plan has demonstrated that such a plan reduces the overall cost of health care because of the dramatic savings that result from eliminating redundant administration—no more billing departments and bureaucrats denying coverage, ramping up copays, and devising ever more complex schemes for taking our money when we or our loved ones are sick and injured.[116]

Abolishing the market in prescription drugs and ensuring that medicines are produced based on people's actual needs will save lives.

The People's Health Administration will also oversee the newly nationalized pharmaceutical industry. Medicines will be free. Pharmacists, scientists, clinicians, and public-health workers will work with communities to assess the use of and need for various medications based on local data and develop a plan for producing them. In the current capitalist system of marketized health care, about $30 billion a year goes to medical marketing. Sixty-eight percent of that, or $20 billion, is spent by health-care companies persuading clinicians of the benefits of certain prescription drugs.[117] Medical marketing convinced clinicians that Oxy-Contin had no abuse potential for chronic noncancer pain. This was a lie. Drug overdose deaths in 2020 hit the highest number ever recorded.[118] According to the Centers for Disease Control (CDC), that year more than ninety-three thousand people died from opiate drug overdoses, most of those with synthetic opiates like OxyContin or fentanyl.[119] Abolishing the market in prescription drugs and ensuring that medicines are produced based on people's actual needs will save lives.

The cost savings from eliminating the current stranglehold that the pharmaceutical industry has on our country will be massive. The industry's pursuit of megaprofits and the mind-blowing compensation awarded to their CEOs will end. On average, CEOs of the top pharmaceutical corporations have annual salaries of around $22 million a year, not including stock options. Stock options enrich them even more. To use a particularly horrifying example: in 2020 the CEO of BioPharma took home $130 million in stock rewards because of the company's role in developing

Regeneron, a COVID-19 treatment.[120] He made out like a bandit because so many people were getting sick and dying.

Nationalizing the pharmaceutical industry under the People's Health Administration further entails the abolition of drug patents, a particularly deadly and insidious form of private property. Under socialism, legal protection of innovation is unnecessary; the goal is sharing and collaboration. Scientists naturally collaborate for the common good. It's corporations that insist on keeping science and innovation under wraps until they secure a profitable corner of the market.

Despite the secrecy of Pfizer and Moderna, for example, scientists from all over the world exchanged their findings as they worked together to research and understand the coronavirus. In the US, scientists formed groups on Zoom; hundreds of people joined these meetings. Within a few months, they were publishing research papers online and in major journals. Working collaboratively allowed scientists to "map out protein interactions and other features of SARS-CoV-2 virus."[121] Because of this work, drug companies quickly identified the best pharmaceutical approaches for targeting the coronavirus. The COVID-19 vaccine is one of the most rapidly developed vaccines in history due to this free collaboration outside the constraints of capitalist preoccupations with patents and secrecy.

The COVID-19 pandemic also ushered in an unprecedented collaboration between researchers based in the US and China. As early as spring 2020, epidemiologists and other medical experts from the two countries were working closely together. Cheng Li and Senqi Ma write that "Within weeks of the outbreak in Wuhan, Chinese scientists successfully determined the pathogen, deciphered the gene sequence, and shared the data on the new coronavirus with international colleagues."[122] Strong international relationships between colleagues will be standard scientific practice under socialism. Freely sharing research findings will no longer be the exception. Under capitalism, US-based researchers who share data with other countries, especially China, are often suspected of espionage—a practice that sacrifices lives for profits.

Sharing knowledge promotes innovation. Cuba began organizing its biotech industry to serve the needs of its people decades ago.[123] The country became expert at making highly affordable generic medications. Cuba helped Iran, China, and Malaysia set up factories and export medications to over fifty countries. At the same time, Cuba continued to innovate. Biotechnology became a pillar of the economy. The Cuban system invested in training doctors and researchers and prioritized patient care. The vision was for science to serve the people, rather than drive big money-making schemes. Sixty years later and despite the ongoing US embargo, this small socialist country has, without assistance or adequate materials, created new vaccines against COVID-19—Soberana 02 and Abdala—that rival the effectiveness of the Pfizer and Moderna vaccines.[124] Soberana 02 and Abdala may even be superior, in that they don't require storage at extremely low temperatures and may have fewer side effects.

Once medicines are produced for people, not profit, that is, once the pharmaceutical sector is socialized, Big Pharma won't be able to exploit people's illnesses through price gouging. One disgusting example of such price gouging involves insulin, the medicine used for treating diabetes. Insulin has existed since the 1920s. In recent decades, its price has skyrocketed. Prices increased 197 percent between 2002 and 2013, and they keep rising. Insulin manufacturers say the increase is due to innovation, but the reality is that they charge whatever they want because they can. They maintain their patents and avoid their medications becoming generic by making minor tweaks to the formulas. This is the ultimate expression of the cruelty of market forces under capitalism. Untold numbers of people with diabetes have died because of their inability to purchase insulin.[125] The socialist government will pay for all necessary prescription drugs and

Insulin Cost Per Vial (Humalog brand), 1996-2016

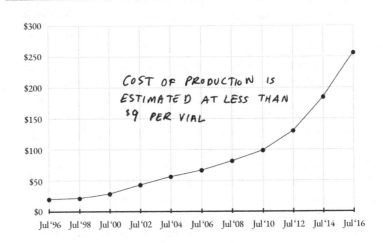

Sources: Truven Health, BMJ Global Health

medical supplies. No one will ever go without needed medications. There will be no marketing or lobbying for drugs. We will create medicines and medical devices to meet everyone's needs and ensure equality.

> ## Those naysayers who say free, high quality, and comprehensive health care is too expensive under socialism have not evaluated the cost savings—to the tune of hundreds of billions of dollars a year—that will come from eliminating the corporate class.

A socialist health-care system will be more efficient and less costly than even single-payer systems are under capitalism. The collectivity of the revolutionary approach will unleash vast human potential and productivity. Millions of people will be part of this new health-care system. They will be mentors, leaders, and health-care activists working to benefit our class and our revolution. The for-profit mentality will be a relic of the past. Those naysayers who say free, high quality, and comprehensive health care is too expensive under socialism have not evaluated the cost savings—to the tune of hundreds of billions of dollars a year—that will come from eliminating the corporate class. Once we abolish capitalism and its costly inequalities, we will be able to deliver high-quality health care to all.

Keeping People Healthy

Under socialism, health will not be defined merely as the "absence of disease." Socialists recognize that good health is a condition of complete physical, mental, and social well-being.

In the capitalist system of market-driven medicine, the typical primary-care visit lasts just fifteen minutes. Because the visit is so short, it only minimally addresses the lifestyle, stress, or environmental factors that may be at the core of a patient's problems. We know that chronic stress in the workplace, at home, or because of financial worries can elevate blood pressure and increase insulin resistance. Over time, chronic stress can lead to hypertension, diabetes, and eventually heart disease. Cardiovascular disease is the number one killer in the United States, so helping people early on with these risk factors is vital. Insurance companies, however, only pay minimally for prevention and certainly don't compensate for in-depth discussions about stress, food, and managing one's environment. Given the deadly prevalence of heart disease, prevention should be a public-health priority. Instead, capitalist medicine manages patients by waiting until they manifest disease or have abnormal lab results and then billing them for tests and medications. By that point, the patient's disease may not be easily reversible.

Because the capitalist system is motivated by market shares and immediate profit, it does not invest in keeping people healthy, even though this would amount to billions of dollars of cost savings to society. Pharmaceutical companies profit from stress-related diseases. For example, migraines are a maladaptive brain response to stress.[126] Repeated stress, like working under oppressive conditions, can lead to chronic migraines. In the US, thirty-nine million people suffer from migraines. The average cost for one eight-tablet box of NURTEC, one of the newer migraine medications, is $1,020.[127] This tells us why capitalist corporations are not interested in preventing disease: there is too much profit to make off of sick people!

Socialism itself is a cure for society's ills because it abolishes the capitalist system that causes them.

Under socialism, preventive medicine will be manifest at a societal level, not just in the clinician's office. The new socialist government will focus on improving everyone's quality of life, increasing free time, and decreasing stress. Healthy food will be widely available. The work week will be shorter and vacation time longer. Day care for children and adults will be freely available, eliminating a significant source of stress for many families. Housing will be free to low-cost, and, as we emphasize throughout this chapter, health care will be free and guaranteed, so people will not have to suffer from anxiety over fears of eviction, foreclosure, and debt. Exploitation, racism, and sexism will be outlawed, again eliminating key sources of trauma and anxiety. Socialism itself is a cure for society's ills because it abolishes the capitalist system that causes them.

After the revolution in Cuba in 1959, health-care workers recognized the need for preventive and integrative medicine. Understanding that many illnesses result from the toll of chronic stress, they developed a

The Cuban health-care system sets an example for organization and the holistic well-being of its population, historically and through the COVID-19 pandemic. (Photo: Matteo Bazzi)

holistic approach to health care. As Don Fitz details in "The Birth of the Cuban Polyclinic," the revolution "inherited a patchwork of unintegrated, overlapping medical structures, including private fee-for-service practices, public assistance for the poor, a few large medical plans, and many small plans."[128] Preventive medicine did not exist. Cuba's socialist government dismantled this ineffective for-profit health-care system and created a person-centered vision. From 1964–69, Cuba "began redesigning medicine as an integrated system."[129] Central to this redesign was the *polyclinic*. Polyclinics brought all the different health services people require into a single location. As Fitz details, polyclinics had staffs of "at least one general practice physician, nurse, pediatrician, OB/GYN, and social worker."[130] Dentistry was also present, and nurses and social workers reached out to people in their homes, workplaces, and schools. Polyclinics were located in each neighborhood, and staff often lived there. Polyclinics provided the organizational basis for health campaigns and vaccinations. The new system was enormously successful: malaria was wiped out by 1967, and diphtheria by 1971.[131] "In 1962, 80 percent of all Cuban children under fifteen were vaccinated against polio in just eleven days."[132] Overall, the polyclinics excelled in continuity of care and attention to the clinician-patient relationship.

Despite sixty years of devastating US sanctions, Cuba still has one of the most effective health-care models. Taking lessons from the Cuban experience, the People's Health Administration will also emphasize the whole person, addressing social, emotional, environmental, and physical determinants of health. Clinicians will have time to discuss patient needs, much more than the fifteen minutes they have now. Each primary health clinician will be part of a larger team consisting of a social worker, psychologist, nurse, and community health worker. Patients will have access, in one place, to the various services that meet their needs. Such services will include massage, acupuncture, nutrition counseling, walking clubs, therapy, and more.

What the Cubans have done with few resources but with significant impact on the health of the population is being emulated in some capitalist countries even now. The Cuban medical system provides primary care within neighborhoods, making it convenient for patients. The system ensures that clinicians have time to see their patients. Clinicians typically have a small number of patients and afternoons off so that they can follow up with patients as necessary. Subspecialists are readily available. Obviously, this is a very different model than primary care in the US. Clinicians in the US are under intense pressure to see patients rapidly. They also endure the enormous administrative charting requirements of the electronic medical records system and the insurance companies. Burnout among primary care physicians is common and has led to increased clinician error and health-care shortages, especially in poor communities.

In the capitalist United States, over thirty million people lack health insurance. Many people living in southern states do not have access to expanded Medicaid, even though they are financially eligible under the Affordable Care Act.[133] Under socialism, health care—inclusive of dentistry and optometry—will be guaranteed to all as a fundamental right. Redeploying insurance and pharmaceutical companies' resources and employees, we will create strong public-health outreach systems. With the polyclinic model, we will bring high-quality health care to rural and underserved areas. The new socialist People's Health Administration will oversee the formation of clinics in the poorest communities. Community members will be developed as leaders to break down barriers to health care. The private practice of medicine will be prohibited. Integrative holistic modalities will be encouraged, supported, and made free and available to all. Currently, services such as naturopathy (herbal medicine) and acupuncture are only accessible to those who can pay for them. Under socialism anyone who wants them will be able to get them.

Food as Medicine

More people in the US are sick than are healthy.[134] The profit fixation of corporate agribusiness and the food industry has targeted the working class with toxic, high-calorie, and diabetogenic foods. As Dariush Mozaffarian and Dan Glickman point out, "More than 100 million adults—almost half the entire adult population—have prediabetes or diabetes. Cardiovascular disease affects about 122 million people and causes 840,000 deaths each year, about 2,300 deaths each day. Three in four adults are overweight or obese."[135] Research shows that diet is the top risk factor for mortality in the US. Over 60 percent of our food is processed—taken apart and put together again with high concentrations of sugar, salt, oil, and additives. Many cancers are thought to be the result of a highly processed diet. There is clear evidence that a plant-based diet can help reverse hypertension, diabetes, and other diseases. Despite the growing literature in this field, the medical establishment shows little interest in promoting the benefits of healthy food.

The concept of *food as medicine* is essential to reversing this trend.[136] The People's Health Administration will make nutrition a central piece of our health interventions, teaching people how to cook nutritiously, making fresh fruits and vegetables readily available, and ridding stores of cheap, highly processed foods. Clinicians will routinely write prescriptions for healthy foods like fruits, nuts, and beans. Public-health campaigns emphasizing the importance of healthy foods for medical treatment will become the norm.

The People's Health Administration will coordinate with the Department of Food Production, discussed in chapter 5, to support people in starting small farms and growing nutritious food for local consumption. Here we will learn from Cuba's approach to rethinking urban landscapes for food production. Green spaces and gardens will be interwoven into the urban architecture, enhancing the quality of life and improving nutrition and social connection, as we detail in chapters 5 and 6.

Public Health

Epidemics

Before the coronavirus pandemic, the US public-health system was already failing. COVID-19 brought the point home: there is no real public-health system in this country. Rosa Luxemburg wrote, quoting Friedrich Engels: "Bourgeois society stands at the crossroads, either transition to socialism or regression into barbarism." Written over a century ago, this sentiment is even more relevant today. The widespread misery and death of over one million people in the US were preventable, as the example of China proves.

Before the coronavirus pandemic, the US public-health system was already failing. COVID-19 brought the point home: there is no real public-health system in this country.

In China, a public-health system that serves the people was able to control the epidemic and save millions of lives. This unique and unprecedented public-health response was possible because the entire country mobilized to deal collectively with the highly contagious coronavirus. Workers and volunteers provided a support system for everyone in quarantine. Over one thousand small public-health teams interviewed people infected with the coronavirus and anyone who potentially had contact with them. Quarantined people had paid leave, job security, and food from local restaurants brought to their doors.

The possibilities for public health in the US under socialism are vast. Like China, Vietnam and even some capitalist countries responded effectively to the COVID-19 pandemic because they had functioning public-health and social-welfare systems. Socialized approaches to public health can control infectious diseases in ways that profit-oriented medicine simply cannot. When saving people's lives is the priority, resources and public involvement can immediately and unquestioningly be devoted to addressing the problem. The US's wealth, knowledge, and technology provide a firm basis for a people-oriented public-health system able to address epidemics and other public-health emergencies before they get out of hand. Socialist organization will make this possibility a reality.

Racism

Racism is a vital public-health issue in the US. Racism takes an enormous toll on people of color, causing toxic stress levels. As mentioned above, high levels of stress hormones can lead to hypertension, cardio-

The Black Lives Matter movement was not just about police violence, but also raised demands related to health care, housing, and poverty. (Photo: Johnny Silvercloud)

vascular disease, stroke, and mental illness. In fact, racism exacerbates all illnesses. Decades ago, frontline health-care workers identified racism and other social inequities as "social determinants of health" (drivers for poor health outcomes). Only in the past few years, as a result of the Black Lives Matter movement and other sustained protests, has the medical establishment recognized racism as a contributing factor to a person's health. Additional social determinants include poor housing, lack of transportation, violence, poor education, low income, food insecurity, poverty, and illiteracy. The American Medical Association (AMA) and the CDC agree that reducing inequities in these areas is an ethical imperative because these factors are killing people. The capitalist system creates these disparities, but neither the AMA nor the CDC recommends abolishing capitalism. They thus fail to address the cause of the symptoms they openly acknowledge. Socialist society takes the elimination of these inequalities as its primary task, understanding that this is the purpose and goal of socialist revolution in the first place.

Racism impacts all areas of public health in the US. The People's Health Administration will rapidly expand medical services to everyone, especially to people from oppressed communities and in underserved urban and rural areas. It will train tens of thousands of clinicians and community-health workers from communities of color to provide high quality medical care. The motto will be "health and quality of life for all." Food deserts will be eliminated and integrative medicine and healthy foods made available free of charge. Staff at neighborhood polyclinics will reflect the racial composition of the communities they serve and, most importantly, treat patients and families with dignity and respect.

Addiction

In *Deaths of Despair and the Future of Capitalism*, Ann Case and Angus Deaton write that between 1999 and 2017 more than six hundred thousand extra deaths occurred among people aged forty-five and fifty-four.[137] Drug companies convinced clinicians that prescription opiates were safe and should be used to treat noncancer pain. These companies told doctors to assure patients that addiction was unusual after surgery and to prescribe opiates routinely. Abuse rapidly became widespread. In regions of the country with high rates of joblessness, overdoses and suicides increased dramatically. This was particularly true among poorly educated and unemployed white people. The combination of mind-numbing and low-paid service jobs, multiple economic recessions, and personal and collective trauma was—and still is—a deadly mix. The instability, stress, and desperation the capitalist system creates lead directly to depression, addiction, and physical illness. Capitalism is to blame for the opioid crisis.

The People's Health Administration will address addiction by confronting the social determinants of health head on, creating supportive community structures and meaningful work while using a trauma-informed approach. We will treat addiction as primarily a biological phenomenon and employ an integrative method that supports mind and body. We will focus on personal trauma, environmental trauma, and the alienation many experience under capitalism. People with addictions will have free access to high-quality rehabilitation programs that are life affirming rather than stigmatizing.

Mental Health

The epidemic of mental illness in the US is astounding. Antidepressant use increased by 65 percent between 1999 and 2014.[138] Even before the coronavirus pandemic, close to 20 percent of US adults reported experiencing mental illness.[139] Writing in *The Selfish Capitalist*, psychologist Oliver James attributes this rise to the intensification of capitalism under neoliberalism. Starting in the 1980s, neoliberalism led to a new level of societal alienation. Job security, unions, community life, and social programs came under intense attack; many were destroyed. With the elimination of workers' rights, the work environment deteriorated. Productivity demands—especially for those in low-wage service-sector jobs—increased. Incarceration rates skyrocketed. At the same time, access to mental-health services declined significantly. The mental-health services that workers were able to access neglected the root causes of their suffering. Mainstream psychiatry fails to appreciate the toll that financial insecurity, unemployment, on-the-job oppression, and alienation take on an individual's mental health. Capitalist mental health care focuses on brain biology and medications. The stress and anger workers feel daily in fast-food service jobs, laboring in Amazon's warehouses, or enduring disrespect and wage theft at Walmart can't be cured by a pill. Capitalist wage slavery is producing a new generation of young people suffering from mental illness.

Socialist society will uplift community involvement, connection, and mental well-being. Because our values will be communal and egalitarian rather than individualistic and consumerist, we will have lower levels of mental illness, greater social cohesion, and deepened mutual trust.[140] The elimination of poverty, foreclosure, and exploitation and the guarantee of meaningful work and abundant free time will go a long way toward remedying anxiety, hopelessness, and alienation. Vibrant communities will provide the cure for the epidemic of loneliness driving so many depression and anxiety disorders. Where there was competition, there will be cooperation and mutual support. Where there was exclusion and disrespect, there will be inclusion and affirmation.

Even with the elimination of the material causes of much mental illness, people will still need mental-health services. The People's Health Administration will establish community mental-health services, incorporating them into the neighborhood polyclinics. Psychiatrists, psychologists, and therapists will be trained to attend to the environmental causes of mental illness. Services will be evidence-based and holistic, inclusive of a wide array of approaches: mind-body, exercise, acupuncture, counseling, group therapy, forest bathing (a treatment that uses the contemplative practice of being immersed in nature), medication, and more. Access to mental-health services will be free and easily obtained.

Offices of the People's Health Administration

Under socialism, health care will be a fundamental right, and any attempt to profit off people's health-care needs will be a crime. The new socialist system will replace the market provision of medical goods and services with a single public system organized under the People's Health

Administration. Divisions will include the Pharmaceutical Planning Agency, the Office for Polyclinic Creation and Support, the Bureau of Food and Nutrition, and the Central Department of Public Health, which will tackle the problems addressed above. Much more needs to be done to ensure the health and well-being of everyone. We conclude this chapter by flagging some of the additional units that we expect will comprise the People's Health Administration.

The Office of Elder Care

The capitalist health-care system neglects the needs of elderly people. During the pandemic, the lack of funding for nursing homes resulted in devastating outcomes. More than 40 percent of US COVID-19 fatalities were residents and employees of nursing homes and other long-term care facilities. Shortages of personal protective equipment and staffing, lack of infection control, underfunding, and complacency led to mass deaths. This was an example of structural ageism: the elderly under capitalism are warehoused in subpar institutions where they are often treated like children. Inadequate facilities are not the only problem. The lack of funding for home care is a major source of financial and emotional stress for tens of millions of caregivers. Unable to afford the high costs of a private senior-housing facility or unwilling to risk a more affordable but lower quality facility or just committed to remaining in their own homes, many working people experience enormous stress and hardship during their retirement years. Socialist society will respect, value, and integrate elders into community life. The Office of Elder Care will develop facilities, networks, and mass organizations designed to ensure that elders flourish, that their last years are vibrant, full of culture and joy. This office will also provide support to caregivers and facilitate the redesign of nursing homes as intergenerational places of creativity and possibility.

Disability Rights and Accessibility Administration

The Disability Rights and Accessibility Administration will serve as a centralized location for handling all issues related to guaranteeing the inclusion and support of people with disabilities. It will develop and implement a plan for eliminating architectural barriers in housing, schools, transportation, workplaces, and public spaces. The plan will also identify ways to create a positive culture around disabilities and encourage the full development of each person's potential. Disabled people will lead this revolution.

The Women's Department

As every woman knows, the current health-care system does not effectively meet the needs of women. The maternal mortality rate in the US is nearly double that of other developed countries. Black women in the US suffer maternal mortality rates three times higher than white women's already high rates. Adequate postpartum care will cut these rates in half, saving women's lives. Misdiagnoses and patriarchal attitudes commonly impact the quality of the medical care women receive, as does a general neglect of women's health. Women often feel unheard and disrespected. Trans women encounter misgendering, bias, and inadequate attention to their specific needs. Trans men face similar problems, which pregnancy amplifies. Historically subjected to forced sterilizations, Black, Brown, and Indigenous women have been especially mistreated. The racism of medical professionals has led to gross underestimation of Black and Brown women's physical pain and general disregard for their symptoms. The capitalist market system for distributing health care makes prenatal and postpartum care inaccessible to many working-class women.

The socialist People's Health Administration will dramatically change all this. A Women's Department will be formed to oversee the education and training of large numbers of doctors, midwives, doulas, nurses, lactation and nutrition consultants, counselors for postpartum depression, and other specialists in women's health. Their orientation will be toward reproductive justice, ensuring that each woman receives conscientious and attentive care. Revolutionary anti-racist and anti-sexist consciousness will transform women's health care. Ensuring that each woman is heard and respected will be the basis for all clinical encounters.

LGBTQ Health Department

Working closely with the Women's Department will be the LGBTQ Health Department. Under capitalism, LGBTQ individuals may avoid seeking medical attention because of discrimination and mistreatment. Transgender people report that they are not only frequently misgendered but that doctors flat out refuse to see them. Because of the bias, ignorance, and cruelty they encounter from medical professionals, nearly 30 percent of transgender people avoided seeking needed health care in 2020.[141] The socialist People's Health Administration will be fully inclusive and supportive of the health-care needs of the LGBTQ community, including free and unrestricted access to reproductive, gender affirmation, and mental/behavioral health-related services. The LGBTQ Health Department will oversee the development of appropriate trainings and protocols as well as their implementation in hospitals, polyclinics, and medical schools.

Conclusion

The leaders of the new socialist health-care system must come from the working class and those with the best track record of serving working-class communities. Racist and patriarchal medical authorities, which are deeply integrated within the whole capitalist power structure, will be removed from their positions of power. We will rid the medical system of the assembly-line approach to patient care, and give clinicians the respect and time they need to care for patients. We will create integrative medicine programs that were previously only available to the rich. Prevention and primary care will be the backbone of health care. Our health-care system will be guided by compassion, revolutionary commitment, and love.

As socialists, it is our responsibility to make the health of all people a priority. In the United States, we have the resources to fulfill this responsibility right now. We have people with the knowledge and skills to create and implement the vision of preventative, comprehensive, and responsive care we outline here. The requisite components already exist. Socialism will enable us to redirect our talents and resources away from capitalist profit and towards people's health and well-being. Lack of health care is a form of oppression, and care for the whole person a form of liberation. When we have a sense of control over our lives and an ability to contribute to something greater than ourselves, we can do more than survive. We can flourish.

CHAPTER 8

SOCIALIST EDUCATION

*A*fter a socialist revolution in the United States, the new state will need to reconstruct public education. A socialist Department of Education will direct this project, beginning with a reevaluation of the prevailing ethos in education. Socialist consciousness and revolutionary spirit will inform a new understanding of what education has been and ought to be. Much can change even in the first decade of socialism.

Vast inequalities plague the current US public-education system. Over 60 percent of students are crammed into overcrowded classrooms, leaving little opportunity for overworked educators to reach every student. School buildings are crumbling: a 2020 US Government Accountability Office report estimated that about half of public schools need major renovations to ensure student and worker safety. Growing numbers of wealthy families, typically white, continue to move away from urban centers in order to send their children to better-funded, de facto segregated suburban schools, while working-class students of various nationalities remain in city schools. Capitalist politicians frequently decry failing schools—a logical conclusion based on the disturbing realities of public school in the US—but the truth is that the capitalist school system is working exactly as it was designed.

In a capitalist economy, the purpose of public education is to produce obedient workers. Job training is an aspect of this purpose: in K-12 schools, students are required to learn foundational reading and mathematical skills, and students who can afford to attend a college or university often choose majors that prepare them for distinct careers. However, the public-school system does more than promote different career pathways: its infrastructure, disciplinary policies, and methods of academic assessment teach young people how to behave as workers, reinforcing the unequal class system. Public schools reward students who comply with rules, listen attentively, and do not question authority.

Education scholars call this behavioral training the "hidden curriculum," referring to the ways public schools teach students to interact with authority. The hidden curriculum, distinguished from the academic content covered in school, reinforces the top-down managerial approach working-class young people will experience at their jobs. By rewarding students who conform to the existing structure of schooling and learn in the manner expected of them, public schools "prepare" young people to submit to the alienating work ahead of them. This is a systemic issue that even the best intentioned and hardest working teachers can only alleviate, but not resolve.

Foundational education exists in large part to establish and reinforce the values and procedures of a larger society. The aim of preparing young people to interact with the world around them will not change after a socialist revolution. Rather, education will prepare students to participate in an entirely different society.

In this chapter, we describe the radical transformation of public schooling and higher education that will follow in the first decade of socialist revolution in the United States. Because the enormity of the tasks of responding to climate change and building socialism requires training and creativity throughout people's lives, we envision education as taking place both in and beyond the classroom. Teaching and learning are practices in which we engage at home and at work, in neighborhoods and communities as well as schools. Therefore, we also promote popular education and community learning as vital for engaging the population in the collective responsibility of meeting social needs.

Our Vision of Socialist Education

Education is necessary for transforming people. Capitalist models of education have indoctrinated many into pervasive and destructive beliefs regarding individualism, moral responsibilities, and social relationships. Elitism, racism, misogyny, and homophobia will not disappear overnight. To combat these destructive beliefs, trusted education professionals will promote the values of a new society: equality, care for the community and the environment, and shared political power to make decisions and create new forms of association. Revolutionary study and learning will engage people throughout society, paving the way for informed and committed participation in the tasks of responding to climate change and building socialism.

Education will be free and accessible from cradle to grave. With a socialist reorganization of society, schools will no longer contend with budget shortfalls. Public education will be fully funded, staffed, and planned. People of all ages will have free and lifelong access to meaningful and personally fulfilling educational experiences. Full access to education requires attending to the diverse needs of the population, responding to historic oppression with reparations, and aligning methods of instruction with specific learning needs. The methods of instructional delivery may be diverse, but the content of the public-school curriculum will incorporate the same history lessons and revolutionary consciousness for all.

Education will prepare students for taking responsibility, engaging problems, and developing solutions. Schools will be institutions crucial to the production of a new generation of socialists able to contribute to and lead in the shaping of the new society. Schools will guide students in determining how best to serve their communities and work with communities to provide educational opportunities designed to train people to meet community needs. At the same time, the greater amount of free time socialist planning provides will create more opportunities for individuals to pursue their own interests. Schools will enhance students' opportunities for creativity, growth, and exploration by exposing them to a wide array of knowledge, cultures, and experiences.

The remainder of this chapter highlights the major shifts in educational policy and understanding needed to realize these principles. It is impossible to predict exactly what education, in all its forms, will look like after a socialist revolution in the United States. Local, regional, and national needs and aspirations will determine the kinds of knowledge and modes of inquiry and problem-solving socialist education will prioritize. Adhering to these guiding principles, though, will ensure that all people have the capacity to participate in the construction of a freer and more equitable society.

The Teacher-Student Relationship

In the capitalist education system, the role of the classroom teacher is complicated, overwhelming, and constraining. To liberate education, teachers too need to be liberated from old ideas about teaching and oppressive traditions which demand they sacrifice their own well-being "for the kids."

On the one hand, educators often play the part of caregivers, especially in the most vulnerable communities. For many children, school is a primary source for nutritious food, mental-health counseling, and primary health care. Because the state fails to provide such basic and necessary services, many students and their families have nowhere else to turn. On the other hand, the classroom is just as often a site of alienation and oppression for working-class students. A complex web of teachers,

Paulo Freire envisioned a new model of education that recognizes students as subjects of their own learning.

administrators, and government officials deprives students of autonomy over body and mind, sometimes treating them as criminals instead of as children in need of guidance and support.

Revolutionary training for teachers will create a new dynamic between students and their schools. Here we can learn from Paulo Freire, who critically described the "banking model of education," the predominant model of schooling in the US and other capitalist countries. The banking model refers to a sharp distinction between teacher and student and the expectation that students arrive at the classroom as empty vessels into which teachers deposit information. This philosophy posits that students' cultural backgrounds and innate ways of learning are at best useless and at worst disruptive in the classroom. To be clear, the classroom teacher in this model is not the ultimate culprit; the state shapes its educational system to serve its needs regardless of the intentions of the individual teacher. Indeed, many individual educators are already doing the necessary work of relationship nurturing, anti-racist curriculum-building, and community engagement; these educators will be at the forefront of socialist education.

To realize the socialist education program, students will be seen not as objects—entities that must be taught—but as subjects of their own learning. Socialist education thus begins with a commitment to deep respect and appreciation for every student's identity, culture, and formative experiences. Students learn and create meaning outside of the classroom by interacting with their communities. They are surrounded by unofficial teachers, including parents, family, friends, and community leaders. Students arrive in the classroom full of learning experiences; in no way are they empty vessels just sitting there waiting to be filled with official "knowledge." For too long, schools have operated under the principle that working-class students can be saved or rescued from their communities by the power of education. In contrast, socialist education will build on and be relevant to the everyday lives of young people. Teachers will be intimately familiar with students' lived experiences, meaningfully connected to students' lives beyond the classroom.

The Cuban literacy campaign during the early years of the revolution exemplifies responsive teaching. Conceived as a way to eradicate illiteracy, the campaign radically reenvisioned education. Urban students—who, prior to the socialist revolution in Cuba, had the greatest access to high-quality formal education—were trained as *brigadistas* (radical educators) and sent to the countryside to labor alongside farmworkers during the day and teach families to read in the evenings after the day's work was completed. The *brigadistas*, most of whom were ten to sixteen years old, were trained to have the utmost respect for the families assigned to them. Requiring the *brigadistas* to assist in the family's labor on the farm served to break down barriers between the formerly privileged urban population and the historically alienated rural communities. Moreover, the curriculum the Cuban government developed for teaching reading was carefully designed with the goal of empowering farmworkers to participate in public life. Details—down to the vocabulary words promoted in the curriculum—were chosen to have the most transformative impact on farmworking families. In fact, the culmination of the curriculum tasked each farmworker with writing an unscripted letter to Fidel Castro with personal reflections about the consequences of the revolution.

A socialist US will follow the spirit of the Cuban literacy campaign. Pedagogy—the tools of instruction and assessment—will change significantly in most schools. Evaluative measures—tests and assessments—cannot copy the assessments which currently exist. In the capitalist United States, assessments create unnecessary and often traumatic anxiety for young people; a high school student who fails a test is subject to shame and negative predictions about the trajectory of their life, as if one "F" dooms them forever. Tests in US schools are coercive mechanisms for enforcing the memorization of content. In the new socialist society, assessments will be authentic opportunities for reflection and growth for students, teachers, and schools. No standardized test will determine any student's fate.

As the Cuban example demonstrates, models for responsive education that instills curiosity and creativity already exist. The Russian Revolution produced new leaps in educational psychology, with Lev Vygotsky, for instance, articulating teaching and learning as a dialectical relationship existing within a cultural and historical context. His ideas are influential today even in capitalist educational circles (although they are stripped of their Marxist underpinnings).

Usually it's the children of parents wealthy enough to pay for private schools that get to experience genuinely responsive education. Working-class children remain stuck in underfunded and understaffed institutions compelled to train students with the "drill-and-kill" tactics that go along with frequent and compulsory standardized testing. In a socialist US, all children will participate in fully funded schooling in which liberatory educational practices prevail. Discussion of relevant and stimulating materials will allow students and teachers to learn alongside and from each other. Meaningful projects rooted in real-world issues will constitute the majority of assessments, and teachers will serve as partners and mentors in such projects. Students will work cooperatively in groups to learn the all-important skills of consensus building, intentional communication, and shared responsibility. The classroom as a place of joyful curiosity will be the rule—not the exception.

Career Guidance and Pathways

Liberatory educational practices will emancipate the working class from the chains of conformity and submission, from the compulsion to follow the dictates of capitalism in order to find a job and earn a wage. Because meaningful work and education will be guaranteed to all, no one will be stuck in endless drudgery for the sake of providing for their families.

Fully funded schools—at the foundational and adult levels—will employ enough guidance counselors to enable every student to meet regularly with their assigned counselor for career coaching. Guidance counselors will know their small assigned cohort of students and will thoughtfully reflect on students' skills and interests along with the needs of the community. As trusted government employees, counselors will direct students into jobs which match individuals' skills with socially important functions. Crucial to this work will be exposing students to and promoting various kinds of manual, trade, and craft labor. The socialist Department of Education will embark on a massive campaign to remove stigmas surrounding manual labor. In a capitalist economy, people who forego postsecondary education in favor of entering the workforce immediately contend with lower pay, demeaning work conditions, and often disparaging judgment from the community. In contrast, socialist society will celebrate the indispensable labor of manual, trade, and craft workers.

> ## In a capitalist economy, people who forego postsecondary education in favor of entering the workforce immediately contend with lower pay, demeaning work conditions, and often disparaging judgment from the community.

Everyone in the socialist US will be called upon to serve the public in myriad ways. For example, a teacher may be in the classroom for twenty hours per week. They may then be tasked with completely different responsibilities, like working in a community laundry or tending the neighborhood garden for an additional five hours a week. Requiring everyone to participate in community work will break down barriers between intellectual and manual labor. It will also ensure that social reproduction tasks are filled equitably and sufficiently to prevent them from being overly time-consuming and burdensome for a few. Ideally, students will choose a career that is personally fulfilling to them from a range of socially necessary options. Under socialism, they will not only be able to change course and engage in different pursuits as their interests change, but they will also be provided with whatever guidance and training they need.

Under capitalism, young working-class people are funneled into low-wage service work in alienating conditions. A relatively small number of workers have the privilege of really "choosing" their line of work based on their desires or passions. Most people find a job opening one way or another that allows them to make ends meet, and then largely stay in the same field for most of their working life. The fear of losing one's job is immense and the prospect of changing careers is an anxious and intimidating one. Where people end up usually bears little resemblance to what they dreamed they would do or even what they studied for when they were younger.

People with college degrees are at the mercy of a job market in which bosses hire and fire as they see fit. Many come out of expensive programs shocked to discover that there are no jobs in their area of expertise—which they often went into debt to acquire. It's an illusion to think that the capitalist labor market is a realm of free choice.

Socialism does not mean that everyone simply chooses whatever job they want. People will still have to fill positions as they open up. But the big change will be that ending the profit motive as the motor force of the economy will create enormous space for far more positions. Under capitalism, the number of workers, especially in positions that require specialized training, is held artificially low so as to reduce labor costs, maximize profits, and reduce government budgets. In contrast, the socialist government will ask: Won't society be better off if we train far more engineers, teachers, social workers, nurses, doctors, carpenters, plumbers, welders, janitors, and so on than we currently have?

No matter what job one has, the dignity of all labor will be respected, wages and labor rights will be vastly improved, and changing careers will be facilitated. Social planning will help guide young people into careers where there will be greater social needs according to local projects and national plans and initiatives. Ensuring an adequate number of trained people to take on the full gamut of necessary labor is too important to be left up to chance. A planned economy that includes personalized career guidance will guarantee that socially necessary roles are fully staffed. While it will be impossible to accommodate every individual's career aspirations, every person can count on work that is useful to their community and respected as such.

Oppressed Groups and Education

Children of color, girls, and LGBTQ kids in the US capitalist educational setting often face extra scrutiny and suspicion, systemic neglect, and institutional violence. Black and Brown students are surveilled and disciplined at outrageously disproportionate rates compared to their white counterparts. The presence of police officers within many working-class school districts compounds these threats.

Additionally, special-education programs within schools (in which Black and Brown children are disproportionately represented) have segregated many children with disabilities into secluded classrooms away from their peers. Some school districts have moved to more inclusive models, but unevenness in policy and funding plagues the country's public-education system. Under special-education law in the US, parents are expected to advocate for their children, a challenge for working-class parents who must balance this advocacy with typically inflexible work schedules. The unevenness in special education results in deeply unequal treatment and inconsistent access to educational content, not to mention to the specially designed instruction students with disabilities need to flourish. While students in dominant cultural groups and nationalities do not have unfettered access to a truthful and meaningful curriculum, students in special-education programs are even further restricted in terms of educational content.

In a socialist US, educators will understand that each student possesses immense potential and will work to draw out that student's talents and skills. The new socialist Department of Education will oversee the transformation of school curricula to be universal in content and appropriately varied in modes of instruction. It will sponsor critical research in educational pedagogy to determine which models of learning empower students to learn relevant content and skills. Community input will be integral to this process, and outcomes will be responsive to the needs of young people in diverse environments. Nevertheless, it is the state's responsibility to ensure that all students are supported and encouraged to reach their full intellectual potential. Local communities will play key roles in implementing the new educational program. The Department of Education will actively monitor implementation efforts, especially with respect to schools' treatment of historically oppressed groups.

The Department of Education will also set standards for the inclusion of language instruction within communities. Currently, language instruction in the US has been limited primarily to English with secondary instruction mainly in Spanish (offered in 46 percent of high schools), French (offered in 21 percent of high schools), German (offered in 8.7 percent of high schools), or Latin (offered in 8.5 percent of high schools).[142] Many students have no opportunity to study a language other than English. US students are expected to be proficient in standardized English regardless of the language or dialect they speak at home. Students who arrive at school speaking a language other than English are compelled to learn English and abandon the use of their native language within the education system. Monolingual English speakers are deprived of the benefits of learning a second language. Socialist education will not favor one language over others.

Diverse languages will be taught in public schools in response to local conditions. Whenever a school community has a significant minority of students who speak a language other than English, instruction will be offered in that language. For example, if a school community has three or more Mandarin speakers, those students will be taught in Mandarin while also learning English. Mandarin classes will be part of the general curriculum for all students in that community so that native Mandarin speakers will have a choice of speaking English or Mandarin in social situations as well as acquiring literacy in both languages.

Students and educators alike will come to appreciate that all languages and dialects are equally valid means of communication. In a racist society, the languages and dialects spoken by the oppressed are devalued. The capitalist education system in the US devalues the language patterns of working-class Black communities in particular. As systemic racism is dismantled in society in general and specifically in schooling, teachers will approach linguistic diversity with respect and genuine interest. In keeping with this aspect of its mission, the socialist Department of Education will train and hire a much more diverse teacher workforce than the US has now, a goal readily achievable once financial barriers have been removed from the teaching profession.

Historically oppressed groups will have their rightful place of honor throughout school curricula, particularly when it comes to teaching and learning history. History in the US tends to be taught as lessons in the achievements of great men—explorers, presidents, and generals. This approach reinforces capitalist individualism, its oft-told myth that only especially brilliant and talented leaders can make change. Not only does this myth diminish the contributions of the diverse multinational working class, but it also inaccurately depicts political change. Political shifts result from collective struggle. New curricula will highlight working-class organizations, social movements, and people's struggles. Celebrations of multinational, LGBTQ, and women's histories will no longer be relegated to superficial monthly recognitions. As the people who have long fought for the public acknowledgment of these histories intended, these diverse contributions will be embedded throughout public school curricula.

Radical curricular transformation will create positive changes in school culture and student understanding of social organization. Still, extra work will need to be done to eradicate biased disciplinary procedures in each school community. The Department of Education will direct a massive reconstruction effort to alter discipline within school communities. Crises among students will be handled with compassion, empathy, and an eagerness for justice. Transformative practices of relationship building, dialogue, written reflection, and connection to social services will replace the use of suspensions, expulsions, and corporal punishment (still permitted in nineteen US states). Students who engage in harmful behavior will be provided counseling and not face isolation from the community except in the direst circumstances and only for a limited time.

The new Department of Education will mandate the democratic construction of community responses to student misconduct. Students themselves will participate in the creation of new school programs—such as peer mediation circles—to address social issues within their school communities. Because disciplinary policy has so often been authoritarian and alienating for students, it is essential that schools involve students throughout the entire process of creating new standards. Wider student consent with regard to rules and responses will help ensure fairness and teach young people the importance of contributing their perspective and talents to community projects.

Adult Education

A massive expansion of adult education programs will be necessary to make education free and accessible from cradle to grave. Most formal adult education in the US takes place in colleges and universities. The new socialist government will transform these institutions, making them free and inclusive. But our efforts will not be limited to this formal sector. On the contrary, we will encourage and support a wide array of popular education initiatives.

First and foremost, the private system of elite universities with billion-dollar endowments will be abolished. Enrollment in any US college or university will be free and accessible to all. This major change will allow students of any age to pursue areas of personal interest and explore new work opportunities throughout their lives. Universities will reform aspects of college life that present barriers to inclusive education by scheduling more weekend and night classes, facilitating work sabbaticals for continuing study, and hiring significantly more staff to support new students in their academic journeys. Given that many currently existing jobs in fields such as advertising, insurance, and financial services will have been eliminated, there is already a large labor force available for taking on this work.

Another change to higher education will be the eradication of competition between schools. As is already done in the State University of New York (SUNY) system, colleges and universities will openly share resources with one another rather than hoarding information, research, and collections. Campus communities will retain their unique cultures, but students will be able to transfer from one institution to the next without fear of losing money or course credits. All colleges and universities will be public and act in accordance with the public good, no longer motivated by financial concerns or the maintenance of elitist class hierarchies.

One final change has to do with academic credentialing. For several generations, getting ahead in the US capitalist economy has required a college education. A bachelor's degree has been necessary for accessing higher paying jobs. In recent years, even this has not been enough and more and more students have assumed large amounts of debt in order to earn master's and professional degrees. Under socialism, mental labor will not be exalted above the necessary and admirable labor of manual workers, agricultural workers, caregivers, and other service providers. Academic degrees will not confer any special prestige or economic privilege. Inquiry for the sake of personal growth and contribution to society will drive educational journeys.

In this spirit of free intellectual exploration, the socialist Department of Education will oversee a robust popular education program. This type of learning will take place in workplaces, neighborhood meeting spaces, religious institutions, and organizational gatherings, bringing together groups of people for the purpose of continued study. Especially in the immediate aftermath of a socialist revolution in the United States, group learning with respect to socialism, collective responsibility, and new cultural norms will help eradicate centuries of capitalist indoctrination. To enhance the appeal of continued study, adult education classes will be celebratory and joyful culminations of socialist consciousness. Art, music, and physical recreation for adults will enrich individual lives and communities while reinforcing key socialist ideals.

In addition to bringing communities together for learning, the Department of Education will respect exclusive spaces as requested. Historically oppressed groups have long created separate spaces in the course of their struggles for liberation. Although capitalism will no longer exist, the cultural consequences of capitalist ideology (i.e., bigotry) will take time to eradicate. Therefore, the new socialist government will support the continued existence of group discussion and learning in more exclusive settings to foster feelings of solidarity for the members of such groups. For example, LGBTQ community centers—sources of pride, solidarity, and warmth for the queer community—will not only remain but receive far greater support from the government.

Like foundational education, adult education will be pervasive, accessible, and inclusive. Diverse applications of a national curriculum will be encouraged so that every person may engage in the shared learning necessary for a cultural revolution.

Universal Design and Learning Infrastructure

The concept of universal design refers to the creation of environments, devices, and lessons modified to facilitate access by the greatest number of people. In education, this concept is important for safeguarding equity with respect to people with disabilities and special needs. For example, a new school building which embraces universal design would not simply supply an elevator for students using wheelchairs. Instead, the school might eliminate stairs from the design altogether, relying on ramps and elevators to get people from one floor to the next. Every student, regardless of their ability to walk, would use the same mechanism to move through the building.

> ## Classrooms and schools in the socialist US will be the gem of every community, the recipients of the best resources that modern technology can offer.

When public education is fully funded, every community will have the resources needed to implement universal design in schools. The Department of Education will guide communities in surveying the diverse needs of their students and forthcoming students. Learning from examples of universal design in action across the country, it will supervise a long-term restructuring process in which school buildings are renovated or rebuilt with more accessible features. Further educational research—another component of fully funding public education—will guide the evolution of universal design in education in ways we cannot know in advance but can confidently predict will be inclusive and inspiring.

Classrooms and schools in the socialist US will be the gem of every community, the recipients of the best resources that modern technology can offer. Rooms will be outfitted with microphones and speakers to ensure that students can clearly hear their teachers' and peers' remarks. High-quality cameras will provide distance-learning opportunities for students who may be unable to attend school in person. Libraries will expand their collections to provide greater electronic book and audiobook access, perhaps one-to-one equivalents for every print book, which will have large-text and multilingual options.

Co-teaching, a model of education where two or more teachers are assigned to a classroom, will be the norm for most classrooms in the socialist US. A content teacher alongside a teacher trained in accessible education, both of whom will be supported by paraprofessionals, will lead small classes which are inclusive of differently-abled students. As stated above, this aim is easily achievable because of the large number of people who will no longer be employed in the soul-crushing office jobs so prevalent in capitalist society.

Finally, greater development of nontraditional classroom settings will constitute another long-term project overseen by the Department of Education. Just as subgroups within the student population won't be isolated from their peers, so the student community itself won't be separated from the wider community. Outdoor classrooms, on- and off-site, will be constructed to provide experiential learning opportunities. For example, community agriculture will be a priority after the revolution. In connection with the imperative of involving everyone in growing efforts, students will spend several weeks at nearby farms, synthesizing their learning about agroecological processes, collective responsibility, and caring for the environment. Students will also engage in service learning, the joining of content knowledge and the application of that knowledge to serve their communities. Partnerships with organizations such as farms, museums, hospitals, and more will create numerous options for experiential learning.

It is exciting but impossible to predict all the ways education will be transformed in the newly socialist United States. Advancements in technology and research will undoubtedly shape this critical public function, but the socialist framework for such changes will remain the same. Education will finally be free, responsive, and fulfilling to all. Liberated from the constraints of capitalism, education will no longer divide people by facilitating class stratification. Schools—in all their forms—will be sites of revolutionary joy and opportunity at last.

REST IN POWER

BREONNA TAYLOR
TRAYVON MARTIN
GEORGE FLOYD

CHAPTER 9

CRIME, POLICING, AND PUBLIC SAFETY

*O*ne of the most explosive issues in society is state violence. The names of George Floyd, Breonna Taylor, Michael Brown, Sandra Bland, Eric Garner, and so many others have come to represent more than individual acts of injustice. They signify the wider unjust system and the deeply rooted phenomenon of police terror, which has killed thousands in recent years.[143] That is why their racist murders sparked rebellions and protests of an unprecedented scale in practically every town and city in the United States.

The mass anti-racist movement of the last decade has revived a widespread social discussion about building alternatives to policing. It sharpened people's consciousness about the role of the police—not as class-neutral crime fighters, but as frontline enforcers of the capitalist system whose daily acts of repression funnel millions into the mass-incarceration system while politically serving to intimidate communities most likely to rise up. The movement led to debates about defunding and even abolishing the police here and now and called on people to imagine a social system where problems are addressed at their root, rather than individualized and jailed away.

Both major parties responded with a substantial counter-offensive to create a divide in working-class communities. They argued falsely that the movement's concepts led to spikes in crime, and that anyone who cares about public safety—and wants killers and rapists brought to justice—should oppose calls to defund the police and divest from mass incarceration.

How would a socialist government satisfy the yearnings of tens of millions of people for a legal and public safety system that genuinely protects and serves them unlike today's system which makes that motto a sick joke?

Under capitalism, the police, prisons, and courts serve to defend above all else the private-property interests and power of the ruling class of corporate owners. The bias of the criminal justice system is hidden by a constant propaganda campaign that in the US we have "equality under the law." This country's policing system originates in slavery, with slave-catcher patrols, alongside for-hire security firms used to suppress strikes and rebellious crowds. The police have always functioned as an especially

More Money Stolen from Minimum Wage Workers Than the Value of All Items Shoplifted

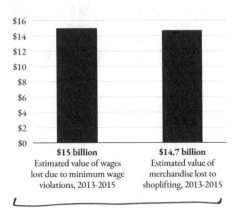

$15 billion	$14.7 billion
Estimated value of wages lost due to minimum wage violations, 2013-2015	Estimated value of merchandise lost to shoplifting, 2013-2015

ESTIMATED RETAILER SPENDING
ON SECURITY: $ 8.9 billion
BUDGET FOR WAGE
ENFORCEMENT: $ 227.5 million

Sources: Demos.org, Economic Policy Institute, The New Barometer

brutal instrument of repression and intimidation against Black, Native, and Latino communities. The prisons likewise function to lock away larger and larger sections of the population that the elite consider "superfluous."

The existing police and courts only retain a veneer of legitimacy because they are also the only institutions tasked with responding to the problems that people naturally *do* care about in their communities, such as violent crimes and the resolution of other disputes. But the truth is that the police do not prevent or reduce such violent crimes, and often aggravate existing problems when they intervene.

The socialist government will abolish policing as we know it. It will replace all capitalist state institutions with new institutions built from the ground up to truly serve and defend the vast majority, the working class and oppressed. Every successful revolution has created new military, self-defense, and community safety institutions to replace those of the prior order. That will be the case here, too.

Socialism will change and drastically reduce what is often described as "common crime." Relieving every person of the struggle for survival—by guaranteeing access to quality food, clothing, shelter, health care, and other social needs—by itself will drastically reduce a whole assortment of "crimes of survival." It will also lift a tremendous psychological pressure imposed on the working class, which often feeds into a range of other crimes against their families, neighbors, and communities. Finally, there is a range of crimes connected to the "get rich quick" culture that values the decadent lifestyles of the superrich. The transformation of this culture, and the drastic reduction of inequality, will reduce such crimes as well.

Still, all the "old crap" left over from the capitalist world will inevitably confront a revolutionary state in subtle and explicit ways: in the habits, consciousness, and culture of broad sections of the population. A whole assortment of destructive, harmful, sexist, bigoted, and antisocial crimes will not disappear overnight simply because the socialist system has changed the economic conditions, the political form of governance, and the rights of the people.

The socialist government will abolish policing as we know it. It will replace all capitalist state institutions with new institutions built from the ground up to truly serve and defend the vast majority, the working class and oppressed.

New socialist institutions will therefore not be able to do away with all policing and corrective institutions at once; so long as grave crimes persist, they will need to have an answer to them. While a socialist society will utilize a broad range of measures as alternatives to incarceration, until society finds other ways to solve such major public safety threats, options such as confinement must remain on the table, and harmed parties will continue to desire it as an outcome. Even in Indigenous societies that inspire today's models of restorative justice, such as the Iroquois, they sometimes used forms of forced residential segregation—in a sense, incarceration—to isolate those who had committed grievous crimes like murder.

Previous socialist experiments provide useful models for how policing can be transformed, and we can even draw some lessons from contemporary capitalism, as we discuss below. Participatory public safety can immediately replace many everyday police functions. Mass women's organizations will be empowered to combat patriarchal violence. The punitive "War on Drugs" will be ended and drug addiction will be treated as a medical issue. We conclude the chapter by turning to the issues of suppressing counterrevolutionary violence and subterfuge and the ultimate goal of the withering away of special armed bodies such as the police.

New socialist institutions will therefore not be able to do away with all policing and corrective institutions at once; so long as grave crimes persist, they will need to have an answer to them.

From Capitalist Rule to Socialist Law

It is important to grasp how what is considered legal or illegal changes from one society to another. Under capitalism, some of the most gratuitous forms of theft—daily exploitation at the job, usurious interest rates, bank bailouts (the theft of public resources)—are legal and perpetrators are in fact rewarded. One can receive a stiff sentence for robbing a bank, but when a bank or insurance company systematically robs society as a whole, no one goes to jail.[144] Class-determined disparities are built into the system of mass incarceration. It is not only socialist radicals who realize this: everyone knows that money buys "justice" in the existing "punishment bureaucracy." The capitalist legal code is systematically shot through with transparent hypocrisies (like the notorious and racist differences in the US legal code between crack and powder cocaine,[145] essentially the same substance). The system's absurd biases in favor of the elite come most clearly to light in the realm of discretionary enforcement and sentencing.

This is the product of centuries of development. US capitalism always ruled through one form or another of legally codified racial apartheid. While decades and centuries of struggle have made it impossible for the legal code to be explicitly racial, its fundamental nature remains the same in practice.

For all these reasons and more, a new legal code will be necessary to fulfill the aims of any socialist revolution. It is impossible to anticipate the specific legal code that will be created via a revolutionary process and the post-revolutionary state, but we can identify a few key principles:

1. The legal code will be organized around principles of accountability and not mere punishment. This means any legal processes will begin with the needs of those directly harmed and the larger affected community.
2. The socialist legal code recognizes that social problems have social solutions. Thus, rehabilitation, education, and the development of new programs and initiatives will be utilized wherever possible in processes of accountability.
3. The socialist legal code does away with the old system's reliance on property and ownership as a measure of legal right and value. For the first time, every person will have equal access and equal opportunity in the legal system, and laws will be applied fairly and consistently. The rule of law will value personhood in place of property.

For example, let's look at housing to see how the notion of "criminal" will be flipped on its head. Under capitalism, it is legal for a person to be homeless. It is legal for a landlord to use police violence to enact an eviction that throws a family out on the street. It is generally legal—either explicitly or implicitly—to leave a family in inhumane housing conditions for the sake of profit. If one tries to move a family which is homeless into an empty home, without the money to pay for it, that can produce serious charges. This system of imposed artificial scarcity is like a whip on the working class to ensure it keeps working. That fear will disappear with the new socialist government, which will guarantee quality housing to all as a constitutional right. We only have to look to one of the first acts carried out by the Cuban Revolution that reduced rents by 40 percent.[146]

In Russia a century ago, revolutionaries faced the terrible quality of housing inherited from capitalist society. They argued that even a short-term forceful redistribution of housing at the expense of the rich would require less physical force than the old regime routinely deployed as a matter of daily reality.

We are in a totally different, and much better, position. There is no significant shortage of housing, or anything else that is socially necessary, in the United States in the twenty-first century. On the contrary, there are plenty of empty houses and apartments immediately available for distribution to those without adequate housing.[147] Empty housing will be appropriated and reassigned where necessary. No one will be denied housing or threatened with the prospect of homelessness. Instead, it will be illegal to be made homeless, a new right the whole working class will be aware of and rally to defend. The need for police repression for tasks such as eviction will be eliminated. The social problems that are currently associated with expanding homelessness will be much easier to treat without requiring the use or threat of violence.

> ## No one will be denied housing or threatened with the prospect of homelessness. Instead, it will be illegal to be made homeless, a new right the whole working class will be aware of and rally to defend.

Under socialism, a vast swath of the capitalist legal code will no longer apply or be enforceable. Activities that were tolerated and even encouraged under the old bourgeois government, like open misogyny and racism, will no longer have the sanction and protection of the law. Racist attacks will require a forceful response. White supremacist terror, a mode of counter-revolutionary activity throughout US history, will be addressed one way while individually held racist beliefs will be addressed in others. Ridding the population of bigoted beliefs and attitudes will take great energy and time, but it will be accelerated through mass mobilization, cultural campaigns, education, accountability processes, and by making racism a disqualification for holding decision-making power. All of this will be underpinned by the universal meeting of social needs, the elimination of job and housing competition, and the experience of living in the new society, which will undercut the material basis of racism. In a phase of protracted peace and stability, the ways in which different problems are treated will adjust as well. Patience, second chances, and creative interventions will be necessary.

Speaking generally, instead of a society that accepts punishment and incarceration as the correct response to common crimes, socialism will create a response that is rehabilitative and comprehensive. Remaking the educational system and popular culture will promote a different set of values. Instead of developing an army of officers who specialize in harassment and brutality, a government of poor and working people will deploy an army of rooted community leaders, including formerly incarcerated people, to function as peacekeepers to address the lingering legacies of gang culture. And this is just the tip of the iceberg; once the resources of society have been liberated from the ruling class, the possibilities are endless.

Participatory Public Safety

Rather than a system that ensures stability through force and intimidation, the new society will adopt a model of participatory public safety. Such an approach means that the majority of the people will be involved in activities that deter, interrupt, and address the root causes of social conflict. From promoting community public health to conflict resolution, local committees will rely on relationship building, not brute force, to address social conflicts. Even under capitalism, it is proven that communities that combine economic security with strong and tight-knit social bonds generally invite much less police intervention.[148]

A participatory public-safety model will also rely on violence interruption as a key practice. Even today, violence interruption is far more effective than capitalist policing—a fact that leads the capitalist state to defund such programs.[149] Violence interruption recognizes that violence acts like a chain reaction: exposure to violence increases one's likelihood of later committing violence, and violence can produce a cycle of retaliation that turns victims into perpetrators and back again. Violence interruption programs rely on community outreach and engagement to stop violence before it starts. They locate ongoing conflicts and respond with conflict mediation techniques. They are premised on activating those with credibility within the community who understand best what people in their community need.

We cannot underestimate the role of media, education, and culture in alleviating interpersonal, community, and counterrevolutionary violence and conflict. No longer will film, television, or music valorize violence, militarism, or war. No longer will mass culture sensationalize and celebrate patriarchal violence and other forms of bigotry and oppression. The changes to society will be immense, brought about by ending the incessant anti-Black violence depicted on the nightly news, the "copaganda" cartoons for children, and the nonstop depiction of male dominance in television dramas. The spectacle of violence will be replaced by mass culture that tells stories involving egalitarian social relations, conflict resolution rather than violence, and holds up the creative power of the people while maintaining a strict prohibition on organized bigotry.

Together, the flourishing of mass culture and models of participatory public safety will inculcate new habits in the people and our institutions. Threatening a neighbor or member of one's family will become anathema as people adopt new habits of being together. Common purpose and collective mission will combat alienation and division. Participation in public safety and other neighborhood activities will act as a central site of community education as the people, together, come to internalize egalitarian social norms and see that we have the power to keep each other safe.

Take, for example, a family that is not sending their children to school. At present, that is a police matter. A participatory public-safety model recognizes that this issue is best addressed via a conversation with a respected community member who lives on the family's block. What barriers to school attendance is the child facing? How might these barriers be addressed together? The conversation might also emphasize the importance of schooling and the seriousness with which the socialist government takes school attendance.

Ending the War on Drugs

The new socialist government will inherit all sorts of social problems from US capitalist society. Emblematic and pervasive in this regard is the problem of substance-abuse disorder. The US is an enormous consumer of psycho-addictive substances and the vast bulk of its police and prison system is ostensibly oriented towards waging war against them. Yet the producers of these substances are integrated at the highest level with the bourgeois government. For example, there was an organized conspiracy within the ruling class to profit from the hollowing out and the physical and human destruction of "postindustrial" areas of the country by hooking millions of people on opiates. The case of the infamous Sackler family profiting from mass addiction to their product, OxyContin, vividly illustrates these dynamics. Not a single one of them spent a day in jail; they instead agreed to settlements and were granted immunity from future lawsuits.[150] The same goes for the big banks that launder billions in drug money for some of the world's largest cartels; they get slaps on the wrist and pay fines that amount to a fraction of what they take in.[151]

These examples of utter hypocrisy characterize the US drug economy, and it would take many books to go over the well-known involvement of the US government in heroin and cocaine trafficking. While corporations that ruin millions of lives go unpunished, a massive legal apparatus exists to catch even the tiniest drug dealer. The bourgeoisie develops a culture around the mindless maximization of profit at all costs and then turns around and wags its finger at a street-corner drug dealer chasing the same dream. The dealer is made to be responsible for the overall social phenomenon.

Under capitalism, which treats poor and working people as disposable, drug rehabilitation programs are often of limited value because they do nothing to alter the underlying social conditions.

The new socialist government will understand the need to separate drug addiction from "crime." As we discuss in chapter 7, the consumption of drugs will be a medical issue, not a police issue. Possessing a psychoactive substance will no longer offer a pretext for indefinite detention—as it does today. Under capitalism, which treats poor and working people as disposable, drug rehabilitation programs are often of limited value because they do nothing to alter the underlying social conditions. Under socialism, a massive public-health campaign, sparing no expense, will be waged against drug addiction. The militaristic "War on Drugs" fought against poor and working people at gunpoint will be relegated to the garbage heap.

Meaningful work and guaranteed housing, education, health care, and provision for basic needs will draw many people involved in the underground drug economy above ground. The material benefits of socialism will also help relieve the persistent anxiety and hopelessness that often lead people to drug addiction. Most impactful, though, will be the broader social transformation redirecting the collective wealth, knowledge, and productive capacity of society toward the satisfaction of collective human needs. Such a transformation sets the foundation for a new culture to emerge based on the values of solidarity and collective purpose, values anathema to the every-person-for-themselves, get-rich-or-die-trying capitalist system.

This is not to say that the international underground drug economy will immediately disappear under socialism or that a socialist state will simply take a hands-off approach to it. But the scale of the drug problem will be greatly diminished; the drug user will be assisted rather than criminalized, and large sections of the working class will be brought into formal work as part of the complete overhaul of social and economic rights. Policing for drug-related crimes will then target the real culprits, the big profiteers.

Patriarchal Violence

So far, we have seen how certain categories of common crime—crimes of survival—will diminish drastically as the social system begins to guarantee everyone's survival. Others, such as drug addiction, will be reframed as public-health matters and shifted away from the punitive incarceration system. Participatory public safety and violence interruption can prevent other conflicts. Certain categories of crime will diminish apace with the larger socioeconomic and cultural transformation but not simply disappear, or at least not for a long time.

Particularly pernicious forms of crime and violence will not be allowed to simply wither away on their own, however; they will be combated with massive people's campaigns, involving both the state and people's grassroots organizations. This is certainly the case with domestic violence, sexual assault and harassment, and femicide, which exist in epidemic proportions under the current system.[152] Ending these forms of violence and the underlying patriarchal norms that sustain them will be a top priority of the socialist revolution, requiring care and attention throughout the building of the new society.

Many of the contributing factors behind domestic violence, especially within the working class, will be addressed through other projects of the new society. These include universal child care, health care, education, housing, and meaningful work, which will go a long way in combating the epidemic of interpersonal violence. While women of all cultural and economic backgrounds are affected by domestic violence, there is a deep correlation between domestic violence and the capitalist economic structure. In an untold number of families, men retain full control of bank accounts and finances, including control over housing, leaving women with no means to survive without their abusers. Since the 1996 legislation cutting welfare, poor women have had even less access to proper assistance.[153] Many women who escape their abusive homes become homeless due to the lack of affordable housing or access to funds. The economic and social reality of capitalist society means that women frequently are forced to stay with or come back to abusive partners because there is no economic or social support for their freedom. All of these restrictions on women's economic and bodily freedom will be eliminated in the new socialist society, leading to a massive reduction in domestic violence and femicide.

Sexual violence, which includes sexual assault, rape, and sexual abuse, is prevalent in our society. In the United States, an estimated one in five women are victims of rape. Almost half of reported female victims were raped by an acquaintance or intimate partner.[154] Some studies suggest that 60 percent of sexual assaults are not reported to the police for fear of retaliation, victim blaming, or the police themselves. Currently, as many as 200,000 rape kits sit unopened in police storage.[155]

The new society, unlike the current racist, sexist, capitalist system, will not just pay lip service to the issue of sexual violence. It will invest resources in education, media, public-health campaigns, and other efforts that address patriarchal violence and work to end it. The socialist government will investigate and adjudicate cases of sexual assault through processes of justice attentive to the needs of those most impacted. There is not likely to be a one-size-fits-all consequence for patriarchal violence. In cases of domestic violence, appropriate remedy and redress will be determined via meaningful consultation with the victim of that crime. Exclusion from certain community activities could be in order or total residential segregation—incarceration, which would be combined with intensive reeducation and rehabilitation.

Addiction services, parenting classes, and mental health counseling may also be suitable accountability measures in some cases. The building and empowering of mass women's organizations will play an instrumental role in all of this and lead the way in deciding outcomes. These organizations will have the protection and support of the government, and in that sense function as quasi-state institutions. By blending popular mobilization with a new legal system, socialism prepares the way for its own state institutions to become obsolete and wither away.

An end to patriarchy is not an inevitable or automatic outcome of socialist revolution. It must be worked on constantly. We can also anticipate that counterrevolutionary activity will be focused on overturning women's equality in society. We will be prepared to treat it as such. Intimidation of emerging women activists, terrorist attacks on abortion clinics, assassination of women leaders, rape as a tool of social control, and the celebration of male chauvinism are tactics already employed by the far right to galvanize their followers and sow terror in the lives of working-class people. One thing is sure: the end of US militarism and imperialism, the abolition of the gender division of labor, and the guaranteed provision for social needs will transform society from one that relies on patriarchal violence into one in which patriarchal violence is actively confronted.

An End to Capitalist Prisons

The new socialist government will release all revolutionary political prisoners, dropping charges and convictions against those who have been persecuted for their commitment to the people's struggles—people like Assata Shakur or those who have put their bodies on the line in the movement for Black lives or against the pipelines at Standing Rock or Line 3.

Beyond the explicitly political prisoners, a socialist victory will initiate a process of the direct release of the vast majority of people still confined in jails and prisons. Over two million people are currently incarcerated in the US, tens of thousands are in Immigration and Customs Enforcement detention centers, and 4.3 million are on parole or probation.[156] With over seven million people currently under the purview of correctional services, the US's addiction to incarceration system has ripped families and communities apart, distorting their development. It is the largest prison system in the world, by far. We cannot underestimate the human potential that will be unleashed with the destruction of the capitalist prison state. Of course, it will be a massive task to address the unmet personal, cultural, health, educational, and psychological needs of those who have been in the dungeons of capitalism for so long—but it is achievable.

Formerly incarcerated people will be integrated into the new socialist society; surplus, not scarcity, is the characteristic feature of US capitalism. There is enough housing for everyone, including formerly incarcerated people. There is enough food. There is more than enough work to be done rebuilding our decayed infrastructure and regenerating our forests, wetlands, and agriculture. And there are enough well-trained people and resources to provide adequate health care, education, and social support for all. Millions of people with direct experiences of the violence of the repressive capitalist state and its institutions will not only be given care and reintegrated, but will be well-positioned to become mentors and leaders of violence interruption and other public safety activities, including health campaigns, to combat the legacy drug epidemic.

From top to bottom and beginning to end, the US prison system is a monstrosity whose physical destruction cannot come soon enough. The most "cutting-edge" prison camps constructed by private contractors and the infamous public ones from Auburn and Attica to San Quentin and the Los Angeles County jail differ in scale and punitive techniques, but they have at least one thing in common: they are not fit places to confine human beings.[157]

Punitive institutionalization will be the last resort and cannot take place in the facilities that currently make up the US prison system. These institutions will be destroyed.

In the postrevolutionary era, there will be a comparatively small number of situations in which confinement will remain necessary for the sake of safety: certain forms of violent counterrevolutionary activity and destructive behaviors to self or others. Punitive institutionalization will be the last resort and cannot take place in the facilities that currently make up the US prison system. These institutions will be destroyed. Temporary confinement or restriction of freedom of movement will generally take the form of house arrest, relocation to a different neighborhood or city, or assignment to a therapeutic or rehabilitative home. Above all, the new socialist system will oppose the "zero tolerance" worldview that slaps the label of "criminal" on individuals to justify their permanent removal or subordination in society and treats poor and working people as disposable and unredeemable. People, especially people learning to live in a new society, may require second and third chances.

Dealing with Counterrevolution

Every postrevolutionary state confronts an inherent dilemma. On the one hand, revolutionaries are motivated by the vision and goal of a new world based on emancipatory principles. On the other hand, they are immediately tasked with fighting off the return of the "old world"—the capitalist world—which does not simply disappear the moment a socialist revolution triumphs. The deposed ruling class, along with their hired hands and those sectors of society still under their influence, inevitably fight rearguard battles to return to power, to sabotage the socialist system. Their allies in other capitalist countries also support counterrevolution from outside. The policing apparatus in the US, if taken as a single unit, would today be the third largest armed force in the world. While this network of police departments and auxiliaries will be dispersed and replaced, it's a fantasy to imagine it will either be annihilated or submit totally to the reconstruction of a new social order. Some devotees of the old order will resort to violence—terrorism—to strike at the new socialist order. Since the new government will be ruthlessly opposed to racism, sexism, transphobia, and all bigotry or chauvinism, reactionary counterattacks can be expected across all of society but targeting the most oppressed groups in the old social order.

A socialist government must possess new state institutions to stop, by any means necessary, those who would otherwise wreck and overthrow it, from outside and from within. It would be a betrayal of the whole revolutionary process to end exploitation and oppression if the new socialist government allowed the old ruling class to regroup, reorganize, and return to power, subjecting hundreds of millions of people to the old system. They would have to be stopped.

The most effective defense against organized reactionary violence is the mobilized masses of people. But when mobilization subsides, as it inevitably will over time, and there is a return to the "normal life" of socialist reconstruction, what agency will maintain vigilance against the emergence of violent contradictions? Responding to some forms of violence, such as counterrevolutionary and white supremacist violence, will require trained community safety teams able to respond quickly. But even those teams tasked with responding to the most serious forms of counterrevolutionary violence will be answerable to the people.

We cannot predict the exact conditions that will characterize the first phases of socialist governance in the United States, but we can look to the long history of revolution for a sense of the choices that will face the new government. In Cuba, for example, the Committees for the Defense of the Revolution (CDR) were founded as local organizations of everyday people working together to fight off imperialist invasion and counterrevolution.[158] As the revolutionary situation developed, the CDR moved from armed groups engaged in community defense, to forms of local self-government planning social and community affairs such as administering vaccines, holding forums and debates, and proposing legislation.

We expect that the organizational forms that emerge to make and defend the revolution will become organs of people's power.

Withering Away of State Institutions

In any society, the main state institutions—the police, prisons, and courts in particular—are specially designated to be able to legally use force and violence, to repress and to incarcerate. They can do things that the rest of society is generally prohibited from doing. In this sense, these "specially armed bodies" stand above the rest of society.

Socialists aim to create a society where human beings live cooperatively and solve their problems without resorting to state violence or incarceration. That may seem like a fantasy, but for thousands of years, our species lived communally without special police and prisons. It is possible for humanity to arrive at such a society in the future—communism—on a new basis of advanced technology, planning, and material abundance. It is only through the mass of people gaining the experience of governing, with all its problems and contradictions, that the reliance on institutions standing above society will diminish by equal measure.

The goal of a socialist government is to so successfully resolve the class inequalities and all the inherited contradictions of capitalism that such special institutions of force no longer are necessary and wither away.

When will this happen? That is impossible to forecast. Unlike other fields of policy where socialist reorganization is fairly predictable and straightforward, such as energy, health care, housing, etc., the question of the scale and functions of the postrevolutionary state apparatus will have to correlate with the relationship of political forces in the United States and worldwide. It will depend on the relative ferocity of counterrevolutionary trends, whether the socialist government will enjoy a long period of peace, and how rapidly the consciousness and culture of the whole people has been transformed. When and under what conditions the state institutions of the police and the prisons will be rendered unnecessary cannot be stated in advance.

What we do know is that capitalism reproduces inequality, dog-eat-dog competition, bigotry, and alienation every day. It breaks down communities and turns them against one another. If people do not know one another and if people understand themselves to be in competition with one another, even small disagreements over, for example, loud music or a blocked parking spot can erupt into conflict. Many projects of the socialist program from housing to education, health care to transportation, will combat alienation.

It will also be necessary to foster people's organizations—in neighborhoods, workplaces, and across different social sectors—that work to combat alienation by demonstrating people's capacity for resolving problems without state intervention. This will include everything from small, interpersonal conflicts to larger social problems such as addiction, truancy, or patriarchal violence. Such organizations will also help unleash the creative power of the people as they work to propose and implement programs and initiatives that address social problems in the new society.

CHAPTER 10

ENDING IMPERIALIST WARS: BUILDING A WORLD OF SOLIDARITY AND PEACE

A socialist United States will turn US foreign policy on its head. Where there has been war, there will be peace. Where there has been enmity, there will be friendship. And where there has been competition, there will be solidarity. Given the obvious desirability of peace, friendship, and solidarity, this hardly appears to be a revolutionary aspiration. But it will take a revolution to become a reality. The capitalist system we live under is based on exploitation, ruthless competition, and domination. War is built into capitalism's DNA, and it is a principal means by which the US capitalist class maintains its global hegemony.

The twenty-year military occupation in Afghanistan ended in defeat, with the squandering of trillions of dollars, the loss of hundreds of thousands of lives, and the devastation of countless more. In spite of that, the US government is spending hundreds of billions to prepare for a new war against Russia and the People's Republic of China, and future interventions in other countries. Short of all-out invasion, US imperialism has a range of tools for making life miserable for the people of targeted countries. In places like Chile, Guatemala, Ghana, Iran, Indonesia, and so many others, the CIA has orchestrated coups that overthrew popular governments and replaced them with brutal dictatorships willing to serve the interests of US corporations. Sanctions, a form of economic warfare, are frequently imposed to bend countries to the will of Washington and Wall Street by depriving ordinary people of the basic necessities of life like food and medicine. It does not have to be this way. Why do we need to compete with China or any other country? In whose interest is it?

Leaders in Washington—Democrats and Republicans alike—constantly promote the idea that we are competing over who will dominate the twenty-first century. Yet it is not in the interests of the working class of any country to "win the twenty-first century" over any other country or group of countries. Working people in the United States have a thousand times more in common with workers in China, Russia, Cuba, and South Africa than we do with the billionaire bankers and bosses here. The idea that we, the people of the United States, are locked in mortal combat with the people of China or any other country is a myth designed to justify wars in the interest of profit and power. The fear and hatred of other peoples, deliberately spread by the capitalist politicians and mass media, must be abolished and replaced by the active promotion of solidarity with working and oppressed people of all countries and all nationalities. Socialism makes these aspirations a reality.

The fear and hatred of other peoples, deliberately spread by the capitalist politicians and mass media, must be abolished and replaced by the active promotion of solidarity with working and oppressed people of all countries and all nationalities. Socialism makes these aspirations a reality.

Imperialism is a stage of the global capitalist system defined by the drive for war, unequal economic and political relations, monopoly control over trade and development, and "the financial strangulation of the overwhelming majority of the population of the world by a handful of 'advanced' countries."[159] US imperialism stands directly in the way of addressing the worsening social and ecological challenges of our time.

Socialist foreign policy will not only dismantle US imperialism but repurpose its institutions and technologies toward correcting historical global injustices and supporting new forms of political and economic integration between countries. Foreign military bases will be shut down and their budget will be converted to pay reparations to nations that have suffered under US militarism worldwide. The right to self-determination for oppressed peoples will be guaranteed and protected. Skills and information will be shared with developing countries, and development will not be based on any "American model" but on supporting each country as

Number of US Military Bases in Other Countries

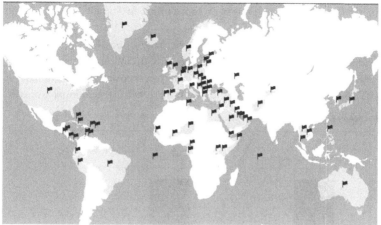

The U S has military bases in eighty-one countries. (Source: World BEYOND War)

it forges its own path forward. Only by working with nations on an equal basis will we be able to address global problems.

The Unbearable Cost of War

The Pentagon is currently the headquarters of a military machine that occupies many lands and has 750 foreign bases—and at least 450 more domestically—in eighty-one countries. The military is the enforcer and protector of US capitalism and its global empire, a role similar to that played by the police and prison system inside the United States. The imperialist occupations of oppressed nations around the world mirror the reality for oppressed communities within the United States.

The territory that formed the basis of the United States was acquired through genocidal wars against one Native nation after another over two-and-a-half centuries. Billions of hours of unpaid, enslaved African and African American labor laid the economic foundation that enabled the US to grow into a world power.

US wars over the past seven decades—from Korea and Vietnam, to Iraq and Afghanistan, to Nicaragua and Libya—have left millions of people dead, tens of millions wounded and displaced, and massive destruction to countries seeking to overcome the already debilitating legacy of colonialism. In each case, war was waged against countries that did not and could not threaten the United States. Every day, bombs are falling in many countries, and casualties go uncounted and largely unknown except for the families and neighbors of those killed in Somalia, Yemen, Iraq, Afghanistan, Pakistan, and elsewhere.

The cost of militarism and war is virtually impossible to wrap one's head around. The Pentagon budget is over $700 billion, but the real cost of wars past and present has been for many years over a trillion dollars—that's $1,000,000,000,000—annually. What is the internal impact of this

US Military Spending Compared to China

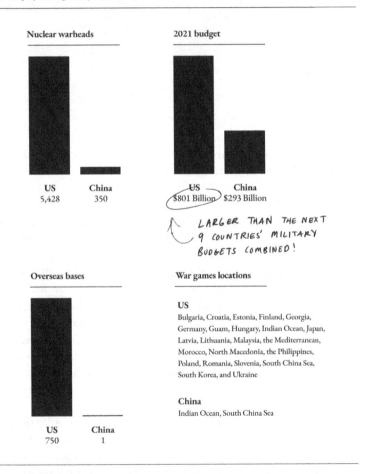

Nuclear warheads

US	China
5,428	350

2021 budget

US	China
$801 Billion	$293 Billion

LARGER THAN THE NEXT 9 COUNTRIES' MILITARY BUDGETS COMBINED!

Overseas bases

US	China
750	1

War games locations

US
Bulgaria, Croatia, Estonia, Finland, Georgia, Germany, Guam, Hungary, Indian Ocean, Japan, Latvia, Lithuania, Malaysia, the Mediterranean, Morocco, North Macedonia, the Philippines, Poland, Romania, Slovenia, South China Sea, South Korea, and Ukraine

China
Indian Ocean, South China Sea

Sources: Federation of American Scientists, SIPRI Military Expenditure Report, World BEYOND War 2020 Report, The Diplomat, NATO, U S Army Europe and Africa, VOA News, Reuters, U S Naval Institute News, South China Morning Post, Peter G. Peterson Foundation

vast spending on war? As Rev. Dr. Martin Luther King Jr. famously said at the height of the Vietnam War: "The bombs in Viet Nam explode at home: they destroy the hopes and possibilities for a decent America."[160] When so much of the limited resources of society are expended on militarism, the result is tens of millions of people deprived of what should be the right of every person: healthy food, clean water, housing, health care, a safe environment, education, and a living income.

Militarism is lethal for the environment and climate. The US military is the number one user of fossil fuel in the world. In 2019, the Pentagon used over 4.6 billion gallons of petroleum, 12.6 million per day, more than most of the countries in the world. The daily training for air, sea, and ground war produces immense quantities of climate-destroying carbon dioxide and other gases. The 750 US foreign bases around the world— and hundreds more inside the country—are notorious for dumping toxic waste that ends up polluting the ground, water, and soil and causing the spread of diseases like cancer, asthma, and more.

Of all the foreign bases in the world, more than 95 percent belong to the United States.[161] No country in history has ever deployed military power on this scale. Maintaining these bases costs hundreds of billions of dollars annually, taxpayer money spent not to defend the US but to protect interests in profit and empire. War and militarism are bad for people and the planet, but great for giant military-industrial corporations like Boeing, McDonnell-Douglas, and Raytheon. There is an infamous "revolving door" between corporate boardrooms and Pentagon offices. A virtual army of lobbyists makes sure the contracts keep coming and the dollars keep flowing. Thousands of politicians have grown far richer over the decades than their salaries alone can explain.

Every year, hundreds of billions of dollars are spent on death-dealing weaponry of all types. For most of it there is only one customer—the Pentagon—and guaranteed profits. The rest is sold, again at a huge profit, to approved allies and client states. In addition to the military contractors and oil companies, the big banks and other investors profit from the hundreds of billions in annual interest payments on the debt from earlier and current wars. The wars in Iraq and Afghanistan will end up costing a minimum of $7 trillion—$7,000,000,000,000—a large part of which has never been accounted for, amounting to corruption on the largest scale in history.[162]

Technology under capitalism expresses its class nature in an especially vivid and repulsive way. Military research projects range from atmospheric water extraction, to self-healing building material that can repair itself on command, to weaponized drones that hunt down and execute people with no human involvement.[163] Robots the size of sugar cubes are being developed with light, sound, and heat sensors to investigate collapsed buildings. Humanoid robots are being developed that can control and operate weaponry. Quadruped robots exist that can carry 400 pounds while following a leader across marshes, fields, and mountains. Systems exist that can control swarms of drones with gestures and facial expressions. Thousands of floating sensors across the oceans enable "persistent maritime situational awareness."[164] The World Modelers program generates early warnings about global supply chain disruption from climate change. Technological advancements which could be used for society's benefit are used for society's oppression. Trillions are poured into developing new means of extermination each year.

'Major Power Competition'—
Pentagon Code Words for World War III

The US military and political establishment are clearly planning for new and larger wars, with the targets being the Russian Federation and the People's Republic of China (PRC). In 2018, the top priority of the official National Security Strategy was shifted from the "war on terrorism" to "major power competition," with China identified as the main "competitor" with the US.[165] It was during the Obama administration that the "pivot to Asia" began, which involved the shifting of up to 70 percent of US overseas military to the western Pacific Ocean.

Starting in 1999, the US government recklessly pursued a policy of expanding membership in the North Atlantic Treaty Organization (NATO) to include former republics of the Soviet Union and the eastern and central European countries that had been the Russian Republic's closest allies during the Cold War. The Russian Federation announced that the incorporation of Ukraine and Georgia into NATO, two former western republics of the Soviet Union, constituted a red line that Russia would never accept. Their argument was a simple one: these countries share a long border with Russia and placing high-tech conventional and nuclear weapons in those areas would constitute a perennial security threat that Russia would never be able to defend against.

Russia's warnings to the US became more threatening toward the end of 2021. Russia began amassing troops near Ukraine and demanded that the US and NATO countries stop militarizing the country. The

Biden administration ruled that Russia's demands were "non-starters" and continued to treat Ukraine as a de facto NATO member. More and more advanced weapons were shipped into Ukraine in early 2022. It is noteworthy that President Obama had refused to send such weapons into Ukraine after a western-backed coup toppled the neutral Ukrainian government in 2014. Having abandoned Obama's cautious policy, Biden and the Pentagon took the opposite tack. In February 2022, almost to the very day of the 2014 coup, Russian president Putin announced that Russia was launching a major invasion of Ukraine to "demilitarize" the country. The horrifying scenes of death, destruction, and long lines of fleeing civilians in Ukraine shocked the world. Predictably, stock prices for corporations that constitute the core of the military-industrial complex soared. Instead of urgently resuming negotiations with Russia on its key demand that Ukraine be neutral and demilitarized, the capitalist government in Washington seized upon Russia's illegal invasion as an additional pretext to prepare for "major power conflict" in the coming period.

The hostility toward Russia and China emanating from political leaders and the capitalist media is aimed at preparing public opinion for a new conflict. Since the fall of the Soviet Union in 1991, US leaders have nearly doubled the number of NATO countries, surrounding Russia along much of its western border from the Baltic Sea to the Black Sea. NATO forces are dominated by Washington, and have joined with the US in Afghanistan, Iraq, and other targets of imperialist occupation. The myth that NATO is or ever was a defensive alliance has been thoroughly demolished. The PRC is accused on a daily basis of stealing "American jobs and technology." But it wasn't Chinese leaders who decided to move production facilities out of the US; it was US capitalists in search of ever-greater profit. They shut down thousands of factories and laid off millions of workers. The amped-up demonization of China in the mass media has resulted in a major surge in violent attacks on Asian Americans and Pacific Islanders inside the US. Relentless anti-China propaganda has persuaded millions of people in the US that China is a military threat to the US and its allies. This is false.

China has no interest in a war with the United States. China's military budget is less than a quarter of that of the US.[166] While China has increased its military spending, it is mainly for defensive purposes and trails far behind the US in nuclear and most conventional weapons. The generals and politicians in Washington do not really believe that China is preparing to attack the United States—that would be suicidal. What they are alarmed about is China taking actions to defend itself in case of attack. They turn reality upside down, presenting China as the aggressor when it is a vast and ever-growing array of US military power surrounding the PRC, not the other way around.

"Major power competition" is the language of the US empire. Since the fall of the Soviet Union in 1991, US foreign and military policy has been based on the idea that there must be one and only one "superpower" in the world. A key 1992 Pentagon strategy document outlined:

> Our first objective is to prevent the re-emergence of a new rival, either on the territory of the former Soviet Union or elsewhere, that poses a threat on the order of that posed formerly by the Soviet Union. This is a dominant consideration underlying the new regional defense strategy and requires that we endeavor to prevent any hostile power from dominating a region whose resources would, under consolidated control, be sufficient to generate global power. These regions include Western Europe, East Asia, the territory of the former Soviet Union, and South-west Asia.[167]

Since the 1990s, China has become an economic powerhouse. Its rapid economic growth has lifted eight hundred million people out of poverty.[168] Through the "Belt and Road Initiative" and other joint initiatives, China has cultivated mutually beneficial relations with many other countries. Washington views these developments with the utmost hostility: they are occurring at a time when the US role in the world economy is declining and the remaining US dominance is military. The threat of a new war on China by the United States and its allies—intent on destroying China's infrastructure and economy—is very real. It has the potential of becoming a nuclear war with incalculable consequences for all of humanity.

The US has made no serious effort to stem the danger of nuclear war. In fact, the US government has proposed plans to expand and upgrade its nuclear arsenal through 2046, including developing new "tactical" weapons that can be more readily deployed in a conflict. According to a 2017 report by the Congressional Budget Office (CBO), these plans will cost US taxpayers $1.2 trillion.[169] Another CBO report from May 2021 indicates that immediate spending over the next ten years will add an additional $140 billion to previous projections.[170] Such colossal spending is furthermore hidden from the public as it is in large part buried in the budget of the Department of Energy.

The US has made no serious effort to stem the danger of nuclear war. In fact, the US government has proposed plans to expand and upgrade its nuclear arsenal through 2046.

From the time atomic bombs were ordered and dropped on Hiroshima and Nagasaki in 1945, the nuclear weapon has been a military and political tool of US imperialism. The United States remains the only country in history to have carried out atomic bombings, which killed, maimed, and poisoned hundreds of thousands of Japanese civilians. The horrific and cruel bombings of Hiroshima and Nagasaki did not just mark the end of WWII, they also signaled the beginning of a new era of US military dominance which has since threatened to carry out nuclear genocide against perceived enemy countries multiple times.

Dismantling US Imperialism

Time and again, the US government has shown no serious concern for the welfare and advancement of peoples around the world—least of all, for the countries on which war and occupation are imposed. The US military is singularly concerned with maintaining global power and hegemony by putting down, oppressing, and stymieing countries and nations perceived to be threats to US interests. And all the while, citizens of the United States have no control or say over matters of war and military expenditure. Such is the brutal reality of US imperialism, which is not—as many might believe—an anachronism, but very much alive and sowing destruction on increasing levels of severity today. Socialism will put a stop to these destructive relations and policies.

The foreign policy of the new socialist government will focus on two immediate objectives: (1) dismantling all US "command" structures that cover the world, and (2) converting the trillion-dollar military budget to meet people's needs.

The first objective is shutting down the Pentagon—the effective center of the global war machine—as well as closing all foreign military bases and withdrawing military forces and weaponry from other countries. The CIA and other instruments of subversion and counterrevolution will be dismantled. The land used for bases will be cleaned up and detoxified for return to the sovereign countries in which they are located. Domestic US bases—hundreds of which are sites that have polluted air and water with extreme levels of cancer-causing chemicals—will also be detoxified and converted to peacetime purposes, turned into facilities for housing, health care, culture, recreation, job training, and education. Domestic communities that have been harmed by bases and militarism will be paid reparations. All nuclear weapons will be decommissioned and deconstructed in coordination with other nuclear weapons states to put an end to the threat of nuclear war.

> ## The foreign policy of the new socialist government will focus on two immediate objectives: one, dismantling all US 'command' structures that cover the world; and two, converting the trillion-dollar military budget to meet people's needs.

The socialist US will withdraw from the imperialist NATO; the Australia, United Kingdom, United States security treaty (AUKUS); and all other overt and covert military alliances. The militarization of space will likewise cease, and all space weaponry and spy satellites will be decommissioned. The US military will be demobilized and a living wage, union jobs, and job training will be provided for all demobilized personnel. Health care programs will be expanded for all veterans, and comprehensive screenings and life-long treatment for physical and psychological injuries suffered on military duty will be provided.

Defense of the revolutionary government will be constructed on the basis of the armed, organized working class. The US's advanced technological research and vast logistical resources will be deployed to provide international assistance. Such assistance will include support for peoples' movements against fascist and far-right governments. It will include pro-viding engineering expertise to aid with infrastructure adaptation and land reclamation, among other projects, that respond to climate change.

The second objective is mobilizing resources to provide food, water, housing, and health care to all people in need, at home and abroad. US military spending will be directed to rectifying historical injustices. The socialist government will recognize special rights for national minorities and oppressed nations' right to self-determination. The US's existing colonial relationships will be dissolved. The independence of Puerto Rico will be immediately recognized. Samoa, Guam, the Virgin Islands, and the Mariana Islands will be free to exercise their right to self-determination, up to and including independence. Native treaties and sovereignty will be honored and restitution provided.

The new socialist government will work ceaselessly to overcome the ravages of US imperialism that have exploited the people, resources, and economies of so many countries of the world. In sum, proletarian interna-tionalism will establish the fundamental principle of the new socialist gov-ernment's orientation to the rest of the world, emphasizing sovereignty, solidarity, revolutionary assistance, and reparations.

A New Era of International Solidarity and Cooperation

There is no hope for pressuring the ruling class and the system they protect toward genuine humanitarian action. Why? Because the close rela-tionship between the US military and arms industry forms an integral part of the US economy. The military-industrial complex is one of the crutches holding up the US economy. The federal government regularly employs enormous amounts of tax dollars to intervene on behalf of the companies that produce munitions, technologies, and other equipment for the mil-itary. The government provides these companies not only with a guaran-teed market but also with guaranteed profits. We cannot and should not expect peace, cooperation, equal exchange, or just development from a system that is not meant to promote these relations.

Economic and financial sanctions provide a textbook example. Usual pretexts for imposing sanctions are that certain countries are becoming too "aggressive" in their regions or are in violation of "human rights." But the most extreme dictatorships, like the absolute monarchies in the Middle East, are among the closest US allies and markets for US-made weaponry. Sanctions are a form of warfare that cause massive death and suffering for entire countries. Dozens of countries have been hit with some form of sanctions, with the most stringent and deadly sanctions inflicted on formerly colonized states that Washington has targeted for "regime change." These include Iran, North Korea, Venezuela, and Cuba. Sanctions, along with bombings, were key to tearing apart Yugoslavia, Iraq, and Libya. Sanctions are not simply embargoes on trade with the US. American embassies around the world follow and seek to block economic relations between their host state and the targeted countries. Because of US financial and economic power, companies and governments that engage in trade with embargoed countries are often subject to a cutoff of trade with the US, huge fines, and sanctions themselves. Smaller and weaker countries are made offers they cannot refuse. It is a form of international gangsterism dressed up as diplomacy. The impact of sanctions on developing countries is devastating, causing widespread shortages of food, medicine, and other necessities, along with soaring inflation due to the disappearance of goods. US leaders cynically claim that food and medicine are "exempt" from sanctions. But if countries that must import such commodities are blocked from selling their own products, they have no means of purchasing what their people need. That the capitalist politicians know what the effects are is beyond question.

We will work ceaselessly to overcome the ravages of US imperialism that have exploited the people, resources, and economies of so many of the world's countries, emphasizing sovereignty, solidarity, revolutionary assistance, and reparations.

The real motivation for sanctions, just like the real motivation for imperialist interventions, has nothing to do with stated reasons and everything to do with power, domination, and empire. Israel, which rules over the Palestinian people through a vicious apartheid system, not only is never sanctioned, but receives more than $4 billion a year from US taxpayers in unconditional grants. No other country comes close to approaching the United States in the number of wars, coups, and other forms of destructive intervention. But, along with its allies, the US is exempt from sanctions under the current global order.

The new socialist foreign policy will immediately end economic sanctions and blockades of other countries. Reparations will be made to countries that have been harmed by US wars. The cost of suffering under sanctions will be paid for from the confiscated wealth of the banks, corporations, and the superrich. Moreover, all aid and international support to regional oppressors around the world will be ended, especially for the apartheid state of Israel. The right of the Palestinian people to return to their homeland will be supported and they will be compensated for their losses.

To oversee the dramatic changes detailed above, the new socialist government will create a Department of International Solidarity and Cooperation. This governmental body will be responsible for developing new relations with other states based on shared principles of progress, equality, common property, and humanitarian aid and assistance. In practice, this work will entail a range of activities aimed at providing nations around the world with the means to create the collective structures necessary for delivering services and meeting needs. Supported projects will include the sharing of various technologies; cultural exchanges for teachers, students, union and peasant leaders, and government officials; farmer-to-farmer programs where agroecological techniques and learning are shared and advanced; and the establishment of educational centers where grassroots organizations and peoples' movements can freely access workspaces, auditoriums, internet, language instruction, and other educational resources. Such support will only be provided at the recipient country's request and on their terms.

The existing State Department already has the infrastructure for carrying out these proposals. Educational centers that can be opened to local organizations and peoples' movements likewise already exist—corporations use them all the time. The Department of International Solidarity and Cooperation will put them in the hands of the working class of the respective countries. Many of the people currently employed and contracted by the State Department are highly skilled and experienced in logistical problem-solving. The new socialist government will not simply discard these workers. It will offer them opportunities to apply their expertise in more meaningful ways: toward peace rather than war, toward responding to disasters rather than causing them.

The Department of International Solidarity and Cooperation will go a long way toward ensuring the success of socialist foreign policies based neither on profits nor market expansion, but on connecting peoples' movements and supporting the development programs autonomously pursued by other countries. Here, "support" and, indeed, "development," are not defined according to Eurocentric models enforced by the International Monetary Fund, World Bank, or other US-dominated global economic institutions. With the exit of the US from them, these institutions will be so greatly diminished as to be effectively demolished. National development agencies like the US Agency for International Development will be dismantled and their resources and logistical capacities repurposed to work cooperatively with desiring countries to develop institutions that hear people's demands, actively meet their needs, and contribute to their flourishing.

Global Cooperation for Addressing Global Problems

Overcoming the destructive legacies of colonialism, capitalist exploitation, and imperialist wars will require a global effort. The new socialist government will encourage the creation of a new institution of international cooperation formed with countries on an equal basis and in line with shared interests. Such a multilateral institution may resemble or even build upon the United Nations (UN) and its various specialized agencies. The UN charter expresses a commitment to upholding international peace, social progress, and prosperity as well as the human rights and dignity of peoples around the world. As it currently stands, however, the US-dominated UN does not live up to the progressive principles outlined in its founding charter. This is why a new institution is necessary.

So long as the United States maintains its permanent seat with ability to veto decisions in the Security Council, the UN will serve as a bulwark for the aggressive and militaristic hegemony of US imperialism and capitalism. A new multilateral institution free from monopoly control by the US or any single country must be created collectively by participating member states, with special attention to the voices of historically oppressed nations and countries. Though it is beyond the scope of this chapter to predict the precise form this global effort will take, it is still possible to highlight what can be achieved in the process. From development programs that strengthen social bonds between workers and peasants in regions around the world; to international laws and agreements that ensure just and fair access to natural resources, technologies, information, communication, and media; to meaningful cooperation on global climate change and issues relating to disaster relief and public health, including the containment of global pandemics to avoid another disaster like the COVID-19 pandemic;

the pressing political, economic, and ecological challenges of our time will be addressed when solidarity replaces competition.

The Party for Socialism and Liberation stands committed to bringing about peace, cooperation, and equality among all nations and peoples, ending once and for all the ruinous wars, racism, competition, and inequality that prevail under the capitalist world order. Peace is not just the absence of fighting at a particular moment. Peace requires justice, particularly for those who for so long have been denied it. Where there is hunger, homelessness, and other forms of deprivation; where there is the denial of self-determination for oppressed peoples; where six billionaires own as much wealth as half the population of a country: there is no justice and there can be no peace.

Peace requires the socialist reconstruction of the United States.

CONCLUSION

The vision of a socialist future for the United States that this book presents is not a utopian daydream based on a wish list of what might be. It is a detailed description of what is realizable in the first period after the diverse working class comes to power. We can end wage slavery and domination by the market, dismantle the structures of special oppression, transform energy production and use, provide universal basic services, expand free time, and engage more and more people in the active reproduction of our common world. The capitalist-imperialist order offers out-of-control climate change, widening inequality, destructive war, increasing repression, and national oppression. Socialist reconstruction offers a future in which people and the planet will thrive.

We can't predict exactly when a revolutionary crisis will erupt in the United States; no one can. What we can say with confidence is that it will and that it is imperative that all who want to see real justice, real equality, real liberation, and real democracy be ready for it. The Party for Socialism and Liberation wrote this book to aid with this preparation and to help overcome the specific ideological baggage designed to keep the US working class here from envisioning and understanding socialism.

This book is informed by a strategic orientation honed in the course of comrades' lifetime commitment to revolutionary struggle. Endless activism without a strategic orientation leads nowhere. A vision for socialist reconstruction that corresponds to reality is essential to the success of the US socialist movement. Socialist transformation will not be possible unless millions upon millions of people have a socialist consciousness. Recognizing that change is necessary in general is insufficient. People have to see what it will look like and how our lives and our children's and grandchildren's lives will be so much better.

The material conditions for socialist transformation exist here and now. The problem is that they are owned and controlled by the capitalist ruling class instead of in the hands of the working class. Fortunately, ever-increasing numbers of people are awakening to the fact that it does not have to be like this. The same material conditions that make socialism possible are creating a new consciousness, a pro-socialist consciousness that extends from support for mainstream political candidates like Bernie Sanders, through the millions in the streets during 2020's revolt against racism, to the wide array of community solidarity projects and mutual aid efforts that emerged to support workers pushed into poverty and unemployment by the inadequate response of the US government to the pandemic and beyond.

Yes, it is true that the ruling class and its capitalist media continue to push their anti-socialist and anti-communist propaganda. But anti-communism has existed for a far, far shorter time than, for example, the bigoted consciousness flowing from patriarchy and the oppression of women. And yet there have been major, dynamic, radical changes in societal consciousness on the status of women and LGBTQ people in a matter of decades. Consciousness changed because of struggle. Furthermore, US capitalism was founded on racism. Racism and white-supremacist consciousness have existed far longer than anti-communism and have even deeper roots in US society than anti-communism. Yet, the heroic struggles of the Black freedom movement in the twentieth century not only ended the system of legal apartheid but changed societal consciousness on a mass scale. None of these emancipatory movements have been carried through to their conclusion. But they left enduring changes in consciousness, as the intensified struggles to deepen and extend them attest. They teach us that revolutionary change is possible when we are willing to fight for it. And they indicate that as long as the US is ruled by capitalists, banks, corporations, and landlords none of our victories are secure. Enduring change requires a whole new system and working-class power: socialism.

The US working class, by virtue of its educational level and training, is fully capable of taking the reins of state power. It does not require a proxy from the "educated elites" or "trained former government bureaucracies" to function as the ruling class. The majority of workers (those who survive primarily based on the sale of their labor) live in cities. Every year some twenty million young people are enrolled in some form of higher education. Most are employed in the service sector rather than industry. And yet most expect their lives to be harder than their parents' lives—saddled with debt, unable to buy a house, unable to afford health insurance, unable to find meaningful work, and overburdened by the uncertainties of a viciously competitive labor market on a warming planet. The general level of education and social consciousness of the working class in the US is so high that it provides a new basis for socialist class consciousness:

we can see with our own eyes that crises facing people and the planet are solvable—all that's required is breaking the 1 percent's hold on political and economic power.

Once again, this book is not a blueprint for everything in the socialist future; it's a realistic demonstration of what socialist reconstruction can achieve. The actual work of planning and building a new society will require the input, creativity, and experience of tens of millions of people, and will always be a work in progress where plans are tested and revised. A genuine, popular democracy of the people; one where we are collectively engaged in the exciting work of transforming our energy, food, and health-care systems, rebuilding our housing and transportation infrastructures, and creating new practices of solidarity and forms of association, is already possible. As socialist consciousness grows among the people, and as we strengthen and expand the organized struggle, we will make it a reality.

ENDNOTES

Chapter 1

1   Albert Einstein, "Why Socialism," *Monthly Review* 1, 1 (May 1949).

2   Fred Jerome, *The Einstein File* (New York: St. Martin's Press, 2004).

3   Martin Luther King, Jr. to Coretta Scott King, July 1952, The King Papers, The Martin Luther King, J. Research and Education Institute, Stanford University, https://kinginstitute.stanford.edu/king-papers/documents/coretta-scott/.

4   Martin Luther King, "Where Do We Go From Here," Speech to Southern Christian Leadership Conference Atlanta, Georgia, August 16, 1967, The King Papers, The Martin Luther King, J. Research and Education Institute, Stanford University, https://kinginstitute.stanford.edu/where-do-we-go-here/.

5   Ibid.

6   Gerald Horne, *Black Liberation/Red Scare: Ben Davis and the Communist Party* (New York: Monthly Review, 1994); Emily Newburger, "A Price Paid for Conviction," Harvard Law Today, July 1, 2009, https://today.law.harvard.edu/a-price-paid-for-conviction/.

7   David L. Dunbar, "The Hollywood Ten: The Men Who Refused to Name Names," The Hollywood Reporter, November 16, 2015, https://www.hollywoodreporter.com/lists/hollywood-ten-men-who-refused-839762/.

8   Richard D. Vogel, "The NAFTA Corridors: Offshoring U.S. Transportation Jobs to Mexico," *Monthly Review* 57, 9 (2006), https://monthlyreview.org/2006/02/01/the-nafta-corridors-offshoring-u-s-transportation-jobs-to-mexico/.

9   An Phung, "Socialism and Capitalism Are Merriam-Webster's Most Searched Words of 2012," NBCDFW, December 5, 2012, https://www.nbcdfw.com/news/national-international/socialism-and-capitalism-are-the-most-searched-words-of-2012/1940193/.

10 "FBI Documents Reveal Secret Nationwide Occupy Monitoring," Partnership for Civil Justice Fund, accessed March 26, 2022, https://www.justiceonline.org/fbi_files_ows/.

11 Ibid.

12 Ibid.

13 Jervis Anderson, *A. Philip Randolph: A Biographical Portrait* (Berkeley: University of California Press, 1986).

14 Philip Foner, *When Karl Marx Died* (New York: International Publishers, 1973).

15 Emily Czachor, "Half of American Workers Made Less Than $35,000 in 2019, Report Shows," *Newsweek*, October 15, 2020, https://www.newsweek.com/half-american-workers-made-less-35000-2019-report-shows-1539503/; "Fifty

percent of the US workforce earned less than $35,000 in 2019, according to the Social Security Administration's (SSA)," *Newsweek* reported in 2019—before COVID-19.

16 George Frisbee Hoar, "Idea of the Senate | A Place of "Sober Second Thought," United States Senate, accessed March 26, 2022, https://www.senate.gov/about/origins-foundations/idea-of-the-senate/1897Hoar.htm/.

17 "Cory Booker Says the US Senate is 'dominated by millionaires' and That He is 'not one of them,'" Politifact, accessed March 26, 2022, https://www.politifact.com/factchecks/2020/aug/13/cory-booker/cory-booker-said-us-senate-dominated-millionaires-/.

18 Gerald Horne, Black Liberation/Red Scare (Newark, NJ: University of Delaware Press, 1994).

19 Hannah Packman, "Juneteenth and the Broken Promise of '40 Acres and a Mule,' " National Farmers Union, June 19, 2020, https://nfu.org/2020/06/19/juneteenth-and-the-broken-promise-of-40-acres-and-a-mule/. Union General William T. Sherman's plan to give newly-freed families "forty acres and a mule" was among the first and most significant promises made—and broken—to African Americans. On January 16, 1865, Sherman issued his Special Field Order 15, which commanded that 400,000 acres of property confiscated from Confederate landowners be redistributed to Black families in forty-acre plots. By June, the land had been allocated to forty thousand of a total of four million freed slaves. But the order was short-lived. President Andrew Johnson—who had owned slaves and publicly shared his beliefs of white supremacy—overturned the order before the end of the year and returned the land to the slaveowners and traitors who had originally owned it. The long-term financial implications of this reversal are staggering; by some estimates, the value of forty acres and mule for those forty thousand freed slaves would be worth $640 billion today.

Chapter 2

20 The 2020 US Census lists 110 metropolitan areas (an urban core with an adjoining suburban area) of more than 500,000 people. In the 2000 Census there were 71 metropolitan areas of more than 500,000, www.census.org/.

21 Diana Fu, "How the Chinese State Mobilized Civil Society to Fight COVID-19," Brookings, February 9, 2021, https://www.brookings.edu/blog/order-from-chaos/2021/02/09/how-the-chinese-state-mobilized-civil-society-to-fight-COVID-19/.

Chapter 3

22 This agreement informed the document Bolivia submitted to the Ad Hoc Working Group on Long Term Cooperative Action under the Convention in preparation for COP 16 in Mexico City, April 30, 2010, https://unfccc.int/resource/docs/2010/awglca10/eng/misc02.pdf/.

23 "U.S. Environmental Footprint Factsheet," Center for Sustainable Systems, University of Michigan, accessed March 12, 2022, http://css.umich.edu/factsheets/us-environmental-footprint-factsheet/.

24 Jag Bhalla and Eliza Barclay, "How Affluent People Can End Their Mindless Overconsumption," Vox, November, 20, 2020, https://www.vox.com/21450911/climate-change-coronavirus-greta-thunberg-flying-degrowth/.

25 Tracey Osborne, "Native Americans Fighting Fossil Fuels," *Scientific American*, April 9, 2018, https://blogs.scientificamerican.com/voices/native-americans-fighting-fossil-fuels/.

26 Peter Beech, "What Is Environmental Racism and How Can We Fight It?," World Economic Forum, July 31, 2020, https://www.weforum.org/agenda/2020/07/what-is-environmental-racism-pollution-covid-systemic/.

27 Casey Berkovitz, "Environmental Racism Has Left Black Communities Especially Vulnerable to COVID-19," The Century Foundation, March 11, 2022, https://tcf.org/content/commentary/environmental-racism-left-black-communities-especially-vulnerable-covid-19/.

28 Larry Edwards and Stan Cox, "Cap and Adapt: Failsafe Policy for the Climate Emergency," *Solutions*, September 1, 2020, https://thesolutionsjournal.com/2020/09/01/cap-and-adapt-failsafe-policy-for-the-climate-emergency/.

29 For an example of a similar such board, as well as other related organizations for implementing a massive national-level climate mobilization see page 33, https://www.theclimatemobilization.org/wp-content/uploads/2020/07/Victory-Plan-July-2020-Update.pdf.

30 Hannah Ritchie and Max Roser, "Energy Production and Consumption," Our World In Data, accessed March 12, 2022, https://ourworldindata.org/energy-production-consumption.

31 Joel Millward-Hopkins, Julia K.Steinberger, Narasimha D. Rao and Yannick Oswald, "Providing Decent Living with Minimum Energy: A Global Scenario," *Global Environmental Change* 65, (November 2020): 102168, https://www.sciencedirect.com/science/article/pii/S0959378020307512

32 Iñaki Arto, Iñigo Capellán-Pérez, Rosa Lago, Gorka Bueno, and Roberto Bermejo, "The Energy Requirements for a Developed World," *Energy for Sustainable Development* 33, (August 2016): 1-13, https://www.sciencedirect.com/science/article/pii/S0973082616301892/.

33 Benjamin Goldstein, Dimitrios Gounaridis, and Joshua P. Newell, "The Carbon Footprint of Household Energy Use in the United States," *Sustainability Science* 117, 32 (July 2020), https://www.pnas.org/doi/10.1073/pnas.1922205117/.

34 Millward-Hopkins, Steinberger, Rao and Oswald, "Providing," 8.

35 Anna Coote, "Universal Basic Services and Sustainable Consumption," *Sustainability: Science, Practice and Policy* 17, 1 (Winter 2020): 32-46. https://www.tandfonline.com/doi/full/10.1080/15487733.2020.1843854/.

36 Ibid.

Chapter 4

37 Alexandra Natapoff, *Punishment without Crime*, (Basic Books: New York, 2018).

38 Ashutosh Pandey, "Is Africa a Victim of Bias by International Investors?," *Deutsche Welle*, August 14, 2020, https://www.dw.com/en/africa-imf-bias-discrimination-debt-international-investors/a-54564359/.

39 David Graeber, *Bullshit Jobs* (Simon & Schuster: New York, 2018), 110.

40 Doug Henwood, *Wall Street: How it Works and for Whom* (Verso: New York, 1997), 4.

41 Karen Petrou, "Only the Rich Could Love This Economic Recovery," *The New York Times, July 21, 2021,* https://www.nytimes.com/interactive/2021/07/12/opinion/covid-fed-qe-inequality.html/.

42 Ibid.

43 J. W. Mason, "Socialize Finance," *Jacobin*, November, 28, 2016, https://www.jacobinmag.com/2016/11/finance-banks-capitalism-markets-socialism-planning/.

44 Ibid.

45 "Evolution of the U.S. Housing Finance System," U.S. Department of Housing and Urban Development, April 2006, 3, https://www.huduser.gov/publications/pdf/us_evolution.pdf/.

46 Jeff Cox, "Household Debt Climbs to $14.64 Trillion, Due to Jump in Mortgages and Car Loans," *CNBC*, May 12, 2021, https://www.cnbc.com/2021/05/12/household-debt-climbs-to-14point64-trillion.html/.

47 "IMB Production Volumes and Profits Reach Record Highs in 2020," Mortgage Bankers Association, April 13, 2021, https://www.mba.org/2021-press-releases/april/imb-production-volumes-and-profits-reach-record-highs-in-2020/.

48 "10 Key Facts About Student Debt in the United States," Peter G. Peterson Foundation, May 5, 2021, https://www.pgpf.org/blog/2021/05/10-key-facts-about-student-debt-in-the-united-states/.

49 Zack Friedman, "Student Loan Debt Statistics in 2021: A Record $1.7 Trillion," *Forbes*, February 20, 2021, https://www.forbes.com/sites/zackfriedman/2021/02/20/student-loan-debt-statistics-in-2021-a-record-17-trillion/.
50 Peterson Foundation, "10 Key Facts."
51 Friedman, "Student Loan Debt."
52 Jenn Jones, "Average Car Payment | Loan Statistics 2022," Lending Tree, March 8, 2022, https://www.lendingtree.com/auto/debt-statistics/.
53 Michael Sainato, "'I Live on the Street Now': How Americans Fall into Medical Bankruptcy," *The Guardian*, November 14, 2019, https://www.theguardian.com/us-news/2019/nov/14/health-insurance-medical-bankruptcy-debt/.
54 Ibid.

Chapter 5
55 Vandana Shiva, *Who Really Feeds the World* (Berkeley: North Atlantic Books, 2016).
56 Nina Lakhani, "One in Four Faced Food Insecurity in America's Year of Hunger, Investigation Shows," *The Guardian*, April 14, 2021, https://www.theguardian.com/environment/2021/apr/14/americas-year-of-hunger-how-children-and-people-of-color-suffered-most/.
57 "The State of Obesity 2020: Better Policies for a Healthier America," Trust for America's Health, accessed March 12, 2022, https://www.tfah.org/report-details/state-of-obesity-2020/.
58 Chris McGreal, "How America's Food Giants Swallowed the Family Farms," *The Guardian*, March 9, 2019, https://www.theguardian.com/environment/2019/mar/09/american-food-giants-swallow-the-family-farms-iowa/.
59 Shiva, *Who Really Feeds the World*.
60 Eileen Crist, *Abundant Earth* (Chicago: University of Chicago Press, 2019).
61 Eric Holt-Giménez, *Foodies Guide to Capitalism* (New York: Monthly Review Press, 2017), 27-28.
62 Paul Gordon, "In the Southeast, Climate Change Finds a Landscape Already Ravaged by Inequality," *In These Times*, June 5, 2021, https://inthesetimes.com/article/southeastern-us-gulf-south-climate-change-black-farmers-green-new-deal/.
63 Holt-Giménez, *Foodies Guide to Capitalism*, 41.
64 Robert Frank, "Why Does the Govt. Pay Farmers to Not Grow Crops?" *PBS News Hour*, August 4, 2009, https://www.pbs.org/newshour/economy/why-does-the-govt-pay-farmers/.

65 Holt-Giménez, *Foodies Guide to Capitalism*, 41.

66 Shiva, *Who Really Feeds the World*.

67 Holt-Giménez, *Foodies Guide to Capitalism*, 47.

68 Ibid, 48.

69 Rob Wallace, "Where Did Coronavirus Come From, and Where Will it Take Us?" Interview on Uneven Earth, March 12, 2020, https://unevenearth. org/2020/03/where-did-coronavirus-come-from-and-where-will-it-take-us-an-interview-with-rob-wallace-author-of-big-farms-make-big-flu/.

70 Shiva, *Who Really Feeds the World*.

71 Tony Weis, *The Global Food Economy* (London: Zed Books, 2007), 15.

72 Susan Kaplan, "Air Pollution From Farms Leads to 17,900 U.S. Deaths Per Year, Study Finds," *Washington Post*, May 10, 2021, https:// www.washingtonpost.com/climate-environment/2021/05/10/ farm-pollution-deaths/.

73 Ibid.

74 Mya Frazier, "The Poultry Workers on The Coronavirus Front Line: 'If One Of Us Gets Sick, We All Get Sick'," *The Guardian*, April 17, 2020, https://www.theguardian.com/environment/2020/apr/17/ chicken-factory-tyson-arkansas-food-workers-coronavirus/.

75 McGreal, "How America's Food Giants Swallowed the Family Farms."

76 Holt-Giménez, *Foodies Guide to Capitalism*, 42

77 Karl Marx, "The Nationalization of the Land," *The International Herald*, June 15, 1872, https://www.marxists.org/archive/marx/works/1872/04/ nationalisation-land.htm/.

78 Karl Marx, *Capital: A Critique of Political Economy*, *Volume 1*, (Moscow: Progress Publishers, 1965), 637.

79 Ivette Perfecto, John Vandermeer and Angus Wright, *Nature's Matrix* (London: Routledge, 2019).

80 Srinivasulu Rajendran, Victor Afari-Sefa, Apurba Shee, T. Bocher, Mateete A. Bekunda, I. Dominick, and Philipo J. Lukumay, "Does Crop Diversity Contribute to Dietary Diversity? Evidence from Integration of Vegetables into Maize-based Farming Systems," *Agriculture and Food Security* 6, 50 (October 2017).

81 Katie Wedell, Lucille Sherman and Sky Chadde, "Midwest Farmers Face a Crisis. Hundreds Are Dying by Suicide," *USA Today*, March 9, 2020, https://eu.usatoday.com/in-depth/news/investigations/2020/03/09/ climate-tariffs-debt-and-isolation-drive-some-farmers-suicide/4955865002/.

82 Vanessa Riba, *On the Line* (Berkeley: University of California Press, 2015); Timothy Pachirat, *Every Twelve Seconds* (New Haven: Yale University Press, 2013).

83 "Agroecology Knowledge Hub," Food and Agricultural Organization of the United Nations, accessed March 12, 2022, http://www.fao.org/agroecology/overview/en/.

84 Susanna B. Hecht, "The Evolution of Agroecological Thought," in *Agroecology: The Science of Sustainable Agriculture*, Second Edition, ed. Miguel A Altieri, (London: IT Publications, 1995), 1-21.

85 R. Douglas Hurt, *Indian Agriculture in America: Prehistory to the Present* (Norman: University Press of Kansas, 1987); Robin Wall Kimmer, *Braiding Sweetgrass* (Minneapolis: Milkweed, 2020); Leah Penniman, *Farming while Black* (Pittsburgh: Chelsea Green Publishing Company, 2018).

86 Miguel A, Altieri, Clara I. Nicholls, Alejandro Henao, and Marcos A. Lana, "Agroecology and the Design of Climate Change-Resilient Farming Systems," *Agronomy for Sustainable Development* 35, 3 (July 2015): 869–90.

87 Miguel A. Altieri and Clara I. Nicholls, "Agroecology and the Reconstruction of a Post-COVID-19 Agriculture," *The Journal of Peasant Studies* 47, 5 (28 July 2020): 881–98.

88 Carey Clouse, *Farming Cuba* (Princeton: Princeton Architectural Press, April 2014).

89 Max Ajl, *A People's Green New Deal* (London: Pluto Press, 2021) 142.

90 Nafeez Ahmed, "UN: Only Small Farmers and Agroecology Can Feed the World," *Ecologist*, September 23, 2014, https://theecologist.org/2014/sep/23/un-only-small-farmers-and-agroecology-can-feed-world/.

91 Eric Toensmeier, *The Carbon Farming Solution* (White River Junction: Chelsea Green Publishing, 2016).

92 Perfecto, *Nature's Matrix*.

93 "The Drawdown Review: Climate Solutions for a New Decade," Project Drawdown, March 2020, https://drawdown.org/sites/default/files/pdfs/TheDrawdownReview-2020-Download.pdf/.

94 R.J. Zomer, D.A. Bossio, R. Sommer, et al., "Global Sequestration Potential of Increased Organic Carbon in Cropland Soils," *Scientific Reports* 7 (2017): 15554, https://www.nature.com/articles/s41598-017-15794-8/.

95 Matt Huber, "Ecosocialism: Dystopian and Scientific," *Socialist Forum* (Winter 2019), https://socialistforum.dsausa.org/issues/winter-2019/ecosocialism-dystopian-and-scientific/.

Chapter 6

96 Alec MacGillis, *Fulfillment: Winning and Losing in One-Click America* (New York: Farrar, Straus and Giroux, 2021) 7-11.

Endnotes

97 Samuel Stein, *Capital City: Gentrification and the Real Estate State* (New York: Verso, 2019) 170.

98 Ibid, 75.

99 "Re-segregation, Black Liberation and Revolutionary Unity," *Liberation News*, February 27, 2014, https://www.liberationnews.org/re-segregation-black-liberation-unity-html/.

100 Gianpaolo Baiocchi and H. Jacob Carlson, "Housing Is a Social Good," *Boston Review*, June 2, 2021, https://bostonreview.net/articles/housing-is-a-social-good/.

101 Ibid.

102 Adam Frost, "Vienna's Affordable Housing Paradise," *HuffPost*, updated February 25, 2019, https://www.huffpost.com/entry/vienna-affordable-housing-paradise_n_5b4e0b12e4b0b15aba88c7b0/.

103 Baiocchi and Carlson, "Housing Is a Social Good."

104 "APTA's Purpose Statement: APTA Leads Public Transportation in a New Mobility Era, Advocating to Connect and Build Thriving Communities, 7th Edition," American Public Transportation Association, March 2020, https://www.apta.com/wp-content/uploads/APTA-2020-Fact-Book.pdf/.

105 Zach George, "U.S. House Approves FY 2021 U.S. Department of Transportation Funding," National Association of Counties, August 26, 2020, https://www.naco.org/blog/us-house-approves-fy-2021-us-department-transportation-funding/.

106 "Transportation," Environmental and Energy Study Institute, accessed March 24, 2022, https://www.eesi.org/topics/transportation/description/.

107 Jeff D. Colgan, "Oil, Conflict, and U.S. National Interests, Harvard Kennedy School, Belfer Center for Science and International Affairs, October 2013, https://www.belfercenter.org/publication/oil-conflict-and-us-national-interests/.

108 "Public Transportation Facts," American Public Transportation Association, accessed March 24, 2022, https://www.apta.com/news-publications/public-transportation-facts/.

109 Laura Bliss, "America Probably Has Enough Parking Spaces for Multiple Black Fridays," *Bloomberg*, November 27, 2018, https://www.bloomberg.com/news/articles/2018-11-27/why-parking-lots-are-not-full-even-on-black-friday/.

110 Adele Peters, "Here's How Much Space U.S. Cities Waste on Parking," *FastCompany*, July 17, 2018, https://www.fastcompany.com/90202222/heres-how-much-space-u-s-cities-waste-on-parking/.

111 Jordan Friedman, "The 10 Most Congested Cities in the U.S.," *U.S. News*, October 13, 2020, https://www.usnews.com/news/cities/ articles/10-cities-with-the-worst-traffic-in-the-us/.

112 André Gorz, *Ecology as Politics* (Canada: Black Rose Press, 1980).

113 Dennis E. Barrett, "Unsafe Streets in Marginalized Communities Lead to Inequitable Traffic Enforcement," Transport for America, March 3, 2021, https://t4america.org/2021/03/03/unsafe-streets-in-marginalized-communities-leads-to-inequitable-traffic-enforcement/.

114 "Solutions: Electric Bicycles," Project Drawdown, accessed March 24, 2022, https://drawdown.org/solutions/electric-bicycles/.

115 Gorz, *Ecology as Politics*.

Chapter 7

116 "Proposal of the Physicians' Working Group for Single-Payer National Health Insurance," Physicians for a National Health Program, accessed March 13, 2022, https://pnhp.org/beyond_aca/Physicians_Proposal.pdf/.

117 Beth Mole, "Big Pharma Shells Out $20B Each Year to Schmooze Docs, $6B on Drug Ads, *Ars Technica*, January 11, 2019, https://arstechnica.com/science/2019/01/ healthcare-industry-spends-30b-on-marketing-most-of-it-goes-to-doctors/.

118 "Drug Overdose Deaths 2020 Hit Highest Number," Worldnewsinpictures. com, March 14, 2020, https://worldnewsinpictures.com/ drug-overdose-deaths-2020-hit-highest-number/.

119 Maggie Fox, "Drug Overdose Deaths in 2020 Hit Highest Number Ever Recorded, CDC data Shows," *CNN*, July 17, 2021, https://www.cnn. com/2021/07/14/health/drug-overdose-deaths-2020/index-html/.

120 Fraiser Kansteiner, "Regeneron CEO Schiefer, Chief Scientist Yancopoulos Bag Massive $270M Payday," *Fierce Pharma*, April 26, 2021, https://www. fiercepharma.com/pharma/regeneron-ceo-schleifer-bags-135m-payday-after-company-s-pandemic-boosted-2020/.

121 Brendan Maher and Richard Van Noorden , "How the COVID Pandemic is Changing Global Science Collaborations," *Nature*, June 16 2021, https://www. nature.com/articles/d41586-021-01570-2/.

122 Cheng Li and Senqi Ma , "How Coronavirus Scientists Offer a Formula for Better US-China Relations," *Brookings*, March 17, 2021, https://www.brookings.edu/blog/order-from-chaos/2021/03/17/ how-coronavirus-scientists-offer-a-formula-for-better-us-china-relations/.

123 Anthony Faiola and Ana Vanessa Herrero, "Against the Odds, Cuba Could Become a Coronavirus Powerhouse," *Washington Post*, March

29, 2021, https://www.washingtonpost.com/world/2021/03/29/
cuba-coronavirus-vaccine-iran-venezuela/.

124 Sara Reardon, "Cuba's Bet on Home-grown Covid Vaccines is Paying
Off," *Nature*, November 22, 2021, https://www.nature.com/articles/
d41586-021-03470-x.

125 Becca Hamberg, "Increasing Insulin Prices Highlight the Prioritization of
Capitalism over the Health of Human Beings in the American Healthcare
System" (paper, Health Humanities, and Humanities, Northeastern University,
May, 19, 2021), https://cssh.northeastern.edu/humanities/increasing-insulin-
prices-highlight-the-prioritization-of-capitalism-over-the-health-of-human-
beings-in-the-american-healthcare-system/.

126 Nasimm Maleki, Lino Becerra, and David Borsook, "Migraine: Maladaptive
Brain Response to Stress," *Headache* 52, no. 2 Supplement (October 2012):
102-106, https://headachejournal.onlinelibrary.wiley.com/doi/10.1111/j.1526-
4610.2012.02241.x /.

127 "Nurtec," Good RX, accessed March 13, 2022, https://www.goodrx.com/
nurtec.

128 Don Fitz, "The Birth of the Cuban Polyclinic," *Monthly Review*
70, 2 (June 2018): 21, https://monthlyreview.org/2018/06/01/
the-birth-of-the-cuban-polyclinic/.

129 Ibid.

130 Ibid.

131 Ibid.

132 Ibid.

133 April Simpson, "'Poor Folks Trying to Make it as Best as We Can':
Surviving Mississippi's Miserly Healthcare System," *The Guardian*,
Dec 16, 2021, https://www.theguardian.com/society/2021/dec/16/
mississippi-miserly-healthcare-system/.

134 Dariush Mozaffarian and Dan Glickman, "Our Food is Killing Too Many
of Us," *The New York Times*, August 26, 2019, https://www.nytimes.
com/2019/08/26/opinion/food-nutrition-health-care.html/.

135 Ibid.

136 David Gorn, "Food As Medicine: It's Not Just A Fringe
Idea Anymore," *NPR*, January 17, 2017, https://www.
npr.org/sections/thesalt/2017/01/17/509520895/
food-as-medicine-it-s-not-just-a-fringe-idea-anymore/.

137 Ann Case and Angus Deaton, *Deaths of Despair and the Future of Capitalism*
(Princeton: Princeton University Press, 2020).

138 E.J. Mundell, "Antidepressant Use Jumps 65 Percent in 15 Years," WebMD, August 15, 2017, https://www.webmd.com/depression/news/20170815/us-antidepressant-use-jumps-65-percent-in-15-years/.

139 Anna Zeira, "Mental Health Challenges Related to Neoliberal Capitalism in the United States," *Community Mental Health Journal* 58, (2022): 205–212.

140 Kate Pickett, Richard G. Wilkinson, *The Spirit Level: Why Greater Equality Makes Societies Stronger* (New York: Bloomsbury Press, 2009).

141 "The State of the LGBTQ Community in 2020," Center for American Progress, October 6, 2020, https://www.americanprogress.org/article/state-lgbtq-community-2020/.

Chapter 8

142 "The National K-12 Foreign Language Enrollment Survey Report," American Councils for International Education (2017), 11, https://www.americancouncils.org/sites/default/files/FLE-report-June17.pdf.

Chapter 9

143 Mohsen Naghavi, "Fatal Police Violence by Race and State in the USA, 1980–2019: a Network Meta-regression, *The Lancet* 398, no. 10307 (October 2021): 1239-1255, https://www.thelancet.com/journals/lancet/article/PIIS0140-6736(21)01609-3/fulltext/.

144 Richard Becker, *The Myth of Democracy and the Rule of the Banks* (San Francisco: PSL Publications, 2012), 17-18.

145 Ibid.

146 Jane Franklin, *Cuba and the United States: A Chronological History* (Melbourne: Ocean Press, 1997), 20.

147 "Quarterly Residential Vacancies and Homeownership, Fourth Quarter 2021," US Census Bureau, Release Number: CB22-10, February 2, 2022, https://www.census.gov/housing/hvs/files/currenthvspress.pdf/.

148 Hanna Love, "Want to Reduce Violence? Invest in Place," *Brooking*, November 16, 2021, https://www.brookings.edu/research/want-to-reduce-violence-invest-in-place/.

149 Wyatt Massey and Michael Dresser, "Advocates rally for Baltimore Safe Streets program after funding cut," *Baltimore Sun*, August 4, 2016, https://www.baltimoresun.com/maryland/baltimore-city/bs-md-ci-safe-streets-funding-rally-20160804-story.html/.

150 Geoff Mulvihill and Jennifer Peltz, "Drug Victims Unload on Purdue Pharma Owners in Court," *The Mercury News*, March

10, 2022, https://www.mercurynews.com/2022/03/10/
drug-victims-unload-on-purdue-pharma-owners-in-court/.

151 Becker, *The Myth of Democracy*, 18.

152 "Statistics," National Sexual Violence Resource Center, accessed March 27, 2022, https://www.nsvrc.org/statistics/.

153 Jacob Passy, "How Welfare Reform Made Women Worse Off," *MarketWatch*, February 27, 2018, https://www.marketwatch.com/story/how-welfare-reform-made-women-worse-off-2018-02-26/.

154 "Statistics," National Sexual Violence Resource Center, accessed March 27, 2022, https://www.nsvrc.org/statistics/.

155 Caroline Mimbs Nyce, "The Atlantic Daily: These Attacks Could've Been Prevented," *The Atlantic*, July 15, 2019, https://www.theatlantic.com/newsletters/archive/2019/07/nationwide-epidemic-of-untested-rape-kits-atlantic-daily/594046/.

156 Drew Kann, "5 Facts Behind America's High Incarceration Rate," *CNN*, April 21, 2019, https://www.cnn.com/2018/06/28/us/mass-incarceration-five-key-facts/index.html/; "Probation and Parole in the United States, 2019," US Department of Justice, July 2021, https://bjs.ojp.gov/sites/g/files/xyckuh236/files/media/document/ppus19.pdf/."

157 "Prison Conditions," Equal Justice Initiative, accessed March 27, 2022, https://eji.org/issues/prison-conditions/.

158 Franklin, *Cuba and the United States*, 29.

Chapter 10

159 Lenin, V.I. (1917). "Imperialism: The Highest Stage of Capitalism," in *Imperialism in the 21st Century: Updating Lenin's Theory a Century Later*, ed. B. Becker (San Francisco: Liberation Media, 2015), 88-89.

160 Martin Luther King, Jr., "The Casualties of the War in Vietnam," February 25, 1967, The Nation Institute, Los Angeles, https://www.aavw.org/special_features/speeches_speech_king02.html./

161 David Vine, "The United States Probably has More Foreign Military Bases Than Any Other People, Nation or Empire in History," *The Nation*, September 14, 2015, https://www.thenation.com/article/world/the-united-states-probably-has-more-foreign-military-bases-than-any-other-people-nation-or-empire-in-history/.

162 "Estimate of U.S.-Post-War Spending, in $ Billions FY2001-FY2002," Costs of War, Watson Institute International & Public Affairs, Brown University, accessed April 10, 2022, https://watson.brown.edu/costsofwar/figures/2021/BudgetaryCosts/.

163 Charles Q. Choi, "AI Drone May Have 'Hunted Down' and Killed Soldiers in Libya With no Human Input," LiveScience, June 3, 2021, https://www.livescience.com/ai-drone-attack-libya.htm/.

164 "About DARPA," Ocean of Things, accessed March 26, 2022, https://oceanofthings.darpa.mil/.

165 Jim Mattis, "Summary of the 2018 National Defense Strategy of the United States of America," Department of Defense, Washington, United States, https://apps.dtic.mil/sti/pdfs/AD1045785.pdf/.

166 "Is China Ramping Up Military Spending?, Xinhua, March 8, 2021, http://www.news.cn/english/2021-03/08/c_139795063.htm/; Kimberly Amadeo, "U.S. Military Budget, its Components, Challenges, and Growth," The Balance, February 22, 2022, https://www.thebalance.com/u-s-military-budget-components-challenges-growth-3306320/.

167 "Excerpts From Pentagon's Plan: 'Prevent the Re-Emergence of a New Rival,'" The New York Times, March 8, 1992, https://www.nytimes.com/1992/03/08/world/excerpts-from-pentagon-s-plan-prevent-the-re-emergence-of-a-new-rival.html/.

168 "Lifting 800 Million People out of Poverty – New Report Looks at Lessons from China's Experience," The World Bank, April 1, 2022, https://www.worldbank.org/en/news/press-release/2022/04/01/lifting-800-million-people-out-of-poverty-new-report-looks-at-lessons-from-china-s-experience/.

169 "Approaches for Managing the Costs of US Nuclear Forces, 2017 to 2046," Congressional Budget Office, October 2017, https://www.cbo.gov/system/files/115th-congress-2017-2018/reports/53211-nuclearforces.pdf.

170 "Monthly Budget Review: May 2021," Congressional Budget Office, June 8, 2021, https://www.cbo.gov/system/files/2021-06/57193-MBR.pdf/.

Made in the USA
Monee, IL
20 February 2024

53821671R00125